Educating Muslim women:
the West African legacy
of Nana Asma'u
1793–1864

Educating Muslim women:
the West African legacy
of Nana Asma'u
(1793–1864)

Jean Boyd and Beverly Mack

Interface Publications Ltd. Kube Publishing Ltd.

Published in the United Kingdom
by Interface Publications and Kube Publishing

Interface Publications Ltd.
5 South Parade, Oxford
Oxfordshire. OX2 7JL. UK
tel: +44 (0) 1865 510251
website: www.interfacepublications.com
email: secretary@interfacepublications.com

Kube Publishing Ltd.
Markfield Conference Centre
Ratby Lane, Markfield
Leicestershire. LE 67 9SY. UK
tel: +44 (0) 1530 249230 fax: +44 (0) 1530 249656
website: www.kubepublishing.com
email: info@kubepublishing.com

Distributed by Kube Publishing Ltd.

ISBN: 978-1-84774-044-1

A CIP data record for this book is available from the British Library.

CONTENTS

List of Maps* and Illustrations

*Maps drawn by Dr. Alexander Kent, FBCart.S., FRGS

Nana Asma'u (1793–1864) was a prolific Muslim scholar, poet, historian, and educator, a legend in her own lifetime. That legend lives to this day; people still name their daughters after her; her poems are read and recited both privately and in public gatherings, and still move people profoundly; the memory of her remains a vital source of inspiration and hope. Asma'u was a devout, learned Muslim who was also courageous and independent-minded, able to observe, record, interpret, and influence the major public events that happened around her. Most important of all perhaps, her example as an educator is still followed: the system she set up in the first quarter of the nineteenth century, for the education of rural women, has not only survived in its homeland – through all the traumas and disruptions of the colonization of West Africa and the establishment of the modern state of Nigeria – but is also being revived and adapted elsewhere, notably among Muslim women in the United States.

In this book, we give an account of Asma'u's upbringing and the critical junctures in her life, described from several perspectives: that of her own first-hand experiences as presented in her writings; that of those who witnessed her endeavours as her contemporaries; and that of travellers to the region. We have relied on a variety of sources, primary and secondary. Of the former, the most important are Nana Asma'u's own works, notably her poetry collected and preserved by her family in their home. For an outsider's view of life at the time, we have referred primarily to nineteenth-century travel memoirs, especially those of Hugh Clapperton and Heinrich Barth. We have of course consulted and benefited from modern scholarship about the peoples, culture, and history of the region, the works in particular of Murray Last, Margery Perham, Mervyn Hiskett and David Muffet. For the account of her legacy, her present influence, and how her example is being sustained and adapted, we have depended on our first-hand experiences and field studies in Nigeria, and documents pertaining to the efforts of women to develop a collective voice and establish their rights as women and Muslims in today's societies. Information about the sources used for this book is set out in the References (pp. 235–45).

The Introduction briefly explains the historical moment of the story recounted in this book, and its cultural setting. We give particular attention to the practice of Sufism in West Africa, its association with Islamic scholarship, the role of the Qur'an in teaching, the pattern and method of education, and the part played by women. That is the minimum of backgrounding necessary to enable a proper appreciation of the achievements of Nana Asma'u and an understanding of why her example should have such resonance today. Thereafter, the main body of the work is arranged as follows:

Chapter 1 narrates and explains the circumstances of the hijra (emigration) of the Fulani community from 'Degel, and the ensuing Jihad which ended with the foundation of the Sokoto Caliphate. The Fodio family, including Asma'u, were actively involved in shaping these events, the understanding of them, and managing their consequences.

Chapter 2 discusses Asma'u's role as a young mother, as senior wife of the Wazir, as the Caliph's sister; her concerns about, and her activism in seeking to meet, the challenges that arose from the social upheavals during and after war.

Chapter 3 explains the origins of the 'Yan Taru, the network of women teachers that Nana Asma'u founded and organized. It remains a model for women's education systems, both in Nigeria and internationally, nearly two hundred years after it was established.

Chapter 4 presents Asma'u's character, using examples of her poems to illustrate her versatility and intelligence. It goes on to recount how, after her death in 1864, her sister, Maryam, assumed her role, and how scholarship among the 'Yan Taru is sustained in an unbroken tradition to this day.

Chapter 5 describes the advent of colonialism, which led to the devaluation and marginalization of Islamic scholarship in West Africa. The negative effects are explained of the abrupt imposition (under British rule) of an alien script, of the illiteracy that followed, and of changes to women's education in the early twentieth century.

Finally, chapter 6 reports the activism of Muslim women scholars in Northern Nigeria in the twentieth and twenty-first centuries, and gives an account of 'Yan Taru organizations, patterned on Nana Asma'u's, established by Muslim groups in various cities in the United States.

This book is the third on which we have collaborated to bring the life and works of Nana Asma'u to the attention of scholars and the wider public. The first was a text with translation in English of over sixty of Asma'u's known works, their sources, historical pedigree, and original manuscripts in facsimile: *The Collected Works of Nana Asma'u Daughter of Usman dan Fodiyo 1793–1864* (1997; Nigerian edition, 1999). The second was a volume that provided Asma'u's perspective on her time and place in the contexts of history, anthropology, religious studies, literature, and women's studies, including representative excerpts of her works: *One Woman's Jihad: Nana Asma'u, Scholar and Scribe* (2000).

In the present book, we have tried to carry the earlier studies up to the present day.

We are mindful indeed of the profound personal debt we owe to the direct heirs of Nana Asma'u, her descendants and other dedicated scholars, who gave so generously of their time and hospitality, who permitted us access to private papers and books, to private spaces, to the precious and fragile heirlooms reverently passed and preserved from generation to generation, and who shared with us their memories and thoughts about Nana Asma'u. It is a rare privilege to have come to know the life and work of this accomplished scholar through the recollections of her direct descendants and, indeed, all those who strive to embody her virtues in their lives. Her involvement in and contribution to nineteenth-century Northern Nigerian history deserves fuller consideration in the field. Her influence on contemporary Muslim women and communities in the international twenty-first century context is irrefutable. As her descendants themselves believe, all who strive to live by her example are of her lineage in the same sense that she was one of a long line of disciplined, ascetic Muslim scholars who embody and keep alive, in word and deed, the example of the *Sunna*, the way of the Prophet.

Jean Boyd, Penrith, Cumbria, UK
Beverly Mack, Lawrence, Kansas, USA
December, 2012

ACKNOWLEDGEMENTS

We would like to record our gratitude for the encouragement, guidance and generosity of the late Alhaji Junaidu, Waziri of Sokoto, who made available many of the rare manu¬scripts concerned with Nana Asma'u, and interpreted and explained them over decades with tireless good humour.

It was our good fortune to benefit from two other Sokoto scholars: Alhaji Sidi Sayudi, Ubandoma of Sokoto, an Arabist, and Alhaji Muhammadu Magaji, an expert in eighteenth- and nineteenth-century Fulfulde. We are indebted to them.

Other scholars who helped over the years were Mallam Boyi of Kofar Atiku Sokoto, Alhaji Shehu na Limam, Alhaji Haliru Binji, Mallam Isa Talata Mafara of Sokoto History Bureau, Professor Sambo Junaidu of Usman ɗan Fodiyo University, Sokoto and his brother Mallam Ibrahim. We wish especially to thank Shaykh Muhammad Shareef for his invaluable efforts to preserve Fodio family manuscripts (Sankore Institute website www.siiasi.org), and his unflagging support for the development of 'Yan Taru sisterhoods in the US; and national Jaji Dylia Camara, who shared her curriculum materials with us for our presentation of the American 'Yan Taru. We appreciate their generosity and energetic perpetuation of the 'Yan Taru model.

This book would have been impossible without the input of the many women who, with patience and understanding, discussed our work. We thank Hajiya Aisha Lemu of the Islamic Education Trust, Minna, Hajiya Sa'adiya Omar of Usman ɗan Fodiyo University, Sokoto along with the FOMWAN leaders, Hajiya Rukkaya daughter of Sultan Abubakar III and in her time the occupant of Nana Asma'u's original room in Waziri's house, and her sister Hajiya Luba, Hajiya 'Yardamu of Dogondaji, *Modibon* Hajara of Kware and eighteen *jaji*s interviewed in villages located in the environs of Sokoto and *Inna* Ta'Allah of Gobir together with her sister *Inna* Ba-Filata. It was a privilege to have met with them all.

We would also like to thank our editor, Jamil Qureshi, for his patience, encouragement and sound advice.

Last, but let it not be said least, our thanks to our husbands Dick Boyd and Bob Henry.

Note on transliteration

We have avoided formal transliteration of Arabic except in the References, where it was necessary to prevent possible misunderstanding of the Arabic titles of some of the works cited. For Arabic names, we have followed the most common usage in modern Nigeria (for example, the spelling 'Aisha' rather than the strictly correct 'ᶜĀ°ishah', or other variants like 'Ayesha'); we have done the same for Arabic or Arabic-origin terms, marking the ᶜayn and hamza characters with an apostrophe. To represent some consonants in Hausa which have no direct equivalent in the standard English alphabet, we have followed the convention of marking those consonants with the addition of a 'hook'. The 'hooked' characters (in lower and upper case respectively) look like this:

ɓ ɗ ƙ ·y Ɓ Ɗ Ƙ 'Y

INTRODUCTION

Historical setting

At the beginning of the nineteenth century, as the Napoleonic wars ended in a peace settlement in Europe, its major powers, with little concern for the rich and diverse cultures of African societies, embarked on one of history's most comprehensive socio-political and economic transformations: they moved into Africa on the pretext of exploration and religious or 'civilizing' mission. These enterprises were funded by governments seeking for themselves, or seeking to deny to their competitors, control of the continent's vast natural resources, which Europe needed to power its incipient industrial revolution. The West African lands around the Niger river were populated by many different ethnic groups who had lived for centuries in fluctuating conditions of peace and conflict. By the early 1800s sub-Saharan West Africa had long established networks of social and commercial exchange, and numerous settlements both urban and rural. These included walled cities able to withstand months-long sieges, rural villages reliant on agriculture, and bands of pastoralists who roamed the region with their grazing livestock. West African cities were by then bustling cosmopolitan centres with their own administrative hierarchies, education systems, and centuries of connection to Mediterranean cultures through trans-Saharan commercial routes. Even in the rural communities the people were neither isolated from, nor unfamiliar with, cultural contexts beyond their own.

13

The Fodio family

The populations of early nineteenth-century West Africa were constituted by the slow consolidation of local ethnic groups, supplemented by migration into the region. The village of Degel was located in the north-western area of what would become 'Nigeria', an entity and a name coined by the British. This area was home to two major ethnic groupings, the Hausa-speaking Hausa, and the Fulfulde-speaking Fulani. Degel is where the family of a Fulani Muslim scholar–preacher named Usman dan Fodio, the father of Nana Asma'u, had settled. Later, he would be known by the reverent title, 'the Shehu'. The name 'Fodio' identified him as belonging to a family long associated with Islamic scholarship. The Shehu's pastoralist ancestors came originally from the region of coastal West Africa, near the Senegal River, called Futa Toro, from which derives the designation of the clan as 'Toronkawa'. Over generations the Toronkawa had migrated eastward, away from internecine warfare and in search of pasture, reaching by about 1500 the area where this history is set. Some Toronkawa clans continued to herd their cattle, while others, like the Shehu's family, had settled into a village-based lifestyle, which allowed them to give more time to intellectual and spiritual endeavours – studying and teaching among themselves, communicating with other scholars across the region, and producing philosophical and theological tracts. The scholarly Fodio family was, in keeping with the ideals of Islam, egalitarian; the Shehu as a young boy had been educated by his mother and grandmother. In *Tazyin al-warakat* (written by his brother, Abdullahi dan Fodio), there is a detailed account of the Shehu's subsequent teachers and the curriculum he followed. His teaching and preaching activities, coupled with his piety and asceticism, made him the most respected scholar in the region.

INTRODUCTION

Islam and Sufism in West Africa

Islam entered West African culture through trans-Saharan commercial relations, beginning as early as the tenth century in places like Futa Toro in Senegal, and carried eastward by migrating clans. By the start of the nineteenth century Islam was closely woven into the fabric of social order and commerce throughout West Africa. The Fulani were commonly seen in cities such as Kano, Katsina, and Alƙalawa, and contributed to the region's cosmopolitan culture. The literacy and numeracy of Muslim traders, an integral part and outcome of their study of the Qur'an, and their familiarity with Islamic cultural norms, were essential to their success as international merchants. The commerce among the Hausa, Fulani, and North African societies fostered a shared understanding whose philosophical and cultural framework was rooted in Islam.

Along with Islam came Sufism. Often described as Islamic mysticism, Sufism was the prayerful pursuit of knowledge aiming to move an individual closer to God. Since the seventh-century origins of Islam, various Sufi groups, eventually loosely organized as brotherhoods (*turuq*; sing., *tariqa*), developed across the Islamic world; they are typically known by the names of their various founding guides. While all Sufis advocate practices that facilitate greater closeness to God, those practices – notably *dhikr* (or *zikr*), the 'remembrance' of God through repetition of words or phrases expressive of the divine attributes – are nevertheless different in their details. Some Sufis engage in communal *dhikr* involving bodily movement and chanting; others prefer private, and silent, invocation. Some groups promote the value of literacy and intellectual examination of the different levels of reality; others practice only oral transmission of knowledge. Some Sufis have been criticized by fellow Muslims for neglecting public norms of behaviour, for not honouring the regulations of jurisprudential schools and the hierarchies attendant on those

15

constructs. Other Sufi groups, actively participant in their local communities and societies, have also taken up overtly political causes. What most Sufis share in common is belief in the importance of prayer, and commitment to the foundational elements of Islam: the sanctity of the Qur'an (i.e. recitation of the word of God), the centrality and value of adherence to the *Sunna* (the life example of the Prophet Muhammad), and the importance of the 'five pillars', the obligatory rites, of Islam.

In Sufi communities, egalitarianism in the pursuit of knowledge is highly valued, and serves as a hedge against patriarchal interpretations of the religion. Sufism intensifies the Islamic sense of a personal connection to God, without the intervention of intermediaries; Sufis are expected to take responsibility for their own lives and behaviour, women just as much as men. Sufis often say that in Sufism 'the soul has no gender'; it is the context in which the egalitarian promise of Qur'anic language can be most readily realized. The Qur'an itself again and again exhorts human beings to seek knowledge of this world in an effort to progress on the spiritual path, and Sufis offer further emphasis to this sentiment, repeating the *hadith qudsi*,[1] in which God said, 'I was a hidden treasure and I loved to be known, so I created the universe'. The sentiment is that, out of His active love, God caused the universe to come into being. Thus, if the universe is viewed as the embodied manifestation of God's love, then seeking knowledge of it can be practised as service on the path to God. The Shehu's nineteenth-century community was exemplary in this regard, valuing scholarship and women's equal participation in it, in their Sufi context. Many Sufis see life as a pilgrimage to a spiritual Makka: for the Fodio family, at the beginning of the

---

1   The term *hadith qudsi* (lit., 'sacred saying') refers to a Prophetic tradition which, on the Prophet's authority, reports God's words. The authenticity of this particular hadith qudsi, as judged by hadith specialists, is not relevant here. It is widely known and circulated among Sufi circles who believe in the truth of its meaning.

nineteenth century, ascetic practice was viewed as a means of inner illumination, complementary to their intellectual endeavours.

The Toronkawa had converted to Islam at a very early date – possibly by the ninth century – since when they have been dedicated to scholarship and devotion to God. They were Sunni Muslims affiliated to the Sufi order, the Qadiriyya, named after 'Abd al-Qadir al-Jilani (d. 1166); born in the Iranian region of Gilan on the shores of the Caspian. His tomb (in Baghdad, where he died) remains, after that of the Prophet and those of certain members of the Prophet's family, among the most visited and venerated sites in Islam. All across the Sahel the earliest Qadiriyya Sufi communities were localized and lineage-based. They were headed by individuals who were spiritually active as teachers, and socially active as advisers, mediators, and medical practitioners: all were devout, men and women. It was customary for subsequent generations to continue the family's affiliation with the Sufi order.

Sufis often explain that the heart is the guide of the spirit; it is the heart that reflects the luminous blessing of God. Negative behaviour deposits on the heart a spiritual rust that blocks the reflection of God's blessings, so the heart must be polished back to its original translucence by prayer. In his book *Kitab 'Ulum al-mu'amala* (*The Sciences of Behaviour*), the Shehu devotes a section to Sufism, opening with the words: 'Every responsible person must learn enough of this science to enable him to acquire praiseworthy virtues and to keep him from blameworthy qualities.' The book explains that the heart must be purified of the whisperings of Satan, of conceit, pride, false hope, anger, envy and showing off. It says one must turn away from all acts of rebellion towards God and learn to do without everything superfluous to a simple lifestyle. The language of the book is direct and clear. Speaking of envy, for example, the Shehu comments that it is harmful because it shows resentment against what God has decreed, and hateful rancour against the blessing that He has given to someone else:

You are always full of grief and sorrow since God does not cease to pour out blessings on your adversaries. Therefore you are punished by every blessing you see... Fear and hope are among the praiseworthy qualities which you must acquire. Fear is achieved by remembering past faults, the severity of God's punishment, your own weakness and the power of God over you. Hope is the joy of the heart when it recognizes the overflowing favour of God and the vastness of His mercy.

(*K. 'Ulum al-mu'amala*, p. 44)

The eighteenth century brought change to Sufi communities throughout the world. In southeast Asia, India, North Africa, and the Sudan a new style of Sufi establishment emerged from about 1750 onwards that marked a significant break with the past. What the renaissance was exactly remains controversial. What is undeniable is that the refashioned Sufism brought a new educational programme, an organizational structure and a sense of belonging to a wider Muslim world. The family of Shehu ɗan Fodio never considered their scholarship to be merely a localized matter. They were very conscious of belonging and contributing to a universal Sufi community, inspired to produce an explosion of literary activity – poetry, treatises, works on grammar and, rhetoric, prayer and praise of the Prophet – in a Sufi context. By the nineteenth century, the literary production of the Sufi groups in the area lying just south of the Sahara was markedly greater in volume than that of previous centuries, and the Fodio clan's contributions to these canons were significant in both quality and quantity.

Although the geographical area was immense, taking very many months on camel to traverse, scholars knew of each other and communicated by sending messages and poetry, some of which have survived and been translated. Shaykh Mukhtar al-Kunti of Timbuktu, praised by the Shehu as 'an excellent scholar, a refuge, a mediator, and a lamp in the darkness', lived about a thousand kilometers to the northwest of Degel. Though the two men never met, the correspondence between them is confirmed in historical documents. Among Sufi communities in the Sudan there is a myth that the Shehu travelled nearly 3000 kilometers east, into the Sudan, to marry a pious woman there. Evidently the Sudanese community felt connected to the distant Sufi groups in Degel and wanted a tangible indicator of that connection.

Politics

The fascination of the Shehu's personality is that it combined the fundamental characteristics of two different kinds of man – on the one hand, the Sufi who strives to be in direct communication with God, and on the other, the lawyer–theologian who derives his authority from his knowledge and understanding of the law. The Shehu was a rare example of a Sufi leader who was also the leader of a jihad. It was the Sufi side of his personality that contributed to his popularity and the reverence in which he was held; his learning and preaching activities were coupled with piety and self-denial. This Sufi-based charisma inspired the loyalty of his followers, leading them to support his jihad in defence of Islamic norms and practices. Both in his preaching and writing, the Shehu devoted himself to campaigning against deviation from Sunni belief and practice. But it was only with his regular students that he discussed advanced theology and Sufism. On their return to their homelands they advocated and diffused his ideas and enhanced his prestige.

Qur'anic education

The Arabic word *qur'an* means 'recitation'. The Qur'an is believed by Muslims to be the recitation of the word of God as it was conveyed to the Prophet Muhammad over a period of twenty-three years, beginning in 610. Comprised of 114 chapters (*suras*) of very different lengths, the Qur'an has always been memorized in full by the pious, as it was among the Prophet's Companions. Memorizing the Qur'an allows a person, regardless of their level of literacy, direct, permanent access to the divine word. For individuals living in a context where there were few written works around them, this was an invaluable means of providing that access. Among contemporary Muslims, memorization is still prized as a spiritual exercise and support. The text of the Qur'an is to be used with courtesy and stored with reverence.

Fig.1 Pages from a loose-leaf ms. of the Qur'an, copied for Malam al-Qadi Ibn al-Husayn by Sayrallah, completed 15 July 1834.[1]

Belief in the *baraka* (blessing) of Qur'anic letters means that one should be careful not to spoil any page of the Qur'an. The text

---

1 Source: Sheila Blair, 'Arabic Calligraphy in West Africa' in Shamil Jeppie and Soulemayne B. Diagne (eds.), *The Meanings of Timbuktu* (Cape Town: Human Sciences Research Council, 2008), ch. 5, fig. 5.2. Free download from www.hsrcpress.ac.za.

is believed to hold the solution to all problems that have arisen and those that will arise. Unknown mysteries are said to be hidden in the sequence of its letters. To come close to it, by touching and reading from it or reciting it by heart, means to enter the divine presence. The single letters or letter clusters in the Qur'an have a sanctity of their own, but even more, certain *suras* or verses carry special *baraka*, particularly the first *sura*, the *Fatiha* (Opening), which is used in all kinds of rites. Among practicing Muslims its use is ubiquitous, perhaps more so than the Lord's Prayer among practising Christians.

Muslims of the Fodio community saw everything in the light of the Qur'an. This constant awareness of the Qur'anic revelation is the reason that allusions to or quotations from it thoroughly pervade the languages of the region, including Arabic, Fulfulde, Hausa, and Tamachek (the language spoken by the Tuareg). It is impossible to grasp fully the range of references in a classical poem or piece of high prose without understanding the numerous references to Qur'anic figures, sentences, or prescriptions. This is true for all the themes in the works of the Fodio family: a single word can evoke a plethora of related ideas and expressions, clear only to the initiated. These evocations are, as the Qur'an itself repeats throughout, 'for those who can understand'. The education processes that led to the kind of scholarship exemplified by the Shehu started at the age of four or five at a school like the one attended by his daughter Asma'u, where the teachers had for their standard text a copy of the Qur'an. Village teachers throughout this vast region which fringes the desert, owned plots of land worked for them by their pupils when not in class. Teachers acted also as dispensers of curative concoctions and amulets, blessed new buildings, advised on family matters and acted as arbiters in disputes. Education, like Islam itself, was integral to all aspects of daily life.

The Qur'anic school was the starting point of all education: there was no such thing as a merely secular approach to learning.

The essential second step, during which basic Islamic principles were studied, was *tawhid* (i.e. the doctrines associated with Islamic monotheism); with the study of books began formal study of the Arabic language.

In the Degel community, lessons proceeded as follows: a section of text was copied out of the book by the student, male or female, who then read it back to the teacher to ensure that any errors were corrected. The teacher would then explain and comment on the text, which the student would study until it had been fully understood. Only then would the student proceed to copy another section of the book. Students, no matter how advanced their level, approached all books studied formally with a teacher in the same way. This approach has always led to a high degree of memorization of prose and poetry, which has a marked effect on intellectual sensibilities: students enjoy being able to hear, recognize and, in displays of virtuosity, recite, streams of text to order. They also learn how to compose, using the internalized texts as models. Furthermore, in the Islamic system, education is a lifelong endeavour. The student can return to school at any time because students in the Islamic system do not progress in year groups. For the Toronkawa, the Fulani clan into which the Shehu was born, there was neither a centralized curriculum, nor teams of inspectors coming to check on activities. If the teacher was no good, the student went elsewhere supporting himself by working at a trade – sewing long strips of cloth together, weaving, making amulets, binding arrow heads to their shafts, copying books, making book covers, working in the fields – Sufis, whether teachers or students, were expected to earn their keep and live simply.

Nana Asma'u and her legacy

The main focus of this book is the enduring legacy, especially as an educator of Muslim women, of Nana Asma'u (1793–1864),

22

daughter of Shehu Usman ɗan Fodio. Her life offers a perspective on the socio-political culture of her time that is rarely available in history books concerned with the doings of indigenous men as complicated by the entail of Western intervention. The historical events surrounding Asma'u's lifetime and legacy are recounted more or less chronologically and, to the extent practicable, through relevant examples of her writings that record and explain those events. Her life cannot be separated from the politics of the time, nor can the politics of the time be separated from her literary output and her activism as a social reformer. Throughout the itinerancy and battles attendant upon the Jihad that ended with the foundation (in 1808) of the Sokoto caliphate, Asma'u was simultaneously active as a social organizer, a scholar, and a poet (to say nothing of her roles as mother, wife, and sister). Everything she did and wrote was aimed at the betterment of society. She worked alongside her father, brother, and husband in war efforts, in administration, in literary and scholarly productivity and in community welfare. In every sphere of activity they all sought to embody the *Sunna*, to establish, through their actions and written works, an ethical community of believers. With her family Asma'u communicated in Fulfulde; with individuals from the wider society she communicated in Hausa. When not engaged in organizing the affairs of her own extended family or her network of women teachers in the countryside, she communicated with scholars across the Sahara in the lingua franca of Islamic scholarship, Arabic.

The literary, political, and social reform activism of Asma'u sustained throughout her life inspired a following sustained after her death, and even after the massive upheaval attendant on colonization by Europeans. Many educational/cultural activities that carry the stamp of Nana Asma'u and are characteristic of the region have found a new relevance in the present century, not only in the region itself but far beyond it. Accordingly, this book traces the continuation of Asma'u's example and practice as an educator in present-day Nigeria and in present-day North America. Women in both Northern Nigeria and North America continue to identify themselves as Qadiriyya Sufi Muslims, and organize in groups of 'Yan Taru, led by women known as *jajis*, explicitly and self-consciously following the example of Nana Asma'u. Their aim, like hers, is to seek knowledge and improve ethical standards in their communities. Some of the inspiration to do so derives directly from the work of the women of the Sokoto caliphate, as led and trained by Nana Asma'u.

Asma'u's experiences and her accomplishments clarify the fullness of her life as a member of a pious, scholarly family that was drawn into the chaos and suffering of politically engaged warfare. Like other struggling societies in the same historical epoch, this Muslim community of Degel sought to assert its independence, maintain its integrity, and live productively. This book tells the story of how integrally involved Asma'u and her community of women were in shaping the society that grew out of the suffering and upheaval of war. It is a story that reaches far beyond the geographical boundaries of its origins.

1

HIJRA AND JIHAD

Asma'u's early years

At the turn of the century, 1799/1800, when the events that would lead to the establishment of the Sokoto Caliphate (1808) began to take shape, Asma'u was five years old. As was the custom for children at this age, she had just begun attending the village school in Degel. The school was inside the large compound of her father, Usman dan Fodio, a renowned scholar and head of the community of Fulanis in the region known as Toronkawa, those who had migrated eastward from Futa Toro. Later, he was consistently, and with reverence, referred to as 'the Shehu'. The school's low walls and floor mats, where the children sat, defined the classroom for Asma'u and the other girls and boys in the class. They used wooden writing boards and black vegetable ink to practice writing out words from the Qur'an, from whose 114 chapters Muslims try to memorize as many verses as they can. When the teacher judged that she had learned to read the words correctly, and that she understood their meaning, they would be carefully rinsed off the board into a basin. The water, now considered holy because infused with the words of God, would be collected for later, medicinal use. Then she would proceed with a new set of verses to write and commit to memory. Asma'u's teacher was Hadija, her eldest sister. Dressed in home-spun robes, like all women and girls in the region, Hadija led the boys and girls in the daily prayers as well as in instruction. Together they performed the afternoon rituals while, simultaneously, the community was also praying – the women privately in their own rooms, the men and older boys in the open air mosque outside the compound, and the children inside their school.

Fig. 2 Learning to read the Qur'an. (Photo: Jean Boyd, 1982)

In 1800 the Shehu had nine children, and he took a keen personal interest in the education of each of them.[1] Several of them, including Hadija and Asma'u, went on to memorize the entire Qur'an. So it would not have been unusual for the Shehu, on his return from the mosque, to catch sight of his daughter Asma'u, call to her, and spend time chatting with her at the entrance to his room. He would have examined her writing board, read the words aloud for her and then listened attentively while she recited the words back to him, slowly and precisely. They would have talked about her concerns, comfortable in one another's company; then he would have blessed her, and sent her back to the womenfolk for the midday meal. Asma'u's mother, the Shehu's first wife and

---

1   By 1800 the Shehu had suffered the deaths of some of his children, and others were born after this time, but in 1800, the number stood at nine.

also his cousin, Maimuna, had recently died, leaving Asma'u in the care of his second and third wives, both of whom lived to see this child become a legend in her own lifetime.

The community in which Asma'u was being raised was a Sufi community. Its leader, the Shehu, modeled his life and urged others to model their lives, as far as possible, on the *Sunna*, the exemplary life of the Prophet Muhammad. Knowing this clarifies many things in the unfolding of the story of Asma'u – to begin with, her name. The Prophet's beloved grandsons were not in fact twins, but it became customary among Muslims to give to twins the names Hassan and Hussein (the feminine forms are Hassana and Hussaina). In the Fodio family, Asma'u was born a twin, and her brother was duly named Hassan but, instead of the name Hussaina, the Shehu chose for her the name Asma'u. This reminded people of the historical Asma, daughter of Abubakar, the Prophet's close friend and Islam's first caliph. That Asma had been heroic in aiding the Prophet and Abubakar as they prepared their escape from persecution in Makka to the relative security of Yathrib (later renamed Madina). Her legacy is one of kindness, honour, courage, and devotion. Puzzling at first, the Shehu's choice of this name for his daughter is explained by the fact that she was born during a time when he was deeply immersed in mystical Sufi devotions. Asma'u's descendants assume that in the course of these devotions a special insight intimated to him, even before she came into the world, a sense of Asma'u's historical importance. Undoubtedly, the circumstances surrounding the naming of Asma'u had deep significance for all in the community. It was an indication from the Shehu that she would be actively involved in the struggle to secure and serve Islam in her time and place.

The Shehu said his aim was the revival of the *Sunna* in the surrounding region, known as Hausaland, for its majority population. His teaching was targeted not at non-Muslims but at people who professed to be Muslims while practising a syncretic form of religion in which Islamic and pre-Islamic (both animist and polytheistic) traditions were mingled. The Shehu's intention in promoting the *Sunna* was to reform local understanding of Islam among the people to whom he took his message – the Fulani and other pastoralists who roamed the savannah with their herds, the Hausa farmers, the elite of the city and marketplaces, and the officials of the local ruler's court. He aimed to be courteous in approach, aware that being confrontational would provoke rejection. The Shehu's son, Muhammad Bello, an eyewitness, said: [1]

You should know that whenever the Shehu was about to go out to the people I used to see him stop just inside the house for a short while, say some words and then proceed. I asked him about this and he replied, 'I am renewing my determination and I am making a promise to God that my intention towards him will be pure. Also I am asking God to open the eyes of those gathered here to the things which I will tell them. And in spite of this I again renew my determination when I sit down and I remember the promise which I have made.'

(Infak, p. 6)

When he went to them he greeted them in a voice that everyone could hear. His face was relaxed and his manner gentle; then he said, 'Listen!' He never grew tired of explaining and never grew impatient with anyone who failed to understand. After he had called to the waiting crowd with a loud greeting that all could hear, he made his explanations plainly in a quieter voice and in the language of the people who had come to listen, whether in Fulfulde, Hausa, or Tamachek. [2]

---

1   Muhammad Bello, *Infaq al-maysur*. Hausa translation by Sidi Sayuɗi and Jean Boyd, *Infakul Maisuri* (Sokoto: NW State History Bureau, 1974) from the original ms. *Infaq al-maysur* (1227/1812-13) by *Sarkin Musulmi Muhammad Bello*. Here and hereafter referred to as *Infak*.

2   This approach is in keeping with the Prophet Muhammad's advice to teach according to the abilities of the student, and thus to use commonsense in addressing people on their own terms, in their own languages.

One of his criticisms concerned the absence among these people of educational opportunities for women. Although there were urban Hausa scholars in the region at the time, not all had a rounded understanding of Islam, and others ignored Islam's egalitarian approach to the acquisition of knowledge, which included the need to educate not only women, but also any individuals of slave status. The Shehu said:

> Most of our... educated men leave their wives, their daughters and their captives morally abandoned, like beasts, without teaching them what God prescribes should be taught them and without instructing them in the articles of the Law which concern them. Thus, they leave them ignorant of the rules regarding ablutions, prayer, fasting, business dealings and other duties which they have to fulfill, and which God commands that they should be taught.
>
> Men treat these beings like household implements which become broken after long use and which are then thrown out on the rubbish-heap. This is an abominable crime! Alas! How can they thus shut up their wives, their daughters and their captives, in the darkness of ignorance, while daily they impart knowledge to their students? In truth they act out of egoism, and if they devote themselves to their pupils, that is nothing but hypocrisy and vain ostentation on their part.
>
> Their conduct is blameworthy, for to instruct one's wives, daughters and captives is a positive duty, while to impart knowledge to students is only a work of supererogation, and there is no doubt but that one takes precedence over the other.
>
> A man of learning is not strictly obliged to instruct pupils unless he is the only person in the country competent to fulfill this office; in any case he owes in the first place his care to the members of his family, because they have priority over everyone else.
>
> Muslim women! Do not listen to the speech of those who are misguided and who sow the seed of error in the heart of another; they deceive you when they stress obedience to your husbands without telling you of obedience to God and His Messenger (May God show him bounty and grant him salvation), and when they say that the woman finds her happiness in obedience to her husband.

They seek only their own satisfaction, and that is why they impose upon you tasks which the Law of God and His Prophet never especially assigned to you. Such are – the preparation of foodstuffs, the washing of clothes, and other duties which they like to impose upon you, while they neglect to teach you what God and the Prophet have prescribed for you. [1]

As for the Fulani clans who were nomadic herders, the Shehu told them frankly that they were wrong if they believed that being a Fulani was the same as being a Muslim, that the two were not in any way synonymous. He explained that Islam had nothing to do with ethnicity; no matter whether one happened to be a Hausa or a Fulani, a Nupe or a Tuareg. He said: 'Religion comes from God and anyone who follows it is my brother.' The Shehu shared the mother tongue of the pastoralists, but he did not, as they did, believe that their social values were superior to those of others. He challenged their assertions, and spent twenty-five years in regular excursions from Degel to the rural areas to teach and preach to whoever welcomed his presence – Fulani pastoralists and Hausa farmers alike – but he always declined to dwell even for a single night within the city walls of Alƙalawa. The city was ruled by a chief or *sarki* who sought to silence the Shehu's preaching. Instead, the Shehu would camp under a tree outside the city – although no longer standing, this tree was still there until the end of the twentieth century.

What the Shehu said to the Fulani and the Hausas is pre-served in a collection of his Fulfulde poetry in the private archive of Waziri Junaidu and his successors (cited hereafter as Waziri Junaidu mss.). In it the Shehu is forthright in his condemnation of non-Islamic behaviour:

---

1   Usman ɗan Fodio, *Islam and Women* in Thomas Hodgkin, *Nigerian Perspectives: An Historical Anthology* (London: Oxford University Press, 1960), pp. 194–5; translated from *Nour el-albab de Cheikh Otmane ben Mohammed ben Otmane dit Ibn-Foudiou* in *Revue Africaine*, 41 (Algiers, 1897–8), pp. 227–8.

These are what I mean by the paganism practised by many Fulani, the evidence is clear. Consider how they manage circumcision. It is quite wrong. They frighten the children by saying if they cry they will be known as cry-babies. They gather them together in remote areas and do not allow them to return home to their mothers until they have recovered. This may please them but it doesn't please the Prophet.

They permit young men to wear necklaces like women and to plait their hair. They see fit to allow a man who is wooing a girl to be alone with her. They humiliate their wives, when it comes to divorce, by speaking ill of them. Some refuse to divorce their wives no matter how much the wives have suffered. They do not teach their wives nor do they allow them to be educated. Their women behave indecorously when they go to draw water at the well. Some women tell tales about a co-wife to their husbands thus transgressing what God has said. All these things stem from ignorance. They are not the Way of the Prophet.

(Waziri Junaidu mss.)

The Hausa village farmers and urban dwellers likewise practised customs that the Shehu condemned. The list was long: farmers deliberately miscounted their bundles of grain, beans and onions at harvest time so they would not have to pay the obligatory alms-tax (*zakah*); weavers cheated their customers by concealing faulty work, rulers illegally took a share of a person's inheritance; some appeased spirits by throwing cotton buds into a heap of stones at the roadside; others wrote words from the Qur'an on impure material. The Shehu said: 'They congregate in great numbers at certain rocks. There they are, putting stones on them and yet from their speech you would take them to be Muslims.' He also condemned practices that were prevalent in the nearby kingdom of Gobir. These practices were co-ordinated by a female court official who was the sister of the *sarki*:

I will tell you what I mean by their paganism – the practice of gathering for *bori* dancing to induce spirit possession. They go to wizards or to those who call up spirits and even boast of knowing the jinns and understanding what they say.

(Waziri Junaidu mss.)

31

Although the Sarki of Gobir is not directly mentioned in this critique, the allusion to him was evident.

Degel, where the Shehu lived, was at the far end of the territory of Gobir ruled from Alƙalawa. It was not a fortified village. The Shehu and his people were unarmed, living with their families and their very few possessions. They had about twenty transport mounts but no armed cavalry or lances, no protective chainmail or ox-hide shields, nor drums or trumpets. Nevertheless, the Shehu was viewed as an increasing threat by a succession of the rulers of Gobir. In 1802 the chief, Nafata, reneged on previous assurances to the contrary by announcing in the Gobir marketplaces that the Shehu's disciples and followers were henceforth forbidden to preach and invite conversions to Islam. Further, those who had not been born Muslims were ordered to recant, and the wearing of turbans was banned because they distinguished people as Muslims associated with the Shehu's Islamic community in Degel.

Nafata was succeeded as *sarki* by Yunfa, who intensified these restrictions by initiating a campaign of attacks on the Shehu's followers in Gobir. The Shehu responded in February 1803 with a declaration warning Muslims that they should not rise against an unbelieving ruler unless they had enough power to do so. However, if they found that they could not practise their religion or that their safety and well-being were in danger, they must migrate to where there was security. The situation as it developed was portending a defensive jihad, the only sort of warfare formally permitted in Islam. News of these plans drew a swift response from Yunfa, the last Sarkin Gobir to live in the capital city of Alƙalawa:

He sent word to the Shehu that he should go away from his community and leave them for a far place; he, together with his own family, but the rest of the people he had to leave behind.

(*Infak*, p. 18)

The Shehu replied: 'I will not forsake my community but I will leave your country for God's earth is wide.' These words make a clear allusion to the Qur'anic verse (4:97), 'Was not God's earth wide so that you could migrate therein [to escape oppression]?' Thus, like the first Muslims who emigrated to Yathrib/Madina to escape persecution and establish the first Islamic society and state, these Toronkawa emigrated together as a community to a location on the far borders of Gobir, a barren area called Gudu. The hijra had begun and hostilities were not far behind.

The four years of warfare that ensued came to be called the Sokoto Jihad, after the caliphal state later set up in Sokoto. Those who survived the warfare had eventually to reconcile and bind together the peoples of Hausaland, an endeavour never fully accomplished. Bitterness and the desire for revenge had to be replaced with compassion and forbearance. The aim was a new society based on Islamic principles. Foremost among those at the helm of affairs in Sokoto were the Shehu's son Muhammad Bello, Bello's friend and chief adviser, the Wazir Usman Gidado, and Bello's sister Asma'u. Asma'u's role, in particular her pioneering work among the families, has become of iconic significance to women of the twenty-first century.

Asma'u in the Jihad

Asma'u was about eleven when the hijra began and so grew up in awareness of political upheaval. Her recollections of these early years of the Sokoto Jihad inform her later poetic output: her eyewitness accounts of battles add depth and dimension to what contemporary historians know about the era. The Sokoto Jihad began in 1804 with the hijra out of Degel. In 1805 the Shehu's forces, including the whole of the community, women and children also, attacked and were pushed back by their enemies in Gobir. Despite the losses they endured, these setbacks were followed in the same year by victories at Birnin Kebbi and Alwasa. Through 1806 battles continued, and in 1807 (the year Asma'u was married to Giɗaɗo, the close friend of her brother, Muhammad Bello) the Shehu's forces attacked Gobir a second time, and in 1808 captured Alkalawa. The fall of Alkalawa was the single most decisive event of the Sokoto Jihad. Asma'u's part in it is celebrated and legendary.

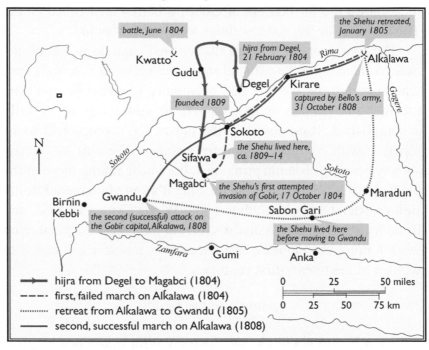

Map 1. The hijra and the marches during the Jihad, 1804–08

According to custom, Asma'u's father chose a husband for her at an early age, the marriage promise marking a long engagement that gave the individuals time to get to know one another and confirm the choice as a fitting one. The Shehu's choice for Asma'u's husband, like his special decision about her name, underlines his respectful relationship with his daughter, and his recognition of her unique value. He planned Asma'u's betrothal

34

carefully, selecting for her a companion who was her equal in character and spirit. Usman Gidado was the best friend of Muhammad Bello, Asma'u's brother and her own close friend and colleague. After years of becoming familiar with her intended husband, Asma'u was about twelve years old at the time of the marriage, a standard age for brides of the period. Gidado was older, as was also common; girls were married when they were able to bear children, but their husbands were usually of an older generation, and more established in life. The Shehu knew that Asma'u had a special destiny; it was therefore important that her husband should enable her character to develop and permit her to go into the world beyond the walls of domestic seclusion. Gidado was affable and good natured – a perfect match for a woman with Asma'u's energy and drive. As a scholar with excellent spoken and written Arabic, he encouraged her intellectual endeavours and, as Bello's closest companion, he was able to foster the convergence of his wife's interests with her brother's .

The orchestration of the hijra is significant in two particular ways that shed further light on the Shehu and the values he promoted in his family. First, it was put in motion only to be delayed for humanitarian reasons. Hadija, the Shehu's eldest daughter and one of Asma'u's teachers, was about to give birth. Her son, the last baby to be born in Degel, arrived on the eve of the date set for the evacuation of Degel, so the Shehu ordered the hijra postponed until after the seventh-day ceremony, when the child was given the name Abdulkadir. Half a century later the traveller Heinrich Barth described Abdulkadir as the finest scholar in the land. It was Abdulkadir who was to translate into Arabic Asma'u's poem about the events of the hijra and the subsequent Jihad.

The second significant aspect of this hijra is the extent to which news of it was spread in the region at a time devoid of modern means of communication. The preparations for departure from Degel had begun several months prior to the anticipated date. Muhammad Bello, the Shehu's twenty-four year-old son, was the liaison officer, in partnership with his friend Giɗaɗo, in charge of contacting allies likely to come to their assistance. The community needed camels and donkeys to transport goods they were taking from Degel, including grain and other foodstuffs to feed everyone. According to Asma'u it was Agali, the Tuareg, who carefully loaded the Shehu's personal effects and collection of books onto his camels. They also needed men with expert knowledge of bivouacking in the wilderness, building shelters, finding water, and knowing how to survive. There was no shortage of volunteers: Tuaregs trekked in from the north leading camels and from the south fellow scholars arrived with food supplies. In addition, Fulani came to the aid of their kinsmen, each with sword, bow, and his matchless experience of living in the bush. It is testament to the Shehu's character that word of his needs spread swiftly and that the popular response was equally swift.

There was not much in the way of clothing and furniture to hoist on to the waiting camels. The Shehu, it is said, had only one set of clothes and tradition holds that when items like his trousers and robe were being washed he stayed in his room until they were dry, quite like similar traditions about some of the Companions of the Prophet. Following the Shehu's example, everyone in the community also dressed with utmost simplicity and propriety. The women wore ankle-length wrappers of locally produced indigo-dyed cloth and a large shawl of similar material to cover the head and shoulders and drape over the hips. There was no furniture, only women's calabashes and cooking pots, mats, pestles and mortars. The most important items were the books which, in the saddlebags of merchants and pilgrims returning from Makka, were regularly transported across the Sahara to be sold or presented as esteemed gifts to scholars like the Shehu. This frontier society at Degel valued books highly. Asma'u, as a major historian of the period, emphasized the part played by the Tuareg ally, Agali, in transporting the Shehu's library, numbering, it is said, up to three hundred volumes, many of which remain in the family compound in contemporary times. These books were not bound. Nearly all were loose-leaf and tied together between special leather covers which held them relatively securely.

It is not known exactly how many people set out from Degel on the 12th Dhu l-Qa'ida 1218 (21st February 1804), but they probably numbered a thousand, more than had been in normal residence because outlying villagers joined them, for example people from Marnona, where Muhammad Bello's grandmother lived. Only the sick, elderly and the very young rode, usually on donkeys already laden with household paraphernalia. It seems likely that Asma'u travelled at Hadija's side to comfort and assist her as she rode with the baby pressed close to her. They journeyed north quite slowly for about five hours, then the signal was given to make camp.

The Fulani who had joined them included women as well as men; they too were expert in bush lore and could help to erect small roofless semi-circular shelters from the branches of thorny trees, hung with grass mats. The older and more vulnerable individuals had similar shelters with the addition of overhead mats. Food had to be prepared. Women pounded millet grain in the heavy mortars heaved off the backs of donkeys, and cooked over open fires to make a porridge which was served with a sauce flavoured with dried onions and *daddawa*, a pungent black paste from the fruit of the tamarind tree. These condiments had been made in advance at Degel, as were nourishing foodstuffs like *murje*, a kind of muesli made from milk thickened with millet flour and sweetened with honey. This was cooked, dried in the sun and finally crushed into granules. There was also thinly sliced meat, *kilishi*, flavoured with oil and mild peppers which was then air-cured making a very tasty accompaniment to the evening meal. At night large

37

fires were lit to ward off wild animals to give confidence to the travellers, because lions and hyenas were not uncommon in the area. The sun was probably high in the sky before the morning activities were completed next day and the pack animals again loaded.

They travelled north for another two days before turning west towards their destination, an infertile desert place called Gudu in the middle of the grazing grounds traditionally controlled by a Fulani ally, Aliyu Jeɗo.

The community heads met to choose their leader. Previously they had been living under the suzerainty of Sarkin Gobir. But now the Shehu, who was already leader in the religious sense and who had renounced any political allegiance to Gobir, was formally chosen as Imam of the community. This was a matter of the utmost importance because, according to the Shari'a, taking part in a jihad becomes incumbent on a Muslim when he is called upon by his Imam to fight. The Shehu as the elected Imam therefore had the right to mobilize all able-bodied Muslim men. Thus they rallied under a single leader with a unifying ideology and shared sentiments.

The Shehu's brother, Abdullahi, was the first to swear allegiance, followed by Muhammad Bello. All this took place under the shade of a tree, the only shelter available in that wilderness. Asma'u later wrote the details of this historic moment, which she had observed as a child, like the name of the tree under whose shade they gathered.

> ...At Gudu God gave him lodging, he and his people.
> There was a *faru* tree there, it was his meeting place
> Beneath it fealty was sworn to him,
> The Shehu, by all including his relatives.
> Everyone resolved to support him.
> Our Shehu appointed his chief officers
> Making ɗan Jeɗo the army commander,

He also appointed a chief judge and a law enforcer …
(CW, #20, vv. 19–23, pp. 137–8)[1]

In the same poem (v. 26) Asma'u went on to say 'the Shehu fought five battles at Gudu', which she later described in detail for her pupils. She had learned by heart what her father had said: 'The Prophet made five raids without the enemy drawing close to his camp and I too made five raids which hurt the enemy'.[2] The analogy with the *Sunna* was obvious to anyone, particularly to the Shehu's students in distant places.

The Hausa leaders were confident that Sarkin Gobir, who had now decided to attack the Shehu, would be victorious once he reached Gudu. In contrast to the Shehu and his followers, the Sarki travelled in style with fine clothes, rugs and a huge ceremonial sunshade to add comfort to camp life. He wore amulets under his robes and turban to protect him from harm, and at his side his sword of German manufacture. As well as foot soldiers, he had a heavy brigade of cavalry – the men protected by chainmail tunics and the horses by padding. He had his own Tuareg allies too. Drummers, mounted on camels or horseback, beat the drums rhythmically as trumpets sounded. In the late afternoon the army made contact with a group of herders grazing their cattle about ten miles from Gudu. The Gobirawa chased the herders who were desperate to escape but caught near a shallow pool of water called Kwatto. Some of the cows were slaughtered and the first cuts to be cooked were juicy chitterlings roasted on sticks around fires. Then, comfortably replete, Sarkin Gobir went to sleep.

At Gudu the Shehu, with the women and children, waited anxiously for confirmation of reports about the Gobir army's

---

1   This and subsequent references marked CW are to *The Collected Works of Nana Asma'u, Daughter of Usman dan Fodiyo 1793–1864* by Jean Boyd and Beverly Mack (East Lansing, MI: Michigan State University Press, 1997).
2   From the Shehu's poem, *'Munasaba'*, v. 14. Waziri Junaidu mss.

approach. Muhammad Bello and Abdullahi had taken up a forward position on a rocky knoll. Whenever they saw the dust devils which, in the hot season, swirl sand into the air signaling an approach, they seized their weapons in readiness, but no one came. Then they heard what had happened from one of the herdsmen who had escaped, and concluded that the Gobirawa had outflanked them. They imagined that the Shehu had been attacked so they galloped back to find to their relief that all was well. However, it was essential to locate the enemy, so with the full moon shining they regrouped and set out, mostly on foot, to find Sarkin Gobir. Muhammad Bello led a surprise dawn attack on a band of men, of whom a hundred had hastily donned their body armour and picked up their shields ready to defend themselves. There was a battle but the Gobirawa were no match for their opponents who were fighting not only for their own lives but also for those of the Shehu and of their wives and children and the community. Asma'u later described this moment:

> There Yunfa [Sarkin Gobir] was driven away and all his army.
> Their horses and their armour were captured and he ran away.
> As well as the royal drums, umbrellas and other paraphernalia,
> They were all taken to the Shehu as spoils of victory.
> Together with Yunfa's personal effects, his boots and sword
> Even his kola nuts were found and seized.
> At the Battle of Kwatto the Haɓe [Gobir army] were in disarray.
> (CW, #20, vv. 28–31, pp. 139–40)

In writing this account, Asma'u knew full well that the enemies of the Prophet had suffered their first significant defeat at a place called Badr even though the Prophet's army numbered only a third of that of his enemies. It was while the full moon, *badr*, was shining that the Shehu's brother Abdullahi led his men to Kwatto. He himself made the connection, writing:

> I said, Quick! Do not let them get before us to our families.
> On the tenth of Rabi – its full moon was rising

40

We came to our families and I passed by my house.
A little before midday our army was drawn up in battle order
Then we drove away the forces of unbelief from their water source
They fled towards the hills, and then they lined up and made their
    drums speak.
While the Muslim army drew near and followed them
Until the moment we saw each other and came even closer
They shot at us and we shot at them, and they turned and dispersed
And there was nothing, except I saw their waterless cloud
Had been cleared away by the sun of Islam which was shining
    through
By the help of Him who helped the Prophet against the foe
At Badr, with an army of angels gathered together.[1]

The defeat of Sarkin Gobir at Kwatto swept over Hausaland like an electric shock. To the Shehu's students news of it was a rallying cry confirming that the Shehu's cause was parallel in justice to that of the Prophet Muhammad. Any account is incomplete which takes note only of logistics, battle formations, siege tactics and weaponry and ignores what the Shehu and his followers believed to be true – that the hand of God was at work.

The fact that the defeat made Sarkin Gobir determined to seek revenge did not cause the community to panic because they were secure in the belief that theirs was a righteous cause. By late August however, with their supply lines broken, they began to starve. There was no alternative but to break out of the noose encircling them. They sought shelter elsewhere, fifty miles to the south where Moyijo, the man who had organized the supply of food to Degel, offered them a well-watered place for their recuperation. Moyijo was able to buy the much wanted grain from the Hausa farmers who were friendly to the Shehu, being familiar with him from his preaching tours amongst them. The future, however,

---

1   Adapted from Mervyn Hiskett (ed. and transl.), *Tazyin al-warakat of Abdullah dàn Fodio* (Ibadan: Ibadan University Press, 1963), pp. 109–10. Cited hereafter as *Tazyin*.

looked bleak. It was clear that they were safe only because Agali and his Tuareg allies were patrolling the wide northern frontier and beating back successive raids from Gobir.

Once they had reached the place Moyijo had prepared for them, the families set to work mending saddles, girths and stir-rups, utensils and mats. They washed and repaired clothes and replenished supplies of the savoury dried ingredients needed in their diet. During the two months spent at Magabci the Shehu sent letters to the chiefs of Hausaland explaining what he was hoping to achieve and inviting their support, much as, in the seventh century, the Prophet Muhammad had sent letters to neighbouring heads of state inviting their support and conversion to Islam. When his emissaries returned with negative answers a decision was taken, according to Muhammad Bello, 'to return with our families to the borders of Gobir in order to find a way of making war on the enemy' (*Infak*, p. 38). From the relative safety of Magabci they decided to march on Gobir – to walk into the lion's den. They took their wives and children with them because without the army the families were defenceless. The camels and donkeys were again loaded and set out with the Shehu in their midst mounted on a white mare, led by his faithful servant. The Shehu, who had indifferent health and suffered periodic longer bouts of illness, travelled with the families and camped at night very close to the military headquarters.

The first and most disastrous defeat they suffered was when the Shehu's eldest brother, the standard-bearer, was killed. On that occasion, when it seemed all was lost, the Shehu, mounted on his horse, rode to the battlefield praying aloud for the enemy to be repulsed. The enemy withdrew but not before they had killed two thousand men of the community, two hundred of whom were men who knew the whole Qur'an by heart. There were too many bodies to bury that night so the task was resumed in the morning. Muhammad Bello wrote 'these martyrs of the faith were buried

42

unwashed to ascend into heaven with the dust of battle on them'
(*Infak,* p. 43). The women, in the tradition of Fatima, the Prophet's
daughter, tended the injured, washing their wounds, staunching
flows of blood and holding water to the lips of the dying. In
adversity the community grew closer together than ever before.
They depended on one another and the fortitude of each man and
woman was equally valued, each person's suffering viewed with
compassion. The lessons learned on the battlefield remained with
Asma'u all her life and moulded her character.

Despite having been badly mauled, the Shehu's army had
no thought of defeat. The decision was made to advance on the
Gobir capital, Alƙalawa. They travelled there with the families
and all their possessions, such as they were, and stayed a month
outside the high walls of Alƙalawa with its deep and slippery
moat, fighting during all this month. The women heard the cries
of attacking horsemen and the howls of men transfixed by spears
and the screams of those having the wounds from barbed arrows
cauterized. They suffered too; there was not a single family left
untouched by death, disease or pain. Among those killed was the
gallant Tuareg Agali who died of wounds sustained in an ambush.

By January 1805 it was clear that unless they obtained food,
the Shehu's people would starve to death, so a retreat was ordered,
a withdrawal covered by a valorous rearguard action mounted
by Muhammad Bello. Men, women and children limped out of
Gobir; they were emaciated and sick, their skin inelastic and
their bodies prone to any infection. Many suffered ulcerated cuts
and contaminated wounds which only a period of rest and an
improved diet would heal. Their sandals and thigh length riding
boots were worn out, their clothing tattered, their saddles in need
of repair, indeed many tools, cooking utensils, rope and water
skins were beyond mending. The Shehu reorganized his forces
in a new camp a hundred miles to the south, deep in the bush –
his simple mosque is still there – and allies arrived with all that

was needed in the way of food, medicines and implements. The outlook brightened and with renewed strength they looked to the future. Only four months later Abdullahi captured the seat of the Hausa state of Kebbi whose chief had refused to come to terms with the Shehu. This was a great morale builder. Asma'u recorded that much booty was obtained; she wrote: 'As Aaron helped his brother Musa, | So Abdullahi helped his brother the Shehu' (CW, #20, v. 60, p. 144[1]) and quoted verses 20:29–32 of the Qur'an:

> And give me a minister from my family, Aaron
> My brother. Add to my strength through him
> And make him share my task.[2]

Despite the victory, the Shehu's company had its own internal problems. News of the Jihad had spread rapidly throughout Hausaland prompting many young men to join the Shehu, who had made new headquarters at Gwandu, in the land recently conquered by Abdullahi. The new recruits were not wholly beneficial to the cause. They were eager to fight but, when put to the test, some of them behaved like hooligans. The lure of adventure and booty, including women and slaves, is what drew some of them to the Shehu's side, and such motives led to serious misconduct on their part. A large army of camel-mounted dissident Tuaregs, together with their Gobir allies, marched on the Shehu's headquarters. In advance of their arrival some of the rash newcomers to the Shehu's army, disobeying their commanders, made an unlawful and brutal attack on a friendly village. Abdullahi later described this debacle, writing: 'And the majority of them have traded their faith for the world, preferring what they desire. And their hearts burn for forbidden pleasures and they devour them as beasts devour grass' (*Tazyin*, p. 118).

---

1   See also p. 65, vv. 18–25.
2   This and all susbsequent citations of Qur'anic passages are from the interpretation given in Abdullah Yusuf Ali's *The Holy Qur'an* (Elmhurst, NY: Tahrike Tarsile Qur'an Inc., 2nd US edn.,1988).

From this point the Shehu's forces were pushed back until their opponents had encircled Gwandu and were clearly visible on the black stony hills. The fighting raged for several days as the enemy closed in. Again all seemed lost but the tenacity of the defenders weakened the attackers who withdrew when they saw one of their leaders crying out with pain as he and his horse were struck down with arrows. Defeat had been narrowly averted. The relief felt in Gwandu would have been especially welcome to the women and children who witnessed everything at close hand. There were about fifty enemy wounded lying close by inside the perimeter of the camp; the women stoned them and left them there exposed in the sun. Asma'u experienced these years of warfare, the movements back and forth and the battles, observed and remembered. Her character, forged by her encounters, developed a steely quality throughout her life and her later military verse needs to be read in the light of her personal experiences; it is stern, sometimes without leniency, when addressing recidivists. It was certainly not the work of a sheltered, untested individual.

Muhammad Bello always lived on the danger side of his father, in the quarter from which an attack was most likely to come. So his camp was about fifteen miles north of Gwandu at a place called Salah. Tucked into the folds of a V-shaped valley it was a stony place with a ribbon of fertile soil in the valley bottom. His neighbour was Gidaɗo and it was to Salah that as a bride in 1807, years after having been betrothed, that Asma'u was conducted by the women she had lived and trekked alongside since they had all lived at Degel. It was at Salah that the standard was raised over the house of Muhammad Bello, where it fluttered for forty days.

Then the army set out for Gobir taking the same route they had followed three years before, in November 1804. Battle commenced; the Sarki and his bodyguards fortified by the rousing words of his sister, the *Inna* of Gobir, put up stiff resistance but were all killed. Sarkin Gobir's mother was captured together with some of his wives and the whole of Alƙalawa torched. The Commander in Chief, Muhammad Bello, sent a messenger post-haste back to Gwandu with the good news of the triumph but when the messenger arrived he found that the Shehu somehow already knew and had told the people who were with him. When the news spread through Hausaland the whole backbone of the enemy resistance was broken and victory assured.

The fall of Alƙalawa was the single most important event of the entire Jihad and, in popular folk-memory it was Asma'u who aided her brother. There is no written source of the story, yet it is the stuff of legend. In towns and villages if you ask if they know about Asma'u they will say, 'Asma'u? Was it not she who helped Bello at Alƙalawa?' Ask further and they will say she hurled a burning brand into the city of Alƙalawa and set it on fire. With slight variations this is the belief of the person in the street and it is essential to know this to understand the veneration in which Asma'u is held today. She is not just a daughter of the Shehu, she is Nana Asma'u, the Lady Asma'u.[1]

---

1   In the twenty-first century an American Shaykh long affiliated with the Fudiawa explains the belief that Nana Asma'u was personally responsible for the turning point in this battle, owing to her deep spiritual powers:

'If you will recall, there is a story circulated among the communities of the Fudiawa (I heard it while sitting with some of the elders in the market in Maiurno on the Blue Nile); that once when the Shehu was in Bodinga with his daughter Nana Asma who was sitting before the fire cooking something for her father; when suddenly, the Shehu pointed at the eastern wall of the compound and said: "Look!" And suddenly they saw her half-brother Muhammad Bello, her two in-laws, Muhammad Namoda, and Ali Jeɗo involved in intense combat against the fortress of Alƙalawa, and they were having some difficulties. [...]

Then suddenly, Nana Asma took one of the hot embers and flung it at the easterly wall through which the time/space continuum had been broken and said: "Burn! Alƙalawa!" Suddenly, at least according to the legend, the western part of the fortress of Alƙalawa burst into flames, and Muhammad Bello and his forces were able to conquer the town. [...]' (Personal communication from Shaykh Muhammad Shareef, 3 September, 2011.)

Asma'u and the establishment of Sokoto

From the smouldering ruins of Alƙalawa there was an exodus; some of the men of Gobir escaped northwards to join up with other dissidents, the rest were taken captive – men, women, and children alike. The city was garrisoned by Bello's forces who bivouacked close by. The walls and principal buildings began to collapse and disintegrate as they were battered season after season by the annual brief monsoon-like rains. Today the remnants of the dye pits and the area of pure clean sand mark the grave of the eighteenth century Sarki Bawa, Jan Gwarzo, famed for his valour and ability. But there are no ruins; it is a quiet empty area where Fulani now graze their cattle, although Gobir people murmur disapprovingly at the sight of such disrespect.

The fate of Alƙalawa was not shared by any of the other capital cities of the Hausa states. In Daura, Kano, Katsina and other places the city walls, impressive gates and nearly all the dwelling houses remained intact. The huge houses of the *sarki*s and their titleholders simply acquired other occupants in the shape of the new emirs appointed by the Shehu. The vanquished *sarki*s were killed or took refuge in remote refuges together with their surviving followers. At the beginning of a new political entity new emirs received letters like this (cited from Jean Boyd's field notes):

> From Imam Usman ɗan Fodio to his brother in Islam, the Emir of Bauci, Yakub.
> I greet you, and all who are together with you.
> This letter is sent to inform you that I have made you Emir of your people. There are seven things I recommend you to do.
>
> Be consistent; agree in objectives, never quarrelling.
> Repair the mosques.
> Pray in them.

Study the Qur'an and its teaching.
Study all aspects of religious learning.
Maintain the markets and prevent wrong doing in them.
Wage the jihad, which is a duty.

The Shehu's position was unassailable. Today scholars who have themselves tried for decades to change things in Nigeria express their amazement at the speed with which the Shehu, a Sufi scholar, living a life of austerity, was able to revolutionize the political system of Hausaland. He was admired, acclaimed, sought after and deeply revered. His personal prestige was unique. By 1807, even before the fall of Alƙalawa, when he was living at Gwandu, people from all points of the compass, including the Sultan of Agadez, journeyed to pledge their allegiance.[1]

After 1808 Muhammad Bello decided to build a *ribat*, a fortified town at Sokoto. The place he chose was on top of a ridge facing north-east in the direction of Gobir. According to tradition, a group of dyers lived there, a belief borne out by the discovery of dye pits during excavations made in 1961. The river which flows past Sokoto provided drinking water, which was transported up the hill in goatskins tied to donkeys, and after the annual flood waters had receded, the flat alluvial plain had as much potential

---

1   Adding to commentary that harked back to the Shehu's example, radical academic, Bala Yusuf, guest speaker at the opening ceremony of the International Seminar on Islam and the History of Learning in Katsina State 1992, said: '…the men ruling us in the last quarter of the twentieth century seem unable to reform this society… [According to] the statement by Shehu Usman ɗan Fodio in his powerful political work *Bayan Wujub* (1806): "a kingdom can endure with unbelief but it cannot endure with injustice." This will not make any sense to the armed forces, the Federal Executive Council, the Presidential Advisory Council and the boards of private companies and banks, but to those who understand the Shehu and his ethics, it is quite clear.' Bala Yusuf, 'The State of Learning, the State of Society: from the Jihad to the S.A.P. [Structural Adjustment Programme]' in Isma'ila A. Tsiga and Abdalla U. Adamu (eds.), *Islam and the History of Learning in Katsina* (Ibadan: Spectrum Books, 1997).

for irrigated farming as did the land surrounding Alkalawa, land which the Gobirawa had tilled so well and to which they returned to farm again, fifty years on.

The pioneer settlers with their wives and families, many of whom had lived at Degel, went to Sokoto in 1809. Muhammad Bello's first wife Aisha was his cousin, the kind of alliance intended to cement families together. He had another wife, also called Aisha, who was Asma'u's best friend and confidante. In a document written at the end of his life Gidado listed the names of all Bello's wives and of some of his concubines. In a separate document he named all the Shehu's wives. Gidado had twenty-seven sons and twenty-one daughters; the names of the children are known, but their mothers' names were not recorded, except for Asma'u's . The names are known of her husband's ancestors and her own ancestors going back for centuries, and that she had six sons. The first died in infancy in about 1815 when Gidado and Asma'u were at the Shehu's house on a day visit. The other five grew up in Sokoto and the names of over five hundred of their descendants have been recorded. All ten of the Waziris who followed on from Gidado have been descended from his wife, Asma'u.

At first the families lived in simple huts while more substantial houses and a town wall were built by the slaves captured during the campaign. Slavery was not introduced into Hausaland by the victors of the Jihad. To go back two thousand years, it seems probable that the Romans traded in slaves from the region south of the Sahara and that later the Arabs and Berbers simply took over a trade which already existed. By the 1600s Hausaland had become involved in the complex trans-Saharan slave trade which persisted along the southern edge of the desert. Some of the slaves captured in raids passed into the northern transit area where Arab and Sudanese middle men took over, but a much larger proportion was absorbed into domestic slavery in Hausaland itself, where the extended family was centred on a large farm tilled by slave labour. The system persisted because the slaves were readily assimilated into the family of the head of the household who assumed a paternal relationship towards them. Large holdings functioned as a single farm unit for the provision and consumption of food, the issuing of tools and seed, the exploitation of economic trees and even the provision of brides for members of the group. When not busy on the farm the workers were free to cultivate, for their own benefit, smaller plots allotted to them, and they were encouraged to practise crafts such as pottery, smithing, weaving, leather-working or mat-making. Others worked as builders, thatchers, dyers or tanners. Post-Jihad women were not allowed to work on the farms as they had been used to doing before they were captured. Otherwise, life after 1808 was for everyone very much like it had been when they lived in Gobir.

The following extract from the diaries of Commander Hugh Clapperton who, as a guest of Giɗaɗo, stayed in Sokoto for eight months makes the point:

> Domestic slaves are generally well treated, the males who have arrived at the age of 18 or 19 are given a wife and sent to live in their new villages to farm in the country (on estates owned by Sokoto notables), where they build a hut and till the land until harvest. They are fed by their owners. The hours of work for their masters are from daylight to mid-day, the remainder of the day is employed on anything he may think proper. At the time of harvest each slave gets a bundle of different sorts of grain for himself. The grain on his own ground is entirely left for his own use... The domestic slaves are fed the same as the rest of the family with whom they appear to be on an equality of footing.[1]

---

1   H. Clapperton, *Journal of a Second Expedition into the Interior of Africa* (London: Frank Cass, [1829] 1966), pp. 213–14. Thirty years later, explorer Heinrich Barth, also noted the same prosperity and remarked that domestic slavery was very little offensive to him as a traveller: see Heinrich Barth, *Travels and Discoveries in North and Central Africa* 1849–55 (New York: Harper and Brothers, 2nd edn., 5 vols, 1857–58).

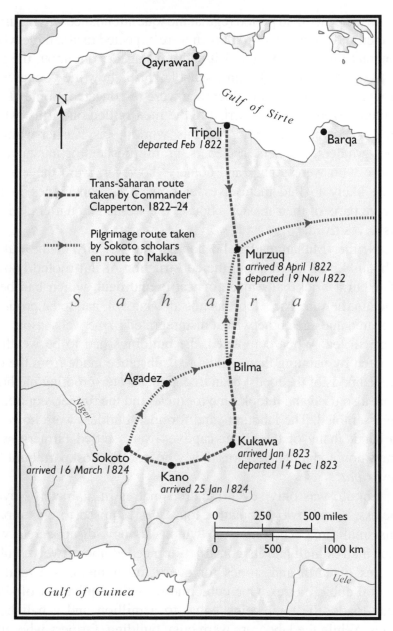

Qayrawan

Gulf of Sirte

Tripoli
departed Feb 1822

Barqa

N

Trans-Saharan route
taken by Commander
Clapperton, 1822–24

Pilgrimage route taken
by Sokoto scholars
en route to Makka

Murzuq
arrived 8 April 1822
departed 19 Nov 1822

S a h a r a

Bilma

Agadez

Niger

Kukawa
arrived Jan 1823
departed 14 Dec 1823

Sokoto
arrived 16 March 1824

Kano
arrived 25 Jan 1824

0   250   500 miles

0   500   1000 km

Gulf of Guinea

Uele

Map 2. Trans-Saharan route taken by Commander Clapperton

In the post-Jihad period regular mosque attendance was required of men and older boys. Adult men were expected to assemble when itinerant preachers paid a visit and boys aged from about the age of five had to attend Qur'anic school. This is how the young were brought up in Islam, and older men were re-educated. Some of the captured women were married to the men settled on farms, while others became household servants working as washer-women, corn-grinders, spinners, sweepers, grain-threshers or nursemaids. Those who were young and comely, however, were the women most likely to find themselves ensconced as concubines in the secure parts of their master's house, the women's quarters, where his wives lived.

Neither Muhammad Bello nor Gidado nor any of the Fulani scholars knew much about the construction of flat-roofed houses of unburnt brick balls made of wattle and daub which had been dried in the sun. The adobe, as it is also known, had to be properly prepared and aged otherwise it disintegrated in the wet season, like sugar in tea. When completed, the buildings had to be weather-proofed by painting them with a red substance made from the de-seeded pods of the locust bean tree. Other water-proofing methods were also used and it took time for these and the timber required to be assembled. The labourers and foremen builders were however to hand, many of the Gobir captives were settled farmers, who knew how to build and it was they who, for the most part, built the new *ribat*.

Sokoto was only seven hundred metres in diameter. Nevertheless, a wall two kilometres long was required to encompass this small area. The city wall, which has now disappeared, was four metres high and its construction needed about twelve cubic metres of earth and stones for every linear metre – a total of 24,000 cubic metres. One cubic metre is the equivalent of sixty head-loads, the total being equal to a million and a half head loads. While the labourers were busy building, farmers who until recently had tended the rich agricultural lands around Alkalawa, were settled on the area between the rivers of Sokoto. They planted sweet potato, rice, sugar-cane, spinach, fruit trees, peppers, onions, cotton, indigo, plantains and pumpkins while on the drier uplands they grew millet and guinea corn. They were good at their occupations and eventually there was a plentiful supply of food.

At the beginning of this new settlement at Sokoto, Asma'u lived with her husband in temporary – and in the wet season quite leaky – accommodation, not dissimilar to the Fulani bivouacs she had been living in since May 1804. Eventually Muhammad Bello's adobe house was finished, parts of it being supervised by a master-builder whose father had learned his trade in Egypt. It is now the home of the Sultan of Sokoto. Gidado's home, now the Waziri's, was situated just round the corner from Bello's. Asma'u's big circular room in which she lived for the rest of her life is still there and houses the regalia of Gidado, including his sword.

In 1812 there was excitement in Sokoto when it was announced that Muhammad Bello's daughter Saudatu was to marry the Emir of Kano, Sulaiman, a very ascetic man who had, at first, declined to live in the vast palace of the previous rulers, believing it to be too ostentatious. The wedding party set out on the seven-hundred mile return journey in about 1813 under the protection of Gidado, the bride herself being accompanied by Asma'u, then aged about twenty. The procession moved slowly because the women, who rode astride, were novices and their horses had to be led by grooms. It took the procession about a month to reach the massive walls of Kano. As they entered the gate they were met by the Emir who, with a throng of followers, escorted Gidado to the palace. The bride and her retinue, surrounded by a crowd of ladies, followed in their wake. It is said that the Emir himself served the food that Gidado and Asma'u ate. The Shehu was not in attendance, but it is recounted by Gidado that the Shehu said to Asma'u when she returned home:

You did not enter the fortress of Kano except that I was with you. When you all had entered, all the men of Kano came out to greet and escort Giɗaɗo and all the women came out to greet and escort you. When you all had reached the palace of the *Amir*, I saw what he did for you in the courtyard of his palace. He was extremely generous toward you by serving you himself. He kept coming to and fro with abundant food and drink the entire day for you. The Shehu then said:, 'The *Amir* Sulaiman exhausted himself on your behalfs that day.'[1]

When the Sokoto visitors began their return journey they did not leave young twelve-year-old Saudatu on her own. She had a few elderly women from home to look after her, as well as several Gobir girl playmates who as each grew into womanhood became a concubine of the Emir. Wives had legal entitlements, the right to a share of her husband's time equal to that enjoyed by any other of his wives, an equal right to prepare his food and equality in the distribution of presents usually made at the Islamic Eid festivals. In contrast, a concubine had no hut or room set aside for her discrete use but shared quarters with the women she served. However, if she bore her master a child she became free – she was no longer a slave and could walk out of the house if she wished, the caveat being she could not take the child with her. On the other hand, all her children, male or female, had equality of status with their siblings born to the husband's wives. A slave's son could become caliph, as for example did Muhammad Bello's son Aliyu, born in 1808 of a Gobir woman concubine called Ladi while Bello was at Salah.[2]

---

1 This citation, from *Rawd al-Jinan* – which, as far as Boyd knows, has not been translated and published – is taken from Sidi Sayudi's translation from Arabic to Hausa, and to English by Jean Boyd. Both these are only in Boyd's notebooks.

2 In contemporary times it remains customary for children of concubines to inherit the social status of their father; several Emirs in Kano have been sons of concubines. Their mothers inherit their own title of Queen Mother and have a separate residence when their son is installed in office.

At sunset in Sokoto the key was turned on the door of the women's quarters of the large houses occupied by the new political leaders, and the women spent their evenings secure together at home. The wives spoke their mother tongue Fulfulde and also Hausa, the lingua franca. The concubines, who in some houses were in the majority, spoke only Hausa. These were difficult circumstances which had to be handled with tact and patience. The wives on the one hand had vivid memories of the years they had spent trekking through lonely and dangerous places; they also remembered the tranquillity of life at Degel. The concubines on the other hand recalled their lives at Alkalawa – their comparative freedom, and their leader, the sister of the *sarki* known as *Inna*. They remembered also the terror of being captured when Alkalawa was sacked. All the women, Hausa and Fulani alike, had suffered; none had remained unaffected by the deaths of relatives and friends and here in Sokoto and elsewhere the women had, by force of circumstances, to live, not adjacent to their former enemies, but together with them while, at the same time, sharing the same husband and bringing up their children in an atmosphere conducive to their development and to household harmony.

While the Shehu was alive, respect for his authority meant that peace reigned. In acknowledgement of his failing health in 1815 he moved to Sokoto into a new house Muhammad Bello had built for him on the western part of the *ribat*. The city wall had to be extended to accommodate all the buildings and the new mosque. Asma'u said: 'He spent two years here. From the beginning of the year in which he died, he was preaching, explaining Islam to the people. Then he passed on to the next world on the 3rd Jumada 1232 (20th April 1817).'[1]

He was 63 years old, the same age as the Prophet Muhammad had been when he died. Hundreds of thousands of people

---

1   Waziri Junaidu, *Tarihin Fulani* (Zaria: Northern Region Literacy Agency, 1957), p. 24. This is a Hausa translation of his *Dabt al-multaqatat*.

travelled to Sokoto to express their condolences to the family. It was then and still is an essential part of Islamic etiquette, a duty. The Shehu's successor, Muhammad Bello, together with other male members of the family and advisers took up their positions, seated cross-legged outside the Shehu's house to receive and respond to the formulaic prayers for the repose of their leader's soul.

Quietly, with heads bowed in acknowledgement of the gravity of the occasion, the mourners left to be replaced by another group and then another. The recipients of the prayers changed as this or that person grew weary. From morning till night, and for days and weeks, they came. Women gave their commiserations to the senior ladies of the Shehu's household in private. Asma'u, her sisters and other senior ladies sat with them giving comfort and support. Then she returned home to receive her own streams of grieving women.

Meanwhile, Muhammad Bello – the acceptance of him as the community's leader after the Shehu could never have been in doubt – became 'Sarkin Musulmi', the Muslims' chief. There was work to do: new emirs and their officers had to be advised on the problems confronting them, taxes collected, the poor fed, booty distributed, legal disputes settled, malefactors punished, mosques repaired, the city walls patrolled and, there being no standing army, householders had to be ready when called upon to repulse raiders. In all aspects of his work Bello was advised by his life-long friend Gidado, now given the title of Waziri in acknowledgement of his appointment as head of the civil service.

The Shehu's library contained many books, some of which were rare and therefore of great importance. Bello, one of the heirs to this inheritance, reached an agreement with his brothers that the library would not be divided between them. He then asked Gidado to supervise a group of scholars as they assembled and listed the books. Asma'u explained that Gidado was concerned about the 'preservation of the Shehu's books which he collected and had copied | Because he feared they would not survive | And if they were not [copied] they would be lost' (CW, #28, vv. 19–20, p. 201). An established tradition among Sokoto scholars likens this to the work of Caliph 'Uthman who ordered the Qur'an to be compiled after the death of the Prophet.

Asma'u was one of the scholars best able to work in the rooms in the women's part of the house, and Gidado himself wrote that the Shehu kept books in each of his wives' rooms. The problem was that books of that era, as already noted, were not sewn into bindings, but left loose-leafed. To keep them safe each was enclosed in a box or leather slip-case which was then tied to keep the pages in position. Pamphlets containing only a few pages would be stacked together. When certain pages needed to be rewritten, due to wear and tear, fire or water damage, a section could be removed and sent to a copyist or parts might be loaned out to fellow scholars. This unfortunately often led to a book's fragmentation. First the library was very methodically checked, then lists made, volumes reassembled, repairs done and then all the items rehoused in the leather satchels, boxes or slip-cases most appropriate to them. Asma'u, in the tradition of the family 'a very neat person' was unusual in dating her compositions, and made a significant contribution to the task.

The new caliph, Muhammad Bello, saw the proof of Asma'u's competence in the work she had done. No one could have done it better. Bello was a man whose pragmatism led him to make bold moves, an example being the ways in which he mentored his sister. Further evidence of her capabilities emerged when she produced in 1820 at the age of twenty-nine a literary piece with the title *The Way of the Pious*. As far as is known, this was her first composition and it is important because it shows how clear her vision was in relation to her life's work. Her piece was patterned on her own priorities which emerge as she wrote:

Affection for the Muslim community [is] shown by working for its best interests and defending it against injuries or losses; [and] asceticism in worldly affairs. … Other signs [of love for the Prophet] are humility towards fellow believers and avoidance of discrimination between them; and keeping good relations with one's relatives, servants and comrades. …This is shown by being cheerful with them, doing good things for them, serving them, never acting as if superior to them, consulting them in many matters, helping them financially and physically, not coveting their possessions, not covering up any of their blameworthy affairs that one may discover, and not excusing them for such things, nor boasting to them of wealth, position, or nobility, visiting their sick ones and offering them advice without any pretense or excessive conceit. … Moderation – the avoidance of ostentation or extravagance – is necessary in food, drink and dress.

(CW, #1, ch. 4, pp. 26–7)

She spent the next forty-five years of her life teaching these virtues to her students.

Asma'u's life in the early years of the Caliphate

It was in October 1821 that all Sokoto heard that the raiding parties headed by Sarkin Gobir Aliyu and a powerful Tuareg chief named Ibra were close at hand. Asma'u knew that Ibra had been at odds with a fellow Tuareg compatriot of his, a religious reformer who had sought safety in Sokoto, whereupon Ibra sent a message to Bello saying: 'I do not wish to fight you. I was hunting and wounded a guinea fowl. It flew off and entered your house; let me have my guinea fowl back.' Bello had then replied, 'Your guinea fowl is in the pocket of my robe. He who tries to take it will have to tear my robe first.'[1] Ibra was now on the warpath.

---

1   Unpublished Hausa translation by Sidi Sayudi, *ca.* 1978–80, of *al-Kashf wa-l-bayan 'an ba'd ahwal al-Sayyid Muhammad Bello* (1254/1838-39). Cited hereafter as *al-Kashf.*

Campaigns in those days were usually mounted after the harvest, because the rains, on which planting depended, made laterite tracks impassable and the wide swathes of guinea corn, with stalks like saplings, made the passage of a large body of men, many of whom were mounted, well-nigh impossible. The invading northerners, moving rapidly, reached a place four miles from Sokoto where they made camp on what is now the site of Shehu Usman ɗan Fodio University. By sitting tight Bello had lured his enemy towards his Sokoto stronghold. An estimated 120,000 people would have been living there at the time, many of whom were of Gobir origin.

Asma'u's husband, Gidaɗo, wrote an account of what happened. He said that when Bello's spies reported that Ibra had actually arrived he went to the war camp outside the Kware Gate, which was about half a mile from his house. Bello coolly decided to return to the city to preach his usual Thursday lesson in the mosque. Gidaɗo reported (*al-Kashf*):

He left me but it was not long before I heard the *tambari* (drums) of the enemy, so I went to the mosque where I found Bello so intent on his preaching that I could not distract him from his address. It was only when he ended what he wanted to say that we returned together to the camp.

According to a family tradition, which Asma'u's great-grandson Waziri Junaidu explained in the late twentieth century, Asma'u went to Bello's house that night – the enemy's camp fires could clearly be seen as she walked there – and she entered the room of her childhood friend, Aisha, Bello's wife, where she was told that Bello had left a message for her. It was a fourteen-line poem, in Arabic, inspired by the Qur'anic text (94:5) well known to Muslims, 'so verily with every difficulty there is relief': 'Are you apprehensive knowing that your Lord is powerful?' wrote Bello, 'Do not be despondent but anticipate the bounties, God's plans are proceeding accordingly. Joyful relief

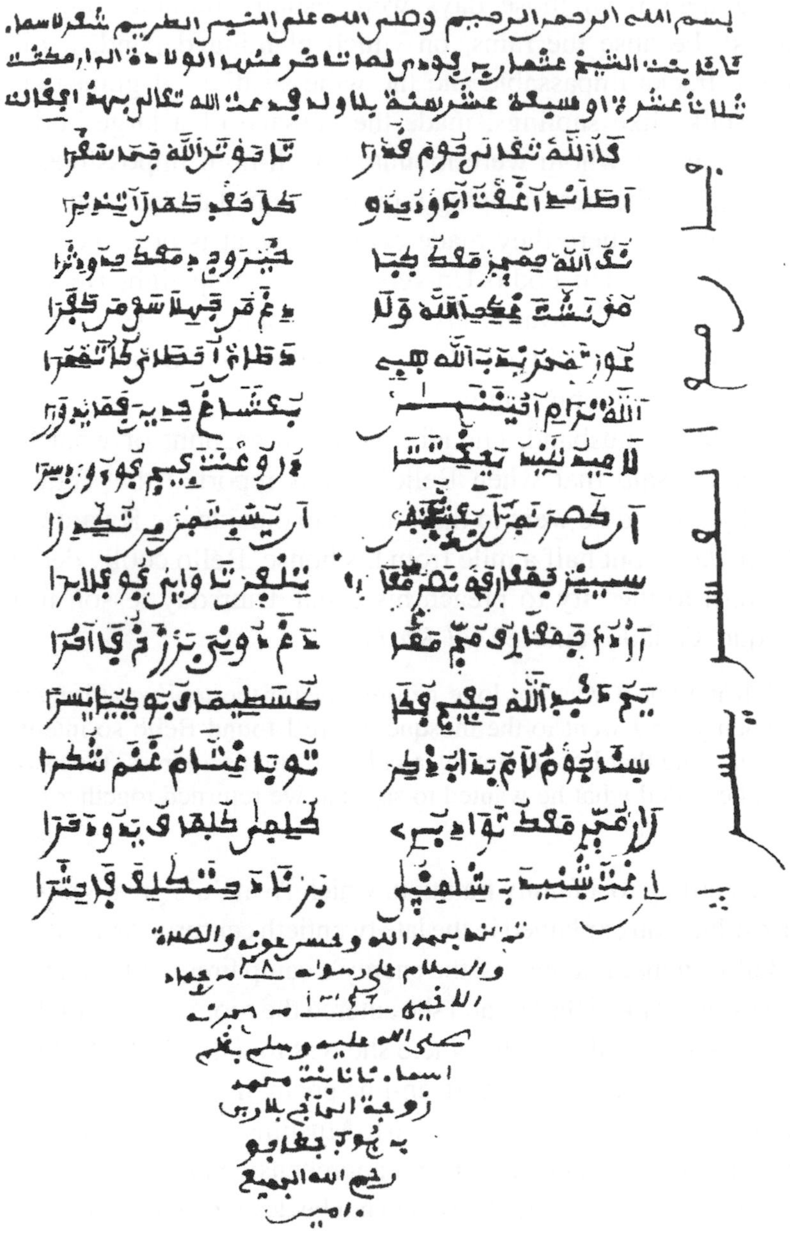

بسم الله الرحمن الرحيم وصلى الله على النبي الكريم شكرا اسما،

كان بعد النبي عشمار بها يؤدي لما تاضر عشبه الولا دة الما، مكث

ثلا نا عشر؟ او سبعة عشر بسنة بلا ولد بعد حمد الله تعالى بها؟ اعقاب

كأن الله تعلم تقوم قدرا	تا تو ترا الله بعد شقر
أطا شد أغث اربو وزيدو	كل مك طها را يدنو؟
شك الله يميز مك بجا	تبيترو م د مك يدوانرا
مؤنشة يكيد الله و لا	د غ قر قيلا سو مر طقرا
غوز تحرز بد الله هيي	د طا م اقطام كا تفعرا
الله ترام آتينف	بعشاع حديد بقدا يد ورا
لا مية لنبذ تبيك شا	درو عنت كيم كو أو وبسا
آر كصر تمتا يعن بب	آر يتشبتمز مر تطدا
سيبيز بقعارقه نعر ما	ينلبرت وايل كو بلا برا
آر دا يمعا ى مم مقرا	ذ م أويز بزر م قا آخرا
يم د نبد الله يعيى قما	كسطيم ا ربو يتبا يسرا
بسد كوم لا م خا بد طر	تو با نشام غنم شكرا
آل قمر مك توا د يس	كليمل طبقا ى يدو وقرا
ا نبذ بنية ب شلهيل	بر نا د تكليك قا يترا

نه انه بحمد الله ويسرعون والصلة

والسلام على رسوله ﷺ مجمد

الا نبيه ١٣٥٢ مد بمرته

صلى الله عليه وسلم بغم

اسما، بابانة مجمد

زوجة النا في بلاري

بد جود بغا بو

رتم الله الجميع

با مين

Fig. 3 Ms. of Asma'u's celebrated poem, 'So Verily'.

will come soon from God.'[1] Asma'u probably spent the night with Aisha and it was during that night, before the battle had been fought and the final outcome known, that Asma'u responded with a fourteen-line acrostic poem in Fulfulde based on the text Bello had given her, 'so verily with every difficulty there is relief'. This is the first example of their shared authorship, their literary collaboration.[2]

The invasion was concluded when Ibra's consultation with soothsayers revealed bad omens, which destroyed his confidence. According to Gidado, Ibra decided that night to head for home, but Sarkin Gobir Aliyu disagreed saying:

> If we try to return immediately we will perish, let us therefore stay here as if intending to attack Sokoto but in the pre-dawn hour we will skirt Sokoto to the west and south and make a raid on Gandi (a few miles to the south east).

(al-Kashf)

Gidado's account continues:

> But when they started to break camp and move away they were detected by our vanguard which attacked them. God caused their defeat and Ibra fled until his horse collapsed and his turban fell off. They left so many mounts and saddles that each of our men took as many as ten camels as his own share of the booty.

By the mid-1820s Sokoto was thriving. Travellers and traders from the entire Sudan region thronged its streets, according to Commander Hugh Clapperton when he made his visits. Staying in Gidado's house he had ample opportunity to learn about the city. There had been bumper harvests and living conditions were good; the rivers teemed with fish and meat was cheap. There were potatoes, wheat, bread made by Arab bakers, fruits of many kinds including figs, onions, *daddawa* – made from the fermented

---

1   From Bello's untranslated, unpublished poem, also titled '*So Verily*'. In the collection of Waziri Junaidu and his successor.
2   See Boyd, *The Caliph's Sister*, pp.35–7.

seeds of the tamarind tree and used in the same way as today's maggi cubes – indigo, cotton lint, hand loomed white cotton cloth, dyed goatskins, considered superior to all other skins in any part of Hausaland, shoes, boots, saddles, bridles, salt and dates from the desert; kola nuts from present day Ghana; swords from Germany; paper from France; glass beads from Italy; china, pewter, umbrellas, Manchester-made cloth from England; and books from North Africa, Egypt and Makka.[1]

It is true that some areas on the frontier were under threat and the Caliph was on bad terms with the Shaikh of Bornu to the far east, but the impression given by Clapperton was that of a prosperous city ruled by a man, Muhammad Bello, who, in Asma'u's words:

...had his affairs in order and had an excellent intelligence service... He was a very pleasant companion to friends and acquaintances: he was intelligent, with a lively mind.

(CW, #14, vv. 28, 30, p. 93)

It was the lively mind which so impressed Clapperton at their first meeting on 17th March 1824. Bello, not surprisingly, as this was the first European he had ever met, asked many questions about England, and then stumped his visitor with the question 'Were the English Nestorians or Socinians?' (Clapperton vol. 1,

---

1   Hugh Clapperton, *Narrative of Travels and Discoveries in Northern and Central Africa: in the years 1822, 1823, and 1824 by Major Denham, Captain Clapperton, and the late Doctor Oudney, extending across the great desert to the tenth degree of northern latitude, and from Kouka in Bornou, to Sackatoo, the capital of the Fellatah empire. Narrative of Travels and Discoveries in Northern and Central Africa* (London: John Murray, 1826).
    Hugh Clapperton, *Journal of a Second Expedition into the Interior of Africa: from the bight of Benin to Soccatoo; to which is added the Journal of Richard Lander from Kano to the sea-coast, partly by a more eastern route* (London: John Murray, 1829; reprinted, London: Cass, 2 vols., 1966). Cited hereafter as Clapperton, vol. 1 or vol. 2.

p. 82). Since the former were followers of Nestorius, appointed Patriarch of Constantinople in 428, and the latter were members of a sect founded by Laelius and Faustus Socinius, sixteenth-century Italians who denied the divinity of Christ, one can hardly blame Clapperton for being perplexed.

In subsequent meetings Bello said he particularly wanted to meet with an English physician who might instruct his people in the healing art, something he himself was deeply interested in, as was his sister Asma'u. Clapperton exhibited his sextant and planisphere of stars. Bello, he found, knew all the names of the zodiac, some of the constellations and many of the stars by their Arabic names. He was just as interested in his visitor's English saddle. 'He examined it very minutely and said it was exactly like the ancient Arab saddle described in one of his books' (Clapperton, vol. 1, p. 94). He had heard of newspapers and asked Clapperton to send him some; he wanted to know about the Greeks and he talked about the Moors of Andalusia. He asked searching questions about the Royal Navy's defeat by an Algerian force in 1816 and, on the subject of British activities in India, amply demonstrated his concerns about long term imperialist ambitions and the likely implications for Muslim Africa. Clapperton chanced on him one day with the Arabic copy of Euclid that he had given to Bello as a present. Bello said his family had once had a copy of Euclid brought by one of their relatives from Makka, which had been accidentally burned the previous year. (Clapperton, vol. 2, p. 198)

Clapperton described men's attire as consisting of a red cap with a blue tassel, white turban, white shirt, long white robe, white trousers trimmed with red or green silk, sandals or boots. Clapperton himself, at least on formal occasions, wore his lieutenant's coat trimmed with gold lace, white trousers and silk stockings, Turkish slippers and a turban. Perhaps he was thus attired when he visited Bello, whom he described as a noble looking man, forty-four years of age 'although much younger in appearance' He was 5ft. 10in. tall, portly in figure, with a curling black beard, a small mouth, a fine forehead, a Grecian nose and large black eyes. When he was at home he dressed in a simple cotton robe with a turban arranged to go round his head and also under his chin so he could draw it up to cover his mouth and nose, a custom still followed, especially when the air is full of dust brought by the harmattan wind. (Clapperton, vol. 1, p. 83)

One day Bello received Clapperton in a part of the palace his visitor had never seen before. He reports (vol. 1, p. 109):

It was a handsome apartment within a square tower, the ceiling of which has a dome supported by eight ornamental arches with a bright plate of brass in its centre. Beneath the arches and the outer wall of the tower the dome was encircled by a neat balustrade in front of a gallery which led to an upper suite of rooms.

Outside the door of this tower was a bell which Bello would ring if he wished to summon his confidential messenger, an old Gobir slavewoman who had occupied a similar position for the last Sarkin Gobir to live at Alƙalawa, the one killed in 1808. Her first responsibility was to take messages back and forth to Gidaɗo, in whose house she also had an apartment, and into whose presence she could enter at almost any time of day or night. The room described by Clapperton disappeared long ago when the palace was undergoing one of the not infrequent improvements. Fortunately, an apartment at Yabo matching Clapperton's account has escaped modernization. Yabo is twenty miles from Sokoto and is near Magabci where the Shehu and his people sought shelter after being forced to leave Gudu in 1804. It is possible that Bello arranged for Clapperton to meet him in the part of the palace he had never visited before so that Asma'u could be present in the gallery and satisfy her curiosity about the visitor.[1]

---

1   Jean Boyd has visited and photographed the room – the gallery is wide enough for one or more persons to observe through the balustrade, without detection, what was taking place below.

Clapperton had taken an instant liking to Waziri Giḓaḓo, whom
he described as 'an elderly man who spoke Arabic well … as polite
and as kind as any man could possibly be' (Clapperton, vol. 1, p. 81).
Clapperton spent by far the greater part of this time with his host.
They became fast friends 'discoursing on every possible subject'.[1]
Waziri took him out riding to see his estates, visit building projects
for which he was responsible and a new mosque being constructed
at his own expense. But the Commander was never invited to see
his family. He thought that when a child died of smallpox in the
house it was Asma'u's and sent his condolences. The child may
have been in her care but it was not hers. Some of his meals were
brought by girls from Giḓaḓo's household who were all allowed to
visit his compound. He wrote, 'inside the house they sat primly but
when outside they giggled and played'.[2] Clapperton observed that
women's activities included: directing female slaves, cooking the
husband's food, cleaning cotton lint and spinning, dressing hair,
teeth and eyebrows, sending slaves to market to sell cotton thread,
cooked food and fried cakes. In other words, their activities were
entirely concerned with the domestic scene.

The entrance hall to Giḓaḓo's house always had a servant in it,
sitting cross-legged on a mat ready to answer visitors' questions
concerning Waziri's whereabouts and the possibility of seeing
him; he would also politely intercept anyone he didn't know, hush
noisy children and turn away persistent hawkers. The big courtyard
had trees at one end under which Waziri's horses were tethered; in
contemporary times a horse is still kept to be ridden on ceremonial
occasions.

From the courtyard there was, and still is, an inconspicuous
entrance to the women's quarters, only accessible by passing
through a number of occupied anterooms. The movement of people

1   J. Bruce Lockhart, *A Sailor in the Sahara* (London: I.B. Tauris, 2008)
     p. 154.
2   *Ibid.*

into the main entrance and thence to the great hall, library and Waziri's private apartments was, in Asma'u's day, regulated by a majordomo figure. In the late twentieth century he was likened by Waziri Junaidu to his own majordomo Shehu Chachaka who served him for sixty years, a man who, with tact, humour, firmness, and dignity kept everything in good order.

Asma'u's room was large and circular. The walls built of adobe were only about five feet high and one had to stoop to enter. The thatched roof was a huge dome which rose high over the centre of the room and dipped to overhang the walls by a good two feet. At the end of the twentieth century there was a threat that the room would be pulled down to be replaced by a modern bungalow-type house but the traditionalist view prevailed. The thatch is covered alas by tin pan and the walls have received a skimming of cement, but the overall effect is much the same as it was. Asma'u's bed, if she followed the Shehu's example, would have been a grass mat. Her husband had his bed to the right of the door; hers was on the left, following the habits of pastoral Fulani.

Asma'u had her dowry, large decorated calabashes, arranged against the far wall, and her library of books stored neatly in ornate goatskin satchels hanging on hooks from the walls. The writing materials she used varied. When drafting her works or putting words down for a grandchild (her first was born in 1829), she used cheap black ink, which could easily be washed from the board she was using. When writing out a poem, or any other composition, she would set it down on paper brought across the desert from the Levant and the best and least corrosive ink available; her pens were quills. Also in her room she had a vessel holding clean water for her ablutions and a brazier on which she sprinkled a little locally available frankincense resin, which lightly scented the air. An oil lamp gave out a flickering light.

Fig. 4 In Asma'u's room: in her day, her dowry would have been 'large decorated calabashes...' (Photo: Jean Boyd, 1982)

Every day she rose before dawn, did her ablutions followed by the morning prayer, then she said her *dhikr*, a litany of praises to God, using her beads. She read aloud from the Qur'an in a low murmuring voice until the sun came up. Then, she signaled that she was prepared to face the day by opening her door, where-upon the womenfolk and children would come in a steady stream to exchange greetings with her. After sipping a bowl of *fura*, a yoghurt type drink thickened with millet flour, she checked that the children were busy with their reading boards – probably calling one or two to her side to hear them read for her – and then entered the schoolroom where girls and women were reading at a more advanced level.

Breakfast of rice with a butter sauce was taken about ten o'clock, according to Clapperton, who ate the same food as the household, after which Asma'u would receive petitioners, women who came to her for advice because she was learned. In the law book written by Abdullahi dan Fodio, it said, 'there is no calamity worse than a ruler keeping aloof from the peasantry'.[1] This advice, it seems, was in Sultan Abubakar III's mind when he wrote the following:

Make a habit of being always available at a given time, either at your office or at home, to listen to the people who wish to speak to you. Ensure no one tries to prevent this from happening by demanding money from the complainants before they are taken to see you.[2]

Asma'u, undoubtedly the leader of women, made listening to the complaints of ordinary women part of her daily routine. They said of her, 'she benefited the aged and indeed anyone who came could depend on Nana because she was generous and also a peacemaker...' (Elegy for Asma'u; CW #65 v. 9, p. 380). When women came, one at a time, they would find her seated on a mat outside the entrance to her room and could see on the lintel over the door the outline of two hand prints. One day the Shehu returning from escorting an illustrious scholar to the North Gate was invited to call at Gidado's house. In an extraordinarily rare gesture the Shehu asked permission to visit his daughter in her room in the women's quarters or *cikin gida*. There he put his hands on the smooth reddish adobe over the door, where the prints remain as a dazzling endorsement of her status. They were visible during the lifetime of Waziri Junaidu and have since been covered for protection.

---

1   Abdullahi Fodio, *Liya' al-hukkami*, Hausa translation by Haliru Binji, (Sokoto, 1965), p. 8.

2   *Mai Rigar Fata*, Sultan Abubakar III, Regulations and advice to District Heads. Undated typescript, locally bound in leather, possibly 1940s, following an earlier version in the 1930s by Sultan Hassan.

2

ASMA'U'S ROLE IN THE CALIPHATE

Nineteenth-century life in the harem

As we noted above, in the 1820s, following the period of the Jihad, Commander Hugh Clapperton recorded some observations about the domestic side of life in Sokoto – the harem. He described the women's roles as active and significant:

> The activities of the wives of the principal people are as follows: directing the female slaves, cooking their husband's food, cleaning cotton lint, spinning thread, dressing hair, teeth and eyebrows and sending slaves to market to sell spun cotton, grain, *fura* (yoghurt like drink), cooked fish and fried cakes.
>
> (Clapperton, vol. 2, p. 207)

Clapperton also commented: 'They are allowed more liberty than the generality of Muslim women' (ibid.). Whether he was comparing these women to other Muslim women that he had observed, or was simply referring to a prevalent stereotype, is unclear. His observation that women had prominent roles in Sokoto society, as they oversaw the production of materials necessary to daily life, certainly challenged the prevailing nineteenth-century image in the West of the harem as a place where women were sequestered, waiting listlessly to be called to provide sexual service to a high-status man. This stereotype was belied by eye-witness reports by individuals like Clapperton in Sokoto, and by others earlier and elsewhere. For example, Lady Mary Wortley Montagu, wife of the ambassador to Constantinople (1716–18), had remarked that it was thanks to seclusion and veiling that women were able to travel incognito, and that Ottoman women had in reality more liberty than English women had. The harem is merely the domestic centre of any Muslim home; inherent in its definition is the idea of sanctity, and protection from intrusion by outsiders. It was a focus of fascination in the West during the nineteenth century in large part because its protected nature veiled it from the eyes of male colonials, who concocted fantastic tales about a sanctum for women they were not allowed to see. In a 1982 article Egyptian scholar Leila Ahmed described the harem as an arrangement that enabled women to have frequent and easy access to other women in their community, a place where women could exchange experience and information, and critically analyse the world of men.[1]

In the nineteenth century the harem was invoked to garner support for missionary work under the guise of restoring women's dignity through Christianity. The popular novelist Joanne Trollope, writing in 1983, quoted from a missionary source as follows:

puerperal fever, after childbirth, was worse in India than in any other part of the Empire, and the evil was compounded by the purdah system, one of the recognised principles of Indian life since the Muhammadan invasion of the eleventh century.

The restrictions of the purdah system imposed upon women are scarcely credible. It did not simply mean that a women might see no man except her husband, or in some cases her nearest relations, but more brutally that she spent her life in a room or a series of rooms often windowless, sometimes with windows too high to see out of, the doorways screened with grass in a most unhappy confinement. There was no air, no exercise, and no occupation. Education was impossible … the female mind was supposed to dwell on the family and religion and the female hands to be idle altogether unless engaged in the simplest household tasks.[2]

---

1   Leila Ahmed, 'Western Ethnocentrism and Perceptions of the Harem', *Feminist Studies*, 8/3 (1982), pp. 521–34.
2   Joanna Trollope, *Britannia's Daughters: Women of the British Empire*,

That picture bears little or no resemblance to the life of women in Sokoto following the Jihad, and since then.[1] The Caliphate household belonged entirely to the women. Husbands did not look after the babies, protect toddlers from the fire, toilet-train the two-year-olds, or teach good manners to the pre-school youngsters. They did not cook, wash the dishes, scour the pans, launder the clothes or sweep the floors. Asma'u may have had servants, but pregnancy, and the bearing and raising of children, each of whom was breast-fed for up to two years, were tasks she could not delegate. She bore six sons, which meant that for twenty years a great deal of her attention and energy were child-centred. The death of her first-born must have had its long-term effects in the way of an increase in the level of anxiety about her infant children and, in due course, her grand-children. Servants in a big household had to be managed, given their orders and supervised, those working in the women's part of the house just as much as those elsewhere in public rooms, courtyards and stables, the world of men. Women in the harem were fully engaged in their work, and the authorities in those circumstances. Most importantly, the domestic context is not to be dismissed, for it was the basis of social life, and provided

---

(London: Hutchinson, 1983), p. 87.

1   The personal contacts of both Jean Boyd and Beverly Mack with Hausa and Fulani women in Northern Nigeria belie this condition of restricted life-experience. Boyd lived in Sokoto and regularly visited the homes of Nigerian friends there throughout the second half of the twentieth century. Mack lived in Kano 1979–1981, and visited royal women in the palace, and other women in their homes. In both Sokoto and Kano women were actively involved in the orchestration of social and domestic work central to the management of the community. Their roles are valued for their importance. It has been alleged by others that Asma'u was privileged: not burdened with domestic routines she could concentrate on enjoyable preoccupations, notably writing, in a way that was denied to many others. Boyd has seen no evidence to support that perspective.

the foundation for any political or battle engagements in which men were involved, providing the food, clothing, and medical care, without which such engagements could not be sustained.

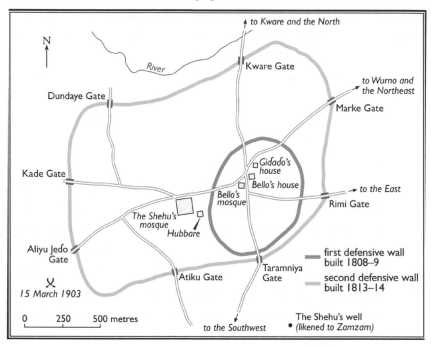

Map 3. Plan of Sokoto, founded 1808/9

In Gidado's house the manager of the harem (*cikin gida*), was his senior wife, the *uwargida*, Asma'u. She did not herself pound grain into flour, pluck and gut chickens or wash pots, but no woman who oversaw such a large community would have done so herself. Instead, Asma'u's portfolio included the overall management of the domestic scene, of which meal production was a significant portion. In addition she had special responsibilities as the wife of the Wazir, the Caliph's prime minister who ran the Chancellery, and travelled to distant emirates on diplomatic errands, as well as taking part in military campaigns. He was a hospitable man who gladly accommodated foreign visitors, like Clapperton. The daily consumption of food was therefore large; the number of chickens and rams, the amount of fish and grain eaten in the household was considerable. Bread was made from wheat, butter, melons, figs – 'some of the finest I have eaten in Africa', said Clapperton – sweet potatoes, rice and plantains. Some visitors travelled long distances and arrived weak and in need of extra care, others had large retinues to be catered for. The women of the household, especially those who prepared the meals, had a major role to play even if they were unseen by male visitors.

Occasions of celebration involved an increased workload for women. During the fasting month of Ramadan the day began long before dawn for those who cooked, because a substantial meal was taken before dawn. During the daylight hours small children and the infirm ate as usual. Meanwhile, adult women who were themselves fasting nevertheless prepared the special food for breaking the fast after prayers at sunset. This was accomplished over open fires, in the heat of the day. At the end of Ramadan, the first of the two Eid festivals was celebrated. For this, everyone who could afford them wore new garments which were stored away until the dawn of the Eid. The men and boys resplendent in their new clothes assembled at the outdoor prayer field beyond the Rimi gate. Headed by the Caliph, his advisers and imams, they prayed in unison then, escorting the mounted Caliph, they returned to the city in a colourful parade complete with drummers and trumpeters and a procession numbering thousands, many mounted on horses or camels. Meanwhile, the household's *uwargida* was responsible for planning and supervising all the work that had to be done by the harem women including the time-consuming tasks involved in the making of the special cakes – those made of wheat, butter and honey, similar to baklava, and called *tsatsafa*, *waina* and *dibla*. These cakes were always in demand, not only for the Eid festivals but also for the celebrations of marriages and births. The work involved was labour-intensive. The *uwargida* was certainly not the stereotype of an inert, bored, oppressed harem captive.

Jean Boyd gives an eyewitness account of what it was like in the women's quarters during the production of a wedding feast fifty years ago in Sokoto:

All the women were at work busy preparing the normal evening meal and there were many fires blazing and pots bubbling. The jobs they did varied. For example two women were grinding peppers; each was kneeling down rubbing a pumice-like rock over peppers, two or three at a time, against a flat slightly tilted stone. Another woman was sorting the wheat from the chaff by cleverly using a large *fai-fai*, a flat tray made of tightly woven grass. She bounced the grains on this device, gradually sorting the heavier wheat grain from the much lighter chaff before gently tossing them into their respective containers.

Yet another woman was pounding millet using a large free standing wooden mortar and a long pestle, the thudding of which added a rhythmical dimension to the workshop.

Uwargida, herself a grandmother, was cutting up onions and toma-toes which she tipped into a huge bowl ready to make soup. But she kept a very close eye on everything that was going on.

Making sweet cakes for the forthcoming feast was Maimuna, a specialist in the art. She was a very big woman with great soft pillow-like shoulders and hair which was puffed into small balls just above her ears. She started off by making the *dibla*. For this she heaped about a kilo of *alkama*, local brown wheat flour, into a bowl and one by one cracked ten eggs into the flour, kneading each one thoroughly with a little water until the mixture stuck together into very dry dough. When she was satisfied with the consistency of the dough she added drops of oil to give the big round ball the elasticity she required. A brazier was then brought which was set on the ground. It was no more than 20 cm in height. A blackened cooking pot of much the same height as the brazier was fitted snugly into it. A fire was lit under the pot which was then half filled with oil. Maimuna started to roll out the dough, a complicated process she was clearly skilled at. She pressed the dough out very gently, rolled it round a rolling pin and then sliced it down and opened it up. Carefully picking each piece of very thin dough she flapped them and they stretched enormously. Each piece she then folded into a loose knot. When a few had been prepared the oil was tested to see if it was hot enough. With Maimuna satisfied on this point she tossed the cakes into the hot oil and they immediately puffed up. After a few minutes they were removed and drained. Finally they were carefully dropped into a dish of deep brown honey before again being put out to drain.

The *tsatsafawa* was different, being made from a batter of flour and water to which an unidentified thin syrup made from soaked tree bark was added. The ingredients were well beaten then poured through a calabash which had holes in it like a colander, into hot oil. Each cake bubbles up but remains flat and resembles a crunchy pancake. The many processes were very time consuming and the heat of the kitchen was overwhelming. [1]

The year's second Eid commemorated the Prophet Ibrahim's obedience to God and perfect trust in Him. Those who were able to do so, made pilgrimage to Makka at this time, but for others, the commemoration was local, and involved a great feast, much as it does to this day. On the morning of the Eid, the symbolic sacrificial ram was taken to the prayer field and slaughtered in the *halal* way, an event witnessed by all who had gathered there, and prayers were said. Then, with the crowd in joyful mood, the Caliph was escorted back home and everyone dispersed to kill their own rams, goats or whatever they could afford. Some would slaughter more than one, depending on the size and wealth of the household. Neighbours helped each other with the flaying and cleansing of the carcasses, then the intestines, the liver, heart, kidneys were sent indoors to the women's quarters where everything was washed and cut into bite size pieces prior to being fried in wide-mouthed pots set on small portable stoves or open fires. As the tantalizing smells of cooking meat wafted from house to house, the job of distributing the delicacies began.

---

1   Observations made by Jean Boyd at the house of Madawaki Abubakar, *ca.*
     1960.

All this took until the late afternoon to complete, by which time the rams had been tied to stakes which were hoisted into place around slow burning fires. Neighbours often shared a fire whereby the evening became a pleasant social affair as men strolled out to view their rams while they cooked and took a turn at conserving the good fat as it melted and ran down the animal or tended the glowing embers. By morning the meat was cooked and could be distributed to friends, relatives and particularly to the sick and the poor. It was a time for everyone to join in the feast, which could not have been enjoyed at all if not for the work of the women.

Fig. 5 Rams roasting in the traditional way. (Photo: Jean Boyd, 1979)

The chief daily activity of women was spinning. Raw cotton was bought, then deseeded, a job for little girls with nimble fingers, and spun using spindles made from a raffia rib stick and a clay whorl. The lubricant came from burned and powdered bones or from gypsum and the sap of a local tree. Two basic kinds of thread were produced, first a tightly spun cotton thread, *zare*, which was used for the warp threads attached to the loom. The second, a more loosely spun yarn, *abara*, was used for the weft. Each type was wound onto storage spindles which, when full, were sent to the market for sale, probably the women's market near Gidado's house, which continued to function until the 1950s. Asma'u would have known how to spin cotton as it was the Shehu's Sufi practice to work at spinning every day until he felt he had earned what he ate. And because she knew how to spin, Asma'u would certainly have recognized faulty goods when she saw them. Any kind of deception or cheating was strongly condemned. No matter which of the servants was in charge of this kind of operation, it was Asma'u who was ultimately responsible for what emanated from her household.

Within the harem, restraint, forbearance, and patience were required of everyone if harmony was to be achieved. Among the women in a large household, this was a tall order, as jealousy was common, despite the ideal of equality that was supposed to be enjoyed by all. The women who comprised the harem were of various statuses, depending on their origins. A typical large harem would include an *uwargida* and up to three other wives, all of whom had Fulfulde as their mother tongue, but who also spoke Hausa. The number of concubines a man took varied considerably. Concubines were captured slaves, or (later) women of slave parentage. After their capture, slaves were, naturally, frightened, apprehensive, and resentful. On arrival at the house of their new master decisions would be taken on their future: this person or that to the farm, those two women to so-and-so's house where triplets had been born and the mother was in great need of assistance, that man to the stables, and this girl to his household as a new concubine. The concubine was a clear outsider, speaking only Hausa, and often the object of the wives' jealousy. Her role in relation to the wives of the household was that of a servant, while her role in relation to the husband was that of an unofficial wife. Any offspring of a husband and concubine inherited the social status of the husband, even up to royal position.[1]

The Shehu had only one concubine, Mariya; in this he was once again following the *Sunna*, the example of the Prophet Muhammad. Bello had six or more. Because the concubines in general spoke only Hausa, they were at a disadvantage; wives, if they wished to be spiteful, could chatter away in Fulfulde. That was something Asma'u warned about in her works. She wrote in 1854, 'Do not utter malicious gossip... Do good works for the day will come when every person will have to look on the actions he has done' (CW #35, vv. 5, 6, pp. 222–3). If a concubine won the deep love of her master, sooner or later, the matter would become apparent to the watchful wives. Tension was inevitable under these circumstances and much depended on the mediatory leadership of the *uwargida*. The husband had a duty to spend an equal number of nights with each of his wives in turn. Wives had separate apartments, unlike the concubines who shared smaller rooms. But the slave girl in favour could be called to his private place, *baraya*, as often as he wished. At another level, an understandable source of irritation in the harem was the jealousy some mothers felt when they saw how well the sons and daughters of others were doing and how indolent were their own children. A child who had read through the Qur'an by the time he or she was twelve years old was obviously very intelligent and might just as easily be a concubine's child as a wife's ; that child

---

1   Any child, regardless of whether the mother was a wife (free-born) or a concubine (slave status) would inherit the social status of the father. In royal circles especially it has long been the case in Northern Nigeria that sons of concubines to the emir are eligible for selection by the committee of king-makers as a successor to the emir. This has happened on numerous occasions. An emir's mother inherits a royal title and her own residence, along with its attendant servants, regardless of whether she was a wife or a concubine

could, if he were a boy, one day succeed to his father's position – everything was possible.

The role of the *uwargida*, in any household, was therefore of crucial importance. Asma'u was the hands-on manager of the harem: the post was not transferable. She had to use tact and persuasion to bring people round. Patience and the importance of reconciliation were lessons learned in the home. Children who grew up knowing that compromise was a useful tactic and not tantamount to surrender, knew better than most how to deal with the problems of the outside world. Things left with Asma'u were in safe hands, and she used her poetry to promote the peaceful attitudes she fostered. Asma'u's role as a social reformer began in her immediate surroundings, the harem, where she dealt effectively with women of a multiplicity of ethnicities, social statuses, traditions, and languages. Her ability to organize and train them is reflected in the advice she offers in her poetry, as is her experience of the political events of her time. Asma'u's role as overseer of the harem is but one of many related facets of her character.

Among the ruling classes, marriage took place within the kinship group which comprised only the descendants of the Shehu and his principal appointees, for example, the Commander in Chief, Chief Imam, and Chief Judge. Girls were spoken for while they were still very young. A contemporary account of the life of Habsatu, the daughter of the Waziri Maccido (d. 1925), helps to clarify the procedure. Habsatu, a great-great-grand-daughter of Gidaɗo and Asma'u, was noticed by Ahmadu Bello, later to become Sir Ahmadu Bello, Sardauna of Sokoto and Premier of Northern Nigeria, when he was in his early twenties and she was a little girl.[1] She was betrothed to him when she was seven and married when she reached maturity at about the age of twelve, around the same age that Asma'u had been when she married

---

1   Ladi S. Adamu, *Hafsatu Ahmadu Bello: The Unsung Heroine*, (Kaduna, 1995), p. 24.

Gidaɗo; consummation of the marriage would not take place until the girl's physical maturity. A recently published book, sanctioned by the Gidaɗo family, shows how the children of Waziri Junaidu (d. 1997) (great-grandson of Asma'u: Waziri Junaidu ɗan Waziri Buhari ɗan Ahmadu ɗan Asma'u) married their kinsfolk just as predecessors had done over many decades.[1] Daughters had married into the families of people in their peer group, like the Imams of the Sultan Bello Mosque or the descendants of senior judges, the *alƙalai*, and the marriage of the Waziri's sons followed the same pattern. Kinship was very important, and nothing much has changed since Asma'u's day.

What has changed since the time of the Shehu is the number of babies that survive infancy; the child mortality rate has declined considerably. In the past, and until the 1980s, many children died before they were five. Asma'u's first-born son died; her own mother Maimuna lost eight children; only the twins, Hassan and Asma'u, and an older sister survived. Some infants died in the birthing process, others because their mothers had post-partum complications. The weaning stage took its toll, childhood illnesses such as measles posed a threat, cerebral-spinal meningitis, smallpox and polo were rife, and dysentery a scourge. High mortality rates among young children remained constant and the traditional solution to the dreadful unhappiness caused by these tragedies was adoption. A woman adopted her younger brothers, sisters, nephews and nieces in the kinship group. She brought them up as her own so that some boys and girls would not know that she was not their natural mother, and no one would tell them. Safe and cared for, they were part of the family. We do not know how many children Asma'u adopted, but her elegy, which was still being sung in the city streets in the 1970s, described how 'she helped orphaned boys and girls' (CW, #65 v. 11, p. 380), yet another facet of her busy life which is hardly ever referred to.

---

1   Ibrahim Junaidu, *Rayuwar Wazirin Sakkwato* (1993). (This biography of Waziri Junaidu was published locally at the Fadama Printing Works.)

Asma'u during Caliph Muhammad Bello's last decade

Until the twentieth century, for most western Europeans (excepting intrepid explorers like Clapperton and Barth), Degel, Sokoto and Hausaland were terra incognita. However, great caravan routes had been established across the Sahara for centuries before Clapperton set out from Tripoli in mid February 1822 heading for Fezzan, a journey of forty days. There he had to wait until 20 May when he and his companions and a two-hundred-strong Arab escort spent another eighty days on the main desert passage before reaching the northernmost fringes of the Sahel. This was a journey regularly made by Arab merchants and scholars; what was difficult for Europeans had been normal for Arabs. In Kano there was a large Arab community; by the 1830s this may have been exceeded by the Arab population in Sokoto, for Arabs liked to 'travel with a purpose' (Ar., *rihla)*, whether for scholarly exchange of ideas, or for commercial exchange of goods, services, and technologies. Travellers may not have known the local languages of the places they visited but they knew Arabic, the *lingua franca* of Muslims. They felt at home and could converse effortlessly with the educated classes. The Sokoto Caliphate was part of Arab civilization stretching from the Atlantic to Asia, a place in which religion, learning, politics, trade and warfare were mutually understood and visitors were well received.

In Sokoto in 1835, the visit of Qamar al-Din, a prominent Egyptian shaykh, was warmly welcomed by the Caliph Muhammad Bello. The Shaykh arrived with gifts, the most important of which were rare and interesting books. Two books in particular seized Bello's imagination: the first was about Sufi women and the second about medicine. He started with the book *Safwa al-*

Safwa, Sufi Women, written by 'Abd al-Rahman Ibn al-Jawzi, who lived all his life in Baghdad and died in 1201. Bello, in the scholarly tradition of his time – recycling works by using them as a template for one's own – copied out parts of the book and added to the lists of saints and saintly women those who had lived at Degel, and some of whom were still alive. The opening remarks following Ibn al-Jawzi's text were taken from well-known Prophetic traditions concerning the dangers of acquisitiveness. Thus the Prophet's injunction to his wives was repeated here over and over again:

> Give alms of your finery and love the very poor. If you want to see the Day of Judgment do not come with possessions – enough only for a journey on horseback for example.[1]

Thirty-seven praiseworthy women were listed from places identified in the present as Iraq, Iran, Makka, and Egypt. The women scholars were all reverently ascetic, fastidious about the origins of any food they ate, and given to long periods of prayer. Some were freed slaves, all were married, a few wrote poetry, and one was a teacher of jurisprudence.

To Ibn al-Jawzi's original list, Bello added Aisha and Hauwa, the Shehu's two senior wives. Hauwa was Bello's mother, and of her he wrote, in *K. al-Nasiha*:

> She was forbearing and of a religious disposition. She was ascetic and always generous with what she possessed. She had the Sufi gifts of insight and perception, constantly in prayer, fasting regularly. She ate nothing except what she had earned by the work she did. She read the Qur'an daily. She conducted herself with decorum and loved her family. Her father, a most upright man was descended from Masirana, a sixteenth-century ancestor. Her mother, Hassanatu, was also of the same lineage, it was she who had raised me until I was ten years old.

---

1   Muhammad Bello, *Kitab al-Nasiha*. This unpublished ms (*Kitab al-Nasihati wa lai'ati* (transl. Sidi Sayudi, Ubandoma) was loaned to Jean Boyd by Waziri Junaidu. Cited hereafter as *K. al-Nasih*a.

Bello continued:

> There were many praiseworthy women in the Shehu's community.
> If it were not for making this book too long I would write down all
> their names as well as the names of his students like Ja'ibatu, Juwaidu,
> Aminatu Luba, Aminatu Adde, Yafunde and others. We should do our
> best to learn from them and their works.
>
> (*K. al-Nasiha*)

It is clear that Bello respected the women and it was at his
request that Asma'u translated his book from Arabic into the two
languages used in Sokoto by the population in everyday speech
– Fulfulde and Hausa. She finished them both within a year, each
with eighty-three verses.

Asma'u's poetic accounts of historic events were intended
to help students remember the facts: they served as a framework
to which the teacher would add details present in Bello's book.
Asma'u would first explain the poem to her student deputies, the
*jaji*s. In the case of Sufi women, Asma'u's translation and versification of the book omitted the section on Prophetic traditions,
and introduced five verses in which she thanked God for the
exemplary lives of women Sufis everywhere, 'for their majesty
will wipe away my sins ...' (CW, #10, v. 59, p. 80). Thus she
allied herself with the righteous women of the wider world of
Islam. The collaboration of the Caliph with his sister to produce
poetry specifically intended to educate both the elite women of
the Shehu's Community and the Hausa slaves was an extraordinary event in the history of the Caliphate and an indication of
the direction in which both wished to move. Reconciliation and
rehabilitation were key strategies.

But war constantly loomed over the Caliphate. The terms of
a truce struck ten years previously with Sarkin Gobir Ali gave
Bello control of the lower end of the Rima valley. To make sure
these approaches to Sokoto were protected, he built a small *ribat*
or fortress at Wurno, on an exposed bluff which had excellent

views over the valley, a sight which was very familiar to him. In a poem about the political situation, Asma'u blamed the Tuareg leader Ibra for the outbreak of hostilities. She said that he had called on all the local chiefs including Sarkin Gobir to rally to his standard. Gobir traditions say that when the message reached Sarkin Gobir he demurred, whereupon the *Inna* sent him a set of butcher's knives. This was insulting because the Fulani never slaughtered their own animals; traditionally they left the job to Hausa butchers. The *Inna* was implying that her brother, Sarkin Gobir, was demeaning himself and at worst nothing less than a collaborator and a traitor. Unable to stomach the criticisms, Sarkin Gobir Ali joined Ibra and they campaigned along the eastern frontier raiding and pillaging.

Bello assembled his army at Wurno with great resolve and rode up the Rima valley towards Alƙalawa. In his day the region was a place of beauty, a haven for migrant bird life – great white

Fig. 6 The Rima river leading to Gobir (Photo: Jean Boyd, 1972)

egrets, spur-wing plovers, and the aquamarine coloured Abyssinian Rollers. Lily trotters with their long splayed feet trod delicately on the lily pads and golden orioles sang their pretty notes after dusk. Pelicans cruised over the pools and the black and white sacred ibis made messy nests in the trees which bordered the river. Bello's army met up with that of the Emir of Kano and, leaving the watered valley behind, they swung due north into the uplands where it was hot and exceedingly dry. Asma'u wrote:

> Thirst tormented the men who were at their limits,
> Frantically they searched for water.
> Bello was told that the army was overwrought because there was
> no water.
> He said, 'Everyone who digs a hole in the hillside will instantly get
> water.'
> Everybody obeyed his instructions, dug and found water.
> We witnessed this extraordinary thing on that mound as water
> poured forth.
> Beyond doubt Muhammad Bello performed a miracle. Water
> bubbled forth.
> I saw it with my own eyes.
>
> (CW, #38, vv. 35–38, p. 237, adapted)

In the late twentieth century, Asma'u's descendant Waziri Junaidu said it was quite possible that Asma'u was with the army, and indeed an eyewitness to this extraordinary event. She rode a horse regularly from Sokoto to Wurno, and had ridden to Kano as a young woman. Comparable accounts are known of the Prophet's wife, Aisha, riding on to the battlefields, and Asma'u certainly would have known this history. Furthermore, Clapperton had observed Gidado riding with a train of attendants – women were behind, some riding horses, others astride camels. Certainly Asma'u's descriptions of the battle have the freshness of an eyewitness account.

Bello ordered the standards to be brought and unfurled,
He told his men, 'Gird yourselves, for today the unbelievers will be
    put to shame.'
Then they made ready, taking up their weapons. The spears looked
    like ripe corn heads.
Madi and 'Danyero raised the standards,
And, with Abduwa, moved into the lead towards the enemy.
With standards flying Bello mounted and rode to the vanguard
You could see nothing but spear heads and swords glinting.
They surrounded the Caliph, the reproachless;
As numberless as flocks of birds or swarms of locusts.
In that year, 1836, Bello thoroughly defeated Gobir.

(CW, #38, vv. 45–53, p.238)

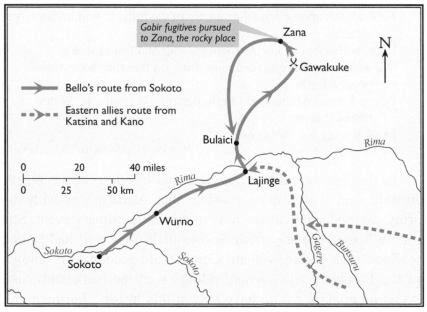

Map 4. Attack on Gawakuke by Muhammad Bello, 1836

Bello continued his search for all the survivors who had fled
to the outlying foothills of the Aïr Mountains, an exceedingly
inhospitable and desiccated area to the far north. He searched
them out until he was satisfied that none of the enemy were left

among the black rocks of the hill of Zana. He then disbanded his men who turned for home, rejoicing.

By November 1836 he had returned to Wurno but four months later, in March 1837, he fell ill with an undiagnosed affliction. When his condition got worse people became fearful. Gidado recorded how he died:

He sent a letter to his brothers telling them of his approaching death. He instructed them to unite together as Muslims and be vigilant. He directed them to follow what God said in the Qur'an [3:103]:

And hold fast
All together by the Rope
of God (stretched out to you)
And be not divided
Among yourselves.

and [4:1]:

Reverence God through Whom
Ye demand your mutual (rights)
And (reverence) the wombs
(that bore you).

In anticipation of death he had a room built and said he should be buried there. He directed that he should not be taken to Sokoto. Before he died he recited the words of the *shahada* three times and also a verse from the Qur'an [16:1]:

(Inevitable) cometh (to pass)
The command of God:
Seek ye not then
To hasten it:

Then he fell on his pillow, but before his head reached the pillow,
    he died.

                                                              (*al-Kashf*)

Asma'u's and Gidado's commemoration
of the Shehu and Muhammad Bello

After the death of Muhammad Bello, Gidado did not wish to act as Waziri under Caliph Atiku. To avoid any rift he gradually relinquished control of the Chancery to his son Abdulkadir, who also took over the Treasury and acted as chief adviser to the Caliph. Muhammad Bello's body was buried at Wurno in the place he had built for the purpose. Gidado then convened the most senior advisers to choose a new Caliph. They chose Bello's younger brother Abubakar Atiku who was religious, brave, and iron willed. What he lacked was his elder brother's enquiring mind, his pragmatic approach to political questions, and his grace of manner. The court moved back to Sokoto where Atiku lived in his own house a mile or so from the homes of Bello and Waziri. This physical divide underlined the profound change which had taken place – the unity of interests and close collaboration of Bello, Gidado, and Asma'u had ended and could not be resumed with Atiku. So Gidado and his wife Asma'u decided to write historical accounts of the lives of the Shehu and Bello for posterity. They collaborated, each working in his or her own distinctive style, each bringing emphasis to bear on different aspects of these lives.

Their enterprise sprang from the crucible of their grief and amounted to the compilation of anecdotal data about the Shehu and Bello, lists of the places they had lived in, of their aunts, uncles, wives, children, advisers and servants, the judges they had appointed, the principal imams of the mosques, the scholars who had supported them, and of the disciplinarians and market supervisors. The aim was to establish a corpus of knowledge that future historians could draw upon. This was a task which could not be done in haste: time had to be spent checking facts and interviewing elderly people some of whom had memories reaching back to the 1780s and beyond. Such people are often

frail, tire easily and argue furiously about events so it is difficult
to reach consensus views, even among people who were present
at the same time and in the same location.

During the preliminary stages of this undertaking, which is
unique in the history of the Caliphate, Asma'u wrote one of her
most beautiful poems, an elegy for Muhammad Bello, recitation
of the original of which has been known to move people to tears.
It conveys a sense of her grief:

> ...I weep [as I]...compose this poem,
> Shedding tears for the passing of the Caliph...
> ...I am alone, missing the eternal love, the companionship
> Of my brother; we were confidantes
> He was my mentor;
> I shall never have that again...
> ...I am like a small chicken
> Whose mother died, leaving him crying forlornly,
> Or like someone abandoned in the wilderness...
> ...He was my teacher...,
> ...Oh God bestow on him your blessings,
> Your mercy, and perfume him
> In his grave with Your favours.
>
> (CW, #12 vv. 3–4, 7, 9, 14, pp. 85–7)

The depth of her loss is evident in these lines.

Gidado and Asma'u writing under the same roof pooled their
resources. They were not engaged in a competition; what each
of them wrote complemented the work of the other. In the same
year, 1838, Asma'u wrote the poem called *Bello's Character*
which dwells on Bello as a man to be emulated. Her praise of
him addressed his learning, level-headedness, uprightness, pre-
paredness, intelligence and resourcefulness. What is omitted
is any reference to Bello's military campaigns, his position as
Caliph, his commanding presence (as reported by Clapperton), or
his swordsmanship: he called his sword *higo*, friend. Instead of
describing Bello's qualities related to his position in the world or

his charisma (*karama*), Asma'u focussed on moral merits valued in the context of Sufism:

> He fulfilled promises and took care of affairs but did not act hastily.
> He shouldered responsibilities and patiently endured adversities.
> He was watchful and capable of restoring to good order matters which had gone wrong.
> He was resourceful and could undo mischief, no matter how serious, because he was a man of ideas.
> He was gracious to important people and was hospitable to all visitors including non-Muslims.
> He drew good people close to him and distanced himself from those of ill- repute.
> These are his characteristics. I have recounted a few examples that are sufficient to provide a model for emulation and benefit.
>
> (CW, #14, vv. 31–7, p. 93)

Gidaɗo's work, *al-Kashf wa-l-bayan*, focused on a different kind of episode in Bello's life. In Arabic prose, Gidaɗo spoke first about Bello's childhood and how he was brought up by his maternal grandmother at Marnona, a village a day's journey from Degel. As a small boy he did not join in boy's games and when he was ten he said he wanted to return to his father. As teenagers Bello and Gidaɗo rode together to visit scholars in search of books, braving wild animals including, on occasion, lions. There is a detailed account of Ibra's attack on Sokoto in 1820, the jinns which played a part in it, and several examples of telepathic communication, or at least a meeting of like minds: for example, upon reaching Daura, an emirate to the east, Gidaɗo found the Emir very sick and installed the Emir's son as his successor. Some days later a letter arrived from Bello instructing him to do just that.

Gidaɗo said Bello was pious and devoted, did not accept bribes, and safeguarded the property of lawful heirs. When he lay mortally ill four thousand birds flew over his house. This was probably the annual arrival of migratory birds which are seen wheeling about in huge flocks over the river at Wurno, but they recalled a similar visitation to the house of 'Ali, when the Prophet's son in-law lay dying. Gidaɗo supplemented *al-Kashf* with a shorter work listing Bello's companions, friends, helpers, regional governors, district representatives, sons and daughters, wives and concubines, the inclusion of the latter being a very unusual event. Some of the people are well known to this day, but many have left nothing behind except their names.

With undiminished zeal Gidaɗo and Asma'u turned their attention to the history of the Shehu. Their works about Bello had been well received by scholars, which encouraged them to do more. Asma'u wrote what is her most famous work in 1839, called *The Journey* (*Waƙar Gewaye* in Hausa). After only two lines of introduction she said, 'Now I am going to explain the practice of the Shehu | For you to hear what was done in his time' (CW, #20 v. 3, p. 134). Having marshaled her facts Asma'u set them down in a typically orderly and straightforward manner. Her skill lay in the way she encrypted information. For example she wrote about one of the major acts of provocation leading to the hijra, explaining that the Shehu had said in 1803 in a letter to all the major towns, 'show by your dress who you are and what you intend' (CW, #20 v.14, p. 136). This succinct directive is replete with meaning, and in Asma'u's day it was up to teachers to explain that the turban had been banned by Sarkin Gobir who was determined to undermine the Shehu's authority; Asma'u's comment echoed that of the Shehu, who said:

Show who you are, wear your turban, gird your bodies for action by tying wide belts round your waists. They are necessary to strengthen your back on long journeys, what is more the belts tie your robes so that your sword arm is free.

(Waziri Junaidu's explanation to Jean Boyd, *ca.* 1980)

Another example is the line, 'The Shehu fought five battles at Gudu' (CW, #20 v.26, p. 139). The significance of five battles is evident in one of the Shehu's own poems. In it he described the opening of the Prophet's jihad, a famous event in history: 'He made five raids without the enemy drawing close' (CW, p. 139, n. 298). Without the explanation, the words have little meaning; once clarified, the poem became a treasure-trove of knowledge, which is why it became so popular, especially when translated from Fulfulde into Hausa by her brother Isa.

Gidado's book about the Shehu was written, he explained, 'to give an account of the unusual perceptions and miracles of the Shehu, qualities which the author himself has observed' (*Rawd al-jinan*, p. 1). Its thoroughness is beyond doubt; he described, sometimes in great detail, unusual happenings – there are more than fifty-four such events. Asma'u must have told her husband about at least one incident which occurred when she was about ten years old (and before her marriage):

One day when they lived at Gwandu Asma'u spoke to the Shehu in Tamajek, the language of the Tuareg. He was curious to know where she had learned the words and she said from Fatima, a concubine of her brother Ali. The Shehu then asked her to translate a series of everyday words for example 'earth, sun, moon, stars, water, and salt'. At the word 'salt' she stopped and said she did not know the Tamajek for 'salt'. Whereupon the Shehu said, 'You have been going not to Fatima but to the Tuareg camp, (implying that he knew without being told what she had done). You have asked them to teach you and you wrote down the words. The rebuked Asma'u promised to be more open and truthful in future.

(*Rawd al-jinan*)

Gidado also described anecdotes more difficult to understand, for example those involving Sufi mystical experiences like the unexplained dispersal of huge rainstorms, the presence of jinns at a meeting, and other paranormal events. Modern academic scholars brush these aside but belief in the Shehu's amazing powers was an important ingredient of the awe in which he was held and should be taken into account. To ignore Gidado's work is unwise because the paranormal was real to him and to many in an age when mysticism was a present force.

Gidado rounded off his work on the Shehu with an astonishingly long list of people who, in, Gidado's view, merited inclusion. They were waziris, disciples, commanders, representatives, the Shehu's teachers, his contemporaries, students, reciters of the Qur'an, judges, wives and children, aunts and uncles: two hundred and forty-two in all. In the hundred verses of Asma'u's poem written at the same time as Gidado's she listed only what were to her the absolute essential names – forty-four – so that her students would, without difficulty, memorize them. To some of those on the list she added thumb-nail sketches like the one about the Shehu's brother

> I will describe his helpers starting with his Chief Ministers [wazirs], there was Bello,
> And the Shehu's younger brother, Abdullahi Bayero, they helped him exceedingly.
> His younger brother acted everywhere on his behalf,
> As for his learning he had no equal.
> Compare him with Aaron
> And how he helped Moses.
>
> (CW, #22, vv. 19–22, p. 165)

Gidado modestly recorded his own name in the list of 'messengers'.

3

ORIGINS OF THE 'YAN TARU

Social Reform, Scholarship, and Teaching: the 'Yan Taru

The pattern of Asma'u's life was shaped by the circumstances in which she found herself. The importance of providing the appropriate Islamic education for refugee women and girls was reinforced by the re-emergence of the non-Islamic *bori* cult, which competed for their allegiance. At the Hubbare in Sokoto, formerly the Shehu's home, lived his widows, all of whom were used to being in a place where books furnished the rooms and students abounded. It was well known that teaching was a regular activity there, and pilgrims were expected and welcomed. The younger women visited each of the senior women, who offered advice, bestowed blessings, and prayed, using their beads in silent devotion.[1] Receiving instruction was part of the reason for the visit.

Teaching was a normal occupation of educated women, including five of Asma'u's sisters, all of whom were learned, and each of whom had written at least one work which has survived. They were: Hadija, Asma'u's teacher in Degel; Faɗima, who married Aliyu Jeɗo, commander of the army; Habsatu, Asma'u's full sister and also one of her teachers; Safiya; and Maryam, who took

---

1   The rosary is called *carbi/carbuna* in Hausa, the 'c' pronounced with a 'ch' sound. The usage is derived from the Arabic *tasbih*, which in Sokoto Hausa is rendered *tasbaha*. *Dhikr* (Ar.) or *zikr* is the devotional repetition of invocations, among Sufis often communal, in which the invocations are counted on the *tasbih*.

over Asma'u's role after her death.

Among the educated women of her milieu, Asma'u was exceptional for two reasons. First, there is the sheer number of her own works and her translations, and their intellectual merit. The second reason for her fame is that she established an organization for women in which they could safely and respectably operate. From the privileged centre of the Caliphate she reached out to unfortunate women who lived hard lives in isolated rural communities. From small beginnings during the reign of Caliph Muhammad Bello, groups of women, who became known as the 'Yan Taru, the Associates, began to visit Asma'u under the leadership of representatives appointed by her. The impetus that propelled Asma'u into initiating this was the growing threat of an upsurge of *bori*, the non-Islamic cult of spirit possession favoured in Gobir. It is important to understand why this was considered dangerous.

Asma'u's twin brother Hassan, a scholarly and reclusive man who had died in 1817, had warned against *bori* in one of his compositions. Asma'u condemned 'the Satan called *bori*' (CW, #1, ch. 2, p. 24). In 1831 she translated a very important work by the Shehu, already famous in his Fulfulde version, *Tabbat Hakika*, Be Sure of God's Truth, a phrase which is repeated in every verse. It became one of the best known poems of the Jihadi period. Of central importance here is verse 31: 'some waste their energy where the music is wild. | Listening to the muse of the *goge* | They find it impossible to return to the Path' (CW, #6, p. 53). The lute, a stringed instrument derived from the oud of the Middle East and earlier Islamic eras, is known in Hausaland as the *goge*, a bowed instrument that is an essential requirement in the *bori* cult. When spirits were summoned the musicians, the *goge* players and the calabash drummers, played the particular beat of the spirit that had been called. Asma'u's translation of *Tabbat Hakika* included a warning against *bori* activity. Singers of religious verse

95

throughout the land disseminated the message to listeners at the mosque, marketplace, or the gate of one's house. Still today the unaccompanied verses sung in a plaintive key fill the air, to be memorized as they enter into a listener's consciousness. So it was the possible re-invasion of the heartlands of the Caliphate by those who promoted the spirits of *bori* – the people of Gobir – that concerned Caliphate leaders.

Fig. 7 Traditional Gobir adobe house (Photo: Jean Boyd, 1957)

The Queen figure in Gobir then, as now, was called the *Inna* (Mother): she had two other titles the importance of which will become apparent later: *uwargida* and *uwardeji*. The *Inna* that Jean Boyd knew in the 1970s and 1980s, who lived in the heart of the present day Gobir, described her work as the same as the Chief's , by which she meant the care of the people, in her case, the women.[1] She said she discussed with him matters to do with the running of Gobir and he sought her advice. 'Everything to

---

1   Commentary here is based on communication between Jean Boyd and the *Inna* of Gobir in the1970s/80s.

do with Gobir is my concern,' she told Boyd. 'Just as the Sarki is given authority, so I am given authority – I am the chief of all women [*masu shan bori*, i.e. those who adhere to the *bori* cult, excluding Muslims; see her clarification below]'. The *Inna* wore male attire on public occasions – trousers, boots, *riga*, a long traditional gown, and a turban over which she wore a straw hat, a *malfa*. The *malfa* is a work of art; at least eighty rows of finely plaited grass are shaped into a hat standing twenty centimetres high with a brim six centimetres broad, and no apparent seam or join in the construction. It is meant to be used over a turban, hence the high dome and is usually worn only by elderly and distinguished men, and surprisingly therefore, also by the *Inna* of Gobir. Ta'Allah, the *Inna* Boyd knew, had male court officials and an impressive praise-song which includes her genealogy and descriptive metaphors which lauded her as *masaka matsera* (the refuge and place of safety), *hankaka mai zaman shiri* (ever vigilant like the black and white crow), *mai damara fama* (always girded and ready for action). As if to demonstrate the role of *Inna*s of the past, Ta'Allah showed Boyd the sword captured from a Caliphate foe a hundred years previously, at a time when the *Inna* was Yarbukuma, whom she described as:

A very commanding figure, her booted feet were not allowed to touch the ground; mats were laid for her to walk on. She was very intelligent and took care of widows and orphans. She was relaxed and pleasant except when circumstances demanded that she behave otherwise. She was generous and distributed booty fairly: she never betrayed any trust placed in her and stood by her kinsfolk.

Another story of the *Inna*s collected by a French colonial official concerned one Sarkin Konni, a subordinate ruler in the Gobir hierarchy, who decided to submit to the Shehu and paid him tribute in accordance with the new Caliphate regulations. However, in order to avoid being raided by the new Sarkin Gobir, now living at Tsibiri, Sarkin Konni continued to pay him homage by sending him a gift of 2,300 kola nuts, worth approximately (according to the season) 'between 120 and 439 French francs', a handsome present. The lists show how the kola were divided:

> 1000 for Sarkin Gobir, the paramount chief at Tsibiri.
> 100 for the *Inna* (the princess having authority over Gobir women, generally the elder sister of the Chief, Sarkin Gobir).
> 100 for the Imam
> 100 for each of the principal officials, eight in number (the Magaji, the Ubandawaki, the Sarkin Rafi, the Sarkin Kaya, the Sarkin Tudu, the Sarkin Baize, the Galadima and the Sarkin Massimo).[1]

The *Inna* was, in her own words, *Sarkin Mata duka*, the leader of all women, but she added 'only those who believed in *bori*' by which she meant Muslim women were not included. The *Inna* had special knowledge and used it to give advice, hold medical consultations and treat illnesses. A sick or depressed woman might be treated with herbal remedies; if she failed to respond, a further diagnosis might deem that the illness had been caused by a spirit which had possessed her. Any long-lasting condition was usually attributed to the penetration of the body by malevolent forces which then had to be exorcised during a function in which the *goge* was played and calabashes drummed. These gatherings varied, men as well as women attended some and took part in dancing purely for the sake of participating in an amusing diversion. For serious devotees like the *Inna* who sponsored these events in their own compounds, the situation

---

1   Tilho, *Documents Scientifiques de la Mission Tilho* (Paris: Centre d'Etudes Linguistiques et Historiques par Tradition Orale, 1911), vol. 2, p. 3. (The Tilho mission gathered oral history in the Niger Republic; the material was made available in typescript form at the C.E.L.H.T.O. library in Niamey, Niger.)

was very different because they venerated the spirits for their usefulness in treating illnesses.[1]

There was nothing wrong with a woman being such an authority figure, but there was everything wrong with belief in spirit possession, which had no place in the reformed Islamic Caliphate. Asma'u realized she needed to redirect the allegiance of women who followed the *Inna*'s devotion to this un-Islamic cult. Therefore, Asma'u made herself knowledgeable about the interests of women and used her intelligence to collate and

---

1   Women-run *bori* spirit possession cults 'purge' malevolent spirits through a carefully orchestrated nocturnal ceremony in which the adept is subjected to entrancement ('possession') induced by physiological changes resulting from increased pulse rate (brought about through increasingly rapid drumming) and body temperature (caused by being covered with a blanket). These changes cause seizures that involve the rolling back of the eyes, foaming at the mouth, and paralysis of the limbs. This is felt to be the physical manifestation of the malevolent spirit that needs to be purged. Beverly Mack has witnessed such events in Kano. For more on bori, see especially Fremont Besmer, *Horses, Musicians, and Gods* (South Hadley, MA: Bergin and Garvey, 1983). The *Inna*s Boyd has read about, and the two that she knew, were authoritarian women of royal birth who were among the principal advisers to the Sarki and benevolent protectors of women; they were also the guardians of non-Islamic spirit possession. In 1972 Boyd met Ta'Allah in Sabon Birni the town built to replace Alƙalawa. Boyd had gone to Gobir in order to ask the Sarkin Gobir for help in locating some of the Jihad battle sites, clearly a matter which had to be handled with tact. That night Sarkin Gobir Ibrahim invited her to his rambling adobe palace where she was led by him into a large room lit by a single flickering oil lamp. She was accompanied by a learned scholar from Sokoto, Ubandoma Sidi Sayuɗi, and the Sarki was attended by a turbaned retainer who sat at his feet. Boyd explained what had puzzled her in some manuscripts and after listening carefully the Sarki said he would provide horses and accompany her to all the places she wished to visit. What she learned from the Sarki that day far exceeded expectations. Ten years later when interviewing Ta'Allah, Boyd was astonished to hear her repeat what she (Boyd) had said all those years ago to the Sarki. 'How do you know?' Boyd asked. Ta'Allah explained that she had been the turbaned retainer who sat at the Sarki's feet that day, his servant, the *Inna*.

corroborate the information she received to benefit the aims of the Caliphate. Thus was she able to conceive of an organization of women with aims different from purging spirits in nocturnal ceremonies. Realizing that many rural women were captives who knew little about Islam, she sought to befriend them in the context of welcoming them into Caliphate culture. This required educating them about reformed Islam and women's rights and obligations in it. The form Asma'u's rural women's organization took had to blend satisfactorily with existing social conditions. It was no good, for example, expecting young women to leave home and come to Sokoto for instruction. Married by the age of twelve, they soon grew into their roles as wives and mothers, and spent the next thirty years bearing, nursing and bringing up children. If they had none of their own, they brought up other people's – a sister's or a cousin's for example. Then, because husbands were often years older than their wives, women were often left as widows. Widows might remarry but many did not, so it was they who were targeted for inclusion in Asma'u's re-education programme, together with the eight- to twelve-year-old girls who were not yet married. What was innovative about Asma'u's organization was the appointment by her of a woman leader to head each village group and to take responsibility for the conduct of its members. Asma'u gave each leader the title *jaji* (caravan leader) and bestowed on her a large hat like the one worn by the *Inna*. Asma'u deliberately adopted the symbol. By giving each *jaji* such a hat, she at once devalued its uniqueness and transformed what it stood for. From being symbolic of the *Inna* the leader of *bori* it turned into an emblem of Islam. To emphasize the transfer of authority Asma'u gave each *jaji* a strip of red cloth to be tied round the brim of the hat. The ceremony of handing over the red cloth was called *nadî*, which was the word used when authority was conferred on a male title holder as the Sarki wrapped the titleholder's turban. Thus, the *nadî* ceremony for a woman leader conferred upon her authority in the 'Yan Taru organization.

Development of the 'Yan Taru

By the 1840s the 'Yan Taru movement had grown as a women's networking organization but how fast and in which geographical areas is difficult to ascertain. The first definite indicator of the movement was an elegy written by Asma'u in 1858 for one of her *jaji*s, which makes it clear that she had known and been close to Asma'u for years:

> [I] remember Hauwa who loved me, a fact well known to everybody.
> During the hot season, the rains, harvest time, when the harmattan blows,
> And the beginning of the rains, she was on the road bringing people to me.
> She warned them to journey in good faith, for she said intention was important.
> As for myself I taught them the religion of God in order to turn them from
> Error and instill in them the knowledge of their obligatory duties.
> Like ritual ablution, prayer, alms, pilgrimage and the fast, all of which are compulsory for adults.
> I taught them what, in the faith of Islam, is permissible and what is forbidden, so they would know how to act.
> I said they must distance themselves from sins such as lying, meanness, hatred and envy,
> Adultery, theft and self esteem. I said they should repent because these things lead to perdition.
> The women students and their children are well known for their good works and peaceful behaviour in the community.
> (CW, #42 vv. 5–13, pp. 253–4)

Who Hauwa was and the names of the home villages over which she seems to have been in charge may never be known. She brought women to Asma'u at all times of the year. If she had been the *jaji* of a single village she would not have needed to travel so very often which means that she could have been a district supervisor of *jaji*s – such people exist in some areas and use the title *Modibo*. The indications are that the 'Yan Taru in Hauwa's domain had been functioning for many years.

'Yan Taru treks to the villages were not for the faint of heart; these women were determined. Trekking through the bush on any occasion presented hardships. During the rains, sudden thunderstorms accompanied by strong winds and driving rain filled gullies in no time, turning paths into mud slides and empty wadis into surging torrents. Anyone caught in the open could easily become disoriented by the blinding rain. After the harvest, when the tall swathes of millet and guinea corn are cut down, travellers would have had to keep an eye open for wild animals which inhabit these savannah lands – lion and hyena were not uncommon. Wild boar were seen on the outskirts of Sokoto as recently as the 1960s and hunters caught wild buffalo, *'bauna*, a very aggressive animal, near Wurno in the 1970s, so there is no doubt that such dangers existed a century prior to this time. The harmattan wind blows when there has been severe weather in the Sahara and the air becomes noticeably cooler as a result. Sometimes the cold wind is transformed at ground level into a dense sandstorm which whips the skin with myriads of sand particles and blinds the eyes. As for the hot season, soaring temperatures in excess of 40 degrees Celsius (110 Fahrenheit) drain people of their energy and render travel in the mid-afternoon a sore trial.[1]

---

1   Asma'u referred to seasons, rather than the months, because in every day speech the names of the lunar months were, as now, rarely used. This is because the year in the Islamic lunar calendar is eleven days shorter than the Gregorian calendar and is not, therefore, synchronized to the seasons. Muslim festivals fall on the same days of the lunar months each year and make the full circle of the seasons every 33 years.

The work was not only physically difficult, but it was also demanding in an intellectual and spiritual way. For success in their work, right intention (*niyya*) on the part of the *jaji*s was essential. '[Hauwa] warned them to journey in good faith for, she said, intention was important' (CW, #42, v. 7, p. 253). If any of the 'Yan Taru set out intending, in their hearts, to use their time in Sokoto visiting friends and shopping in the market they had definitely not travelled in good faith. The *jaji* would ask them, before they set out, 'Why are you going? Who do you wish to see? What do you wish to learn?'[1] As they trekked, no matter what the season, they would sing the songs Asma'u had taught them. Always in the centre of the thin column of 'Yan Taru was the *jaji* wearing her distinguishing emblem, the *malfa* hat. Immediately next to her, in front and behind, were the pre-pubescent girls and beyond them and in the rear travelled the older women, senior in years and experience, who had made the journey many times over the years.

The procedure for the 'Yan Taru has not changed over the years. In 1983 when the 'Yan Taru arrived at the house of a *Modibo*, a district supervisor, they left their sandals outside, entered the courtyard where the *Modibo* was sitting and bent their knees to the ground to greet her. It would have been an act of discourtesy to look down on her from a standing position. She answered them in a kindly manner before waving them on to the rooms of her eldest daughter, who was in line to become the next *Modibo*. There they handed over the small gifts they had brought – grain, butter, honey, small hand-woven mats and some coins. These were given for redistribution to the poor and needy but part of the grain was for their own sustenance while they were in residence. According to the rule about giving, each item had been lawfully obtained and was without taint. This contemporary example of a 'Yan Taru visit parallels what happened in Asma'u's time.

---

1   Jean Boyd's observation, 18 April 1984.

The young girls who travelled with the *jaji*s were expected to learn the songs that Asma'u wrote. Some would memorize as many as twenty verses at a time; others could manage only a few. Grandmothers and great aunts, the older women, travelled with the younger *jaji*s. When they reached Sokoto, whether at Asma'u's house or the Hubbare, they brought news of their localities, what was going right and what was not. There might be concern about the outbreak of a disease, the rise in the price of food, the departure of a merchant to North Africa or the arrival of a swarm of locusts. The *jaji*s took with them the problems entrusted to them by the young mothers who could not make the trek to Sokoto. At the Hubbare, or when meeting Asma'u, the *jaji*s explained the personal anxieties troubling those at home, often to do with marital affairs, illness and matters to do with sickly infants and children. The *jaji*s asked for prayers to be said for individuals by name. In these ways women kept in contact with each other and were not isolated from one another in seclusion, as is often said about the lives of the women of the region.

Asma'u's aim in creating the 'Yan Taru was to educate and socialize women, unifying them under the banner of reformed Islam, regardless of their ethnicity, age, or first language. Asma'u said, 'I taught them what in the faith of Islam is permissible and what is forbidden so they would know how to act' (CW, #42, v. 10, p. 253) .The young girls were very important to her because they were the community's future. Asma'u cradled her hands over the heads of each of them and prayed that they would be blessed with good husbands. In the 1970s Jean Boyd interviewed a woman living in a remote village who said that in the reign of Caliph Abdurrahman (1891–1902), she herself made a visit to the Hubbare with the 'Yan Taru of her area. Her memory was very clear – she remembered for example the year 1892 when the Caliph fought a campaign against the Kebbi people and some of the leaders camped at their home en route to the battle. She described the paths the 'Yan Taru followed to Sokoto and the kind of alms they carried, using old-fashioned words to describe the receptacles they were held in. For example some items were taken in a *tandu,* a vessel made of dressed hide; small sizes were for storing ointment and larger ones for butter. Grain was carried in a *taiki*, a large leather bag. Another woman of much the same age, ninety plus, told Boyd that as a girl at the Hubbare her head had been stroked and a prayer said over her by the Shehu's granddaughter, Ta Modi.

The messages conveyed by Asma'u in her poetry, and spread by the work of the 'Yan Taru, reverberate through the generations. What she wrote then is relevant now: 'Repent, worship, give alms and fast. Do not turn to *bori*, do not boast or be greedy. Do not steal or be miserly. Instead be patient and generous, compassionate and forgiving, cheerful and forbearing, to the end' (adapted from CW, #1, chs. 2 and 3, pp. 24–6). Asma'u never ceased to advocate ethical behaviour. At the age of sixty-eight, in 1861, she wrote a poem in which she said: 'Lying, whispering slander, spreading rumours, jealousy, self-esteem and boasting are all forbidden. And so are adultery, theft, the seizing of property and oppression' (CW, #46, v. 19, p. 266). In an elegy written two years later she praised her niece Fadima for her generosity, serenity, pleasantness and courtesy. (CW, #48, vv. 9–11, p. 271).

Such diligent advocacy of good behaviour had its effect in shaping the community, allowing Asma'u to write with confidence 'the women students and their children are well known for their good works' (CW, #42, v. 13, p. 254). Some *jaji*s and 'Yan Taru that Jean Boyd visited in different villages in the 1980s said that senior members of the 'Yan Taru routinely washed the bodies of deceased women before burial and assisted at the birth of children, often by cutting the umbilical cord.[1] All taught reading and writing of the Qur'an at a primary level using the customary wooden board, the *allo*. Many taught women how to say their prayers correctly, a few swept the mosque, and all gave advice and sorted out disagreements. In these ways women played a significant role, their work being part of the warp and weft of the fabric of society. Within the 'Yan Taru organization women found the kind of help and support the *Inna* had offered to all who lived in Gobir, while leaving behind the non-Islamic spirit possession activity that had once been a significant part of their social life. Asma'u was the voice of women at the very heart of government. She listened to her students, weighed their reports, checked on the facts and, if so minded, raised issues directly with the Caliph, person to person, first with Muhammad Bello and then his successors.

Asma'u's life in the 1840s

In 1843, when Caliph Aliyu moved his headquarters to Wurno, to be closer to enemy territory in Gobir, his Waziri, Abdulkadir, joined him there. Gidado, Abdulkadir's father, remained with Asma'u in Sokoto; he was in his late sixties and she was by then aged about fifty. Away from the centre it might be assumed that Asma'u would lose some of her authority, but her position in the Caliphate did not depend on her closeness to powerful people. It derived from the authority of her scholarship and charisma. She was a polymath able to speak informedly on a wide range of topics including spirituality, medicine, politics, history and issues of social concern. Her charisma came in large part from her numinous quality of *baraka*, blessedness. Her attributes, as one who had *baraka,* included piety, spirituality, moral fibre, and therapeutic gifts. She also shared with the Shehu a sense of

---

1   In Islam, the washing of a corpse proceeds in a particular fashion, with specific prayers, and is a means of obtaining grace for the washer.

obligation to use her special talents for the benefit of the Jihad. The breadth of her knowledge and her magnetism were alike focussed on the well-being of her community.

Asma'u's abilities allowed her to become an active member of the intelligentsia and her personality made her an effective teacher of both men and women, as well as a leader of women educators. People within her community and those far off in other countries recognized her special character and they had extraordinary respect for her. 'Greetings to you O woman of excellence and fine traits!' wrote her kinsman Shaykh Sa'ad on his return from the hajj in Makka. 'In every century there appears one who excels. The proof of her merit has become well known, east and west, near and far. She is marked by wisdom and kind deeds; her knowledge is like the wide sea.' (CW, #55, vv. 1–3, p. 285). The scholar Ali Ibrahim from Masina (in the far west) wrote:

> [Asma'u] is famous for her erudition and saintliness which
> are as a bubbling spring to scholars.
> Her knowledge, patience and sagacity she puts to good
> Use as did her forebears.
>
> (CW, #56, vv. 3–4, p. 289)

From her family home in Sokoto she allowed nothing to stand in her way. Among the works that she produced in her maturity and which are still in daily use in the twenty-first century, is *Yearning for the Prophet* (*Begore*). The original work was written in Fulfulde by an eighteenth-century scholar Muhammad Tukur, and reproduced by Asma'u in Hausa translation for the edification of the masses, who spoke only Hausa.

Composed in the classic style, *Yearning for the Prophet* is first of all a condensed yet extremely detailed history of the Prophet, focusing on battles he fought and the tactics he used in promoting Islam. This is a poem which again shows how a parallel was easily drawn between the Prophet's endeavours and those of the Shehu.

An uneducated person would not have been able to understand this poem without scholarly help, which indicated that the women leaders, the *jaji*s, Asma'u's 'friends' as she called them in the text, would have been given intensive training to enable them to explain the poem to others back home. However, this particular work had talismanic properties and its recital alone would have been deemed to be meritorious. For people knowledgeable about the Qur'an, the poem would have been a joy to recite, with the familiar miracles, victories, names and events falling agreeably on the ear, reminding them of the Shehu's own deeds. It is a very popular poem in contemporary times. In the 1980s on a visit to Dange, a village south of Sokoto, a *jaji* showed Jean Boyd her handwritten copy of *Begore*. It was in a very fragile and tattered condition. Gently she turned the pages where the faded ink and crumbling paper gave clear evidence of decades of use. A poem as long as this – 318 verses – demanded perseverance and one can almost imagine her in her room as she translated the original into Hausa: 'Bring water to refresh me as I faint, | Today I am weary, longing so much for [Muhammad]' (CW, #60, v. 260 pp. 338–9).

Gidado became much more frail as he grew older, and died in 1848. The man Asma'u described as 'my beloved' had been her husband for forty years. She wrote a very personal poem for him, an elegy in which the intensity of their companionship can be discerned:

We remember the deaths of Bello and Atiku, and now the Reconciler
    has also gone.
He worked conscientiously to put things right and benefit Muslims.
    He was untiringly hospitable to strangers.
He honoured all the senior members of the Community and pro-
    tected the rights of everyone regardless of their rank or status.
He honoured the Shehu's womenfolk, his children and his relatives.
    He neglected none of them.
He was close to the Shehu and Bello and explained their affairs…

He provided accommodation for all who came. He was the same
    with everyone, strangers and kinsmen alike.
He constantly tended to the needs of the people, making sure they and
   had food and drink. Tirelessly he helped them to endure misfortune.
Likewise he explained about affairs known to him, sent gifts to
    those in need, never seeking recompense.

He was in charge of repairing the Shehu and Bello mosques, and other
    city buildings, tasks he never tired of.
He was also in charge of repairing the city gates and tombs [the Hubbare,
    where the Shehu was buried and where other members of the family
    lived]. He was their guardian and acted punctiliously.
He stopped corruption and wrongdoing in the city. He acted sternly
    about such matters.
He held fast after Bello's death, honouring his purpose and explaining
    it to the people.
As for the Shehu's message, whenever the people gathered together,
He reiterated it to them. He was very serious about this...
The Shehu had certain attributes of the Prophet, by the grace of the
    Prophet.
His books were written [to guide] Muslims: O God ensure their useful-
    ness.

(CW, #28, vv. 6–18, 21, pp. 200–2).

    She ended the poem thus:

O God, bless Gidado and grant him a peaceful rest in the grave
    until the Day of Judgement.
And on that Day O God may he be given shade
And may he be saved by the Best of Mankind [the Prophet] ...
And on that Day when deeds are weighed
May his good deeds exceed his bad...
May he drink the water of *Kauthara*, together with Bello;
Reunite them with the Shehu in Paradise, where there is no parting.
Unite him with Bello, who was his friend
In the place of contentment where joy is forever.

(CW, #28, vv. 22–4, 26–7, p. 202)

109

In this work Asma'u concentrated on Gidaɗo's attributes, just as she had focused on Bello's character in the elegy she wrote for him. She did not even mention Gidaɗo's position. As Waziri he was second only to the Caliph and his authority, as the leader's deputy, in theory, covered everything. In practice, because the Caliphate was so vast, certain geographical areas and commands were delegated to others who were responsible directly to the Caliph. But the Waziri retained his overall authority. Above all he was the senior councillor and met with the Caliph early every morning of every day.

Asma'u's works show that she herself was well informed about the state of the Caliphate and was fully aware of political events and military clashes. She also understood what Gidaɗo was trying to achieve as he 'constantly tended to the needs of the people, making sure they had food and drink [...helping] them to endure misfortune': rehabilitation and reconciliation.

Asma'u and the problems of the 1850s

Political problems arose during the 1850s. Asma'u's nephew, Aliyu, succeeded Atiku as Caliph. Aliyu's personal qualities were recounted by the German traveller Heinrich Barth (1849–55). Aliyu was a stocky man of middle height. His mother was a Gobir concubine, his father Muhammad Bello. He had good features and a fine beard; according to family tradition he was nicknamed Mai-Saje, 'the man with whiskers', because of his luxuriant side whiskers. He was intelligent and well-read, very genial, good natured, and fond of laughter. He treated all men alike and had the gift of remembering the names of people he had previously met. He was devoid of malice and remained uncorrupted by power. He did not stand on ceremony and was always accessible to people who wanted to see him. When he rode, he often sang Fulfulde poetry and was considered an accomplished exponent of the art.

It is clear to see why he was remembered affectionately by the people of Sokoto.

However, Aliyu was not very good at countering the strategies devised by the clever and daring Mayaƙi, the chief of Gobir, who had built a fortified town at Tsibiri, which still exists, to the north east of Alƙalawa, and consolidated his power base there. He then made alliances with other dissidents to the south and west with a view to disrupting trade routes to Sokoto, the heart of the Caliphate. Aliyu's response was to move his own headquarters closer to Tsibiri, the source of his troubles, Gobir. He re-established the Wurno *ribat* and together with his Waziri, Abdulkadir, and the court, moved there.

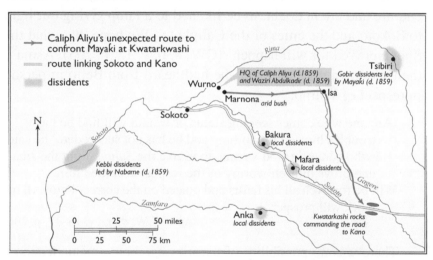

Map 5. Caliph Aliyu's unexpected route to confront Mayaƙi

All towns in the region were protected by walls, and the larger villages by wooden stockades. Unprotected villages were usually sited within easy reach of walled towns so that their inhabitants could take refuge when threatened. Travellers noticed the tall silk-cotton trees growing near every town gate. These provided look-out points from which the men on watch could give the alarm as soon as raiders appeared on the scene. Sure enough in Sokoto at the gate opening eastwards and looking towards Gobir, there is a silk-cotton tree (*rimi*), hence the gate is called *Kofar Rimi*.

In the big walled towns there were many acres of farmland and grazing grounds to accommodate refugees in times of trouble and to make cultivation possible if ever the town was besieged. Small walled and fortified garrisons had a different role. It was the job of the men living there to protect the hinterland. However, Wurno, the garrison town built by Bello, was another matter, a fact made plain in 1849 when Asma'u described how the Shehu himself had foretold the building of Wurno; it was meant as a rebuke intended for Caliph Aliyu. 'It is a place for those who enquire and are in doubt, to be likened to a lamp giving out light to Sokoto and the cities of the Caliphate.[1] We hope that what the Shehu prayed for will happen' (CW, #30, v. 12, p. 205). Asma'u then set down what she said she had heard from Bello in person in respect of Wurno:

'Anyone who comes seeking status or wealth will find he has
   troubled himself for nothing and he has not succeeded,' he said.
'He who comes in God's name to revive the *Sunna*, fight the Jihad
   and prove himself worthy of the respect accorded him,
Will be forgiven all his faults and placed on the correct Path. All his
   work will prosper.'

(CW, #30, vv. 15–17, p. 206)

There was no possibility of the message being misunderstood. It was a warning to Caliph Aliyu and his advisers, including the Wazir Abdulkadir, to pull themselves together. Asma'u was prompted to write the poem because of the defection of a certain prominent young prince, Nabame, who, had been captured as a boy,

---

1   This reference would be familiar to those who know the Qur'an, recalling 24:35: 'God is the Light of the heavens and the earth. The parable of His Light is as if there were a niche and within it a lamp: the lamp is enclosed in a glass: the glass as it were a brilliant star...'

when his father, the chief of Kebbi, was killed fighting against the Jihad. Instead of being enslaved, he was adopted by Muhammad Bello who, because his father had been a chief, accorded him the privileges that befitted his birth, no doubt in the hope that the boy would one day be made chief himself and bring the small state he was heir to into the fold. He was treated as one of the family. Eventually he went on expeditions, fighting shoulder to shoulder with the forces of the then Caliph Aliyu; he even saved the life of Aliyu's son. When Nabame requested permission to return to his own country, Kebbi, Aliyu was unable to refuse, saying he had every confidence in Nabame and wished him well. However, back home Nabame remembered the taunts hurled at him on the battlefield accusing him of colluding with his father's murderers. He renounced his allegiance to Aliyu, and proclaimed himself Chief of Kebbi.

Naturally this put Aliyu in the firing line; people demanded to know what he had been thinking in releasing Nabame, and made remarks about his ineptitude and incompetence. They did not consider that things might have turned out differently, with a permanent peace, had Nabame proved loyal. The whole affair was thrown into sharper relief when in a raid by Kebbi on an outlying village, a widow of Muhammad Bello was killed. There is nothing to suggest that it was by Nabame's own arrow that she was hit, but he was held responsible for the incident. The Caliph, realizing that he had to deal with the principal protagonist, Mayaƙi, made his plans. Nabame was not the central character; the main target was Mayaƙi because it was he to whom many others looked for leadership.

The massive granite inselbergs at Kwatarkwashi provided the scene of the next major confrontation. Rising abruptly from the plain they are an unmistakable landmark. From most angles they are difficult to climb, but once there the view from the top is commanding. Strategically the rocks were important because they lay athwart the main route from Sokoto to Kano. Mayaƙi, a superior strategist to Aliyu, persuaded the local people to ally with him. Audaciously, he then occupied the hill forts and set men to guard all the wells on the normal approach roads. Local historians say that until recently Kwatarkwashi was home to baboons, crested duikers, red-fronted gazelles, leopards and eagles, to say nothing of hyenas and snakes.

Fig. 8 Descendant of Mayaƙi, Ibrahim Chief of Gobir (Photo: Boyd, 1972)

In 1853/54 Caliph Aliyu responded swiftly to Mayaƙi's bold move by mobilizing a large force which set out for Kwatarkwashi at the height of the hot season with temperatures soaring into the forties Celsius. In an extraordinary way he planned to outflank his enemy by marching across a waterless desert. As recorded in Waziri Junaidu's history (*Tarihin Fulani*, p. 53), 'His people murmured amongst themselves questioning his wisdom', but he refused to deviate from his plan. Some sources say sixty people died of thirst on the march. When he reached the great rocks he found that his quarry had flown; Mayaƙi had had plenty of warning from his spies; what is more, the dust raised from a thousand water-bearing camels in Aliyu's horde would have been seen tens of miles away. Aliyu decided to make the best of a bad job; he destroyed the hill forts, and then followed the main route home, collecting plenty of booty en route, and finally arriving in Wurno with an army of men who were content with the outcome of the campaign.

Asma'u, however, was not placated; to her mind, this was not the way things should be. She opened her poem abruptly, in urgency: 'God the Beneficent, destroy Mayaƙi and Nabame!' (CW, #31, v. 1, p. 208). It omits the standard opening invocations, which gives the impression that she wrote it in the heat of the moment. In it she prayed that God might give Aliyu future success and named all the trouble spots. She stressed also the importance of unity of purpose and disciplined order. She appealed for supplies: strong horses, food, clothing, safe roads, and good pastures:

> [O God] give us fat cattle, goats, sheep and camels
> For our satisfaction.
> May the wildernesses have in them prosperous settlements
> So people can travel without fear.
>
> (CW, #31, vv. 18–19, p. 209)

The last words best sum up her feelings: 'without fear'. The home of Mustafa's widow Hadiza, whom Asma'u had assisted when making the hijra from Gudu, was attacked and her books scattered. A girl, said by Gobir sources to be a granddaughter of Asma'u, was abducted and given to Mayaƙi at Tsibiri where she bore him three sons. People wanted an end to fear of such attacks.

Following the failure to deal with Mayaƙi and the attacks on the Caliphate heartlands, the foremost scholars in Sifawa met in the mosque and demanded action. The place of the meeting was where the Shehu had lived for several years prior to moving to Sokoto and where he had written *Be Sure of God's Truth* (*Tabbat*

Hakika) in 1812, which Asma'u had revised in her own version in 1831: 'Whoever seeks a position of authority | So that he can get rich or become powerful, | Or slyly allies himself with wrong-doers, | And those who pay money for titles of authority | Without doubt will burn hereafter' (*Be sure of God's Truth*') CW, #6, vv. 8–12, p. 48]. The venue had symbolic significance for all those involved. In this case, Asma'u wrote to reinforce confidence in Aliyu, based on his character.[1]

In another powerful poem, *The Battle of Gawakuke II* (1856), Asma'u reinforced Bello's place in history as a forceful and charismatic leader, as is evident in the work's opening statement:

I give thanks to Allah, who neither slumbers nor dies,
    I greet the Prophet, the Chosen One, the Saved
The blessing and peace of Allah be upon him,
    His companions and kinsmen
And so, now listen, for it is my intention in this poem
To say what I have heard of the deeds of Bello the peerless
    And what I have witnessed of his miracles
Thereby soothing my broken heart which longs for Bello.
                    (CW, #38, vv. 1–4, p. 233)

---

1   Ever-willing to comment on the political situation – and perhaps to draw a parallel with effective leadership, thus bolstering trust in Aliyu – she went on to list Bello's attributes in an account of the Battle of Gawakuke, which had taken place in 1836. In full flow, she described the battle in some detail ending with the prophecy: 'I keep remembering how he preached | For a whole month warning of the drought which would come' (CW, #38, v. 64, p. 240). Indeed, by the end of the decade the drought was upon them. It was a time like no other to pull together, because the cyclical droughts which occur in the Sahel are scourges that are not selective of whom they affect; town dwellers, nomadic herders and arable farmers all suffer alike as food runs out and people become emaciated and die. When the Sahel was gripped by drought in 1859 Gobir savants believed supernatural forces were involved; people shrugged and said, '*shin yaƙi na yiwuwa ba ruwa?*' – 'How can we wage war if the wells are dry and there are no watering holes?'

Then death came to the four leading figures in the struggle between the followers of the Shehu and the Hausa nationalists. Nabame, Chief of Kebbi, the man who had reneged, was killed in a skirmish, and Mayaƙi Sarkin Gobir died in Tsibiri of natural causes. Their deaths were followed in October 1859 by that of Caliph Aliyu, unexpectedly at Wurno, and then of Waziri Abdulkadir, Asma'u's son.

The people of Gobir had battled on against Sokoto, even after having been dispossessed of their homeland, seen their capital, Alƙalawa, burned down, and been forced into exile. The Gobir leader, Mayaƙi, was a thorn in the flesh of the Caliphate for twenty years. He and his predecessors throughout the first half of the nineteenth century fought to retain the mode of living they had inherited from their forebears. According to Gobir sources, Mayaƙi was the 329th chief in line, reaching back name by name to the very distant past when they had lived, it is said, in the Middle East. Their way of life, grounded in a blend of native customs and traditions and Islam, dated back at least 400 years and, significantly, had been tolerant of any Muslims in their midst who wanted nothing to do with *bori* tradition. The people of Gobir believed they had a balanced and just society and were not content to take the Shehu's reformist views on board. In this they gained some support from a very eminent scholar in Bornu, El Kanemi, who was at loggerheads with Bello at the time of Clapperton's visit. El Kanemi argued that 'though idolatrous sacrifices were great evils, it was not right to say that those guilty of them were heathens […] it were better to command them to mend their ways than to make war on them'.[1] Unfortunately, there is nothing from the Gobir side to explain their perspective, nothing to match the massive documentation of the Sokoto Caliphate's records. Defenders of Gobir blame the Jihadists who, they say, burned everything, but it is not remotely

1   S. J. Hogben and A. H. M. Kirk-Greene, *The Emirates of Northern Nigeria* (London: Oxford University Press, 1966), pp. 325–6.

credible that every single document written over fifty years in a wide variety of locations was destroyed by Caliphate officials. For seventeen years, from 1842 to 1859, the situation did not change, and the raids and campaigns continued.

The Waziri Abdulkadir presided over the burial arrangements for Caliph Aliyu. Aliyu was laid to rest in a room north of his father's tomb. Abdulkadir then convened the electors. Contenders for the position of Caliph rode post-haste to Wurno to present their credentials. As recorded by Sokoto historians, Asma'u made known to her son, Waziri Abdulkadir, that she supported the candidacy of Ahmadu, son of Caliph Atiku. She pointed out that fifty years previously, when Ahmadu was only six years old, she had been present when the Shehu foretold good news about him, predicting that he would be a man of honour, one who would act purposefully and uphold the Prophet's *Sunna*. Her testimony on this occasion was the deciding factor: before the election was decided, leading figures said that the Shehu when at Sifawa had indicated Ahmadu's qualities as a follower of the *Sunna* of the Prophet and his aunt Asma'u also said the same. (Waziri Junaidu, *Tarihin Fulani*, p. 55)

On the day the new Caliph Ahmadu was installed in office, at the ceremony in the mosque, he addressed his governors, advisers, and the populace, commending them to follow the *Sunna*, root out unacceptable innovations and customs, and deal decisively with all acts of tyranny and corruption. He said they must stop selling off land, stop demanding rewards for finding missing animals or slaves, and respond to any summons issued by judges. They must obey the Caliph with alacrity and readily perform collective duties like jihad and the repair of city walls.

Forty days later people were still arriving in Wurno to present their condolences on Caliph Aliyu's death when another shocking event occurred: Waziri Abdulkadir died. How his mother coped we can only deduce from the elegies she wrote when other loved ones died – she felt sorrowful and lonely and let her tears flow, while accepting what had happened with humility, and praying that God forgive his sins and unite him with the Shehu in Paradise.

The new Caliph appointed Ibrahim Halilu, Abdulkadir's son and Asma'u's eldest grandson, as his Waziri. Though a young man, Ibrahim had served as his father's deputy and so had some experience of the work involved. Asma'u insisted however that he make his uncle his deputy. She was a determined woman who made her views known, and her wishes were usually acted upon.

The family chart (below) shows the direct descendants of Asma'u who have served as Waziri. By the year 1859, three of Asma'u's and Gidado's sons were dead; the first as a baby, the second, Ahmadu, of illness in 1832, and the third, Abdulkadir, in 1859.

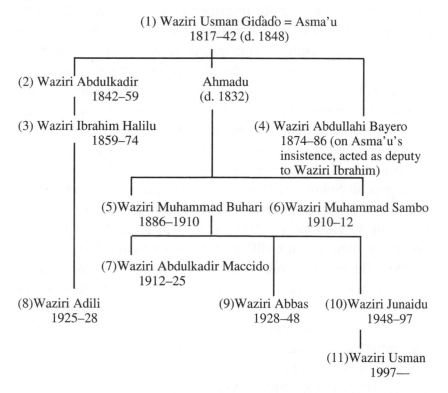

The Hubbare

The tomb of the Shehu Usman dan Fodio lies within the compound where the Fodio family lived. When he moved to Sokoto in 1814, he came with many followers all of whom were settled within the new city walls. Great numbers of scholars and students visited him daily, and congregated in the large empty space seen in the compound today. The graveyard proper is where the Shehu's harem (*cikin gida*) was; however, after his death the whole compound came to be known as the Hubbare. Asma'u's tomb, in honour of her, was placed adjacent to that of the Shehu. Over the Shehu's tomb there is an elevated platform covered with a black cloth inscribed in gold-threaded Qur'anic passages. Otherwise, it is unremarkable, plain. Asma'u's tomb too is plain, in keeping with tradition; it is covered in sand, unmarked, but indicated by the head-high concrete-block wall that protects it. Nearby there are many other graves that are unmarked but known to *Mai Hubbare* (the custodian), to scholars and frequent pilgrims. Waziri Junaidu wrote a *Handbook for Pilgrims* (*Bughyat ar-ragibin bi-ziyadi is'afi z-za'irin*), translated into Hausa by Kadi Haliru Binji and published by Sifawa Printing Enterprise in Sokoto, with the support of Alhaji Ahmadu Bello, Premier of Northern Nigeria, in 1961. Jean Boyd has two faded photos of the Hubbare *ca.* 1960, which appear in *Tarihin Fulani*. The place then was not different from when she last visited it in 2003. Beside the tombs mentioned, there are, on one side, a row of unmarked graves of esteemed relatives, and, on the other, several round huts with small patches of vegetation around them. The huts were the apartments of family members and the women associated with Asma'u. Some details of their histories. as entrusted to us by their descendants, may be of interest to future researchers (see Appendix, below p. 232).

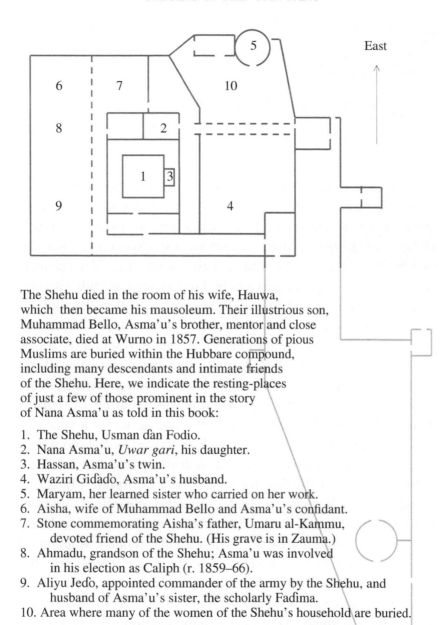

The Shehu died in the room of his wife, Hauwa,
which then became his mausoleum. Their illustrious son,
Muhammad Bello, Asma'u's brother, mentor and close
associate, died at Wurno in 1857. Generations of pious
Muslims are buried within the Hubbare compound,
including many descendants and intimate friends
of the Shehu. Here, we indicate the resting-places
of just a few of those prominent in the story
of Nana Asma'u as told in this book:

1. The Shehu, Usman dan Fodio.
2. Nana Asma'u, *Uwar gari*, his daughter.
3. Hassan, Asma'u's twin.
4. Waziri Gidado, Asma'u's husband.
5. Maryam, her learned sister who carried on her work.
6. Aisha, wife of Muhammad Bello and Asma'u's confidant.
7. Stone commemorating Aisha's father, Umaru al-Kammu,
    devoted friend of the Shehu. (His grave is in Zauma.)
8. Ahmadu, grandson of the Shehu; Asma'u was involved
    in his election as Caliph (r. 1859–66).
9. Aliyu Jedo, appointed commander of the army by the Shehu, and
    husband of Asma'u's sister, the scholarly Fadima.
10. Area where many of the women of the Shehu's household are buried.

*Fig. 9 Plan of the Hubbare (adapted from the sketch, not to scale, in
Waziri Junaidu's handbook for visitors to the site).*

4

POETIC WORKS

Asma'u's character

It is evident that Nana Asma'u was a figure to be reckoned
with – her strength of character is clear but with what other
qualities was it combined? It is not her copious output, as much
as her Sufi affiliation that can support the expectation that she
was held in affection as well as being respected. Her spiritual
beliefs likely led her to strive to be kind as well as authoritative,
forgiving as well as unbending, forbearing as well as demanding.
Her strength is reflected in the epithets associated with her, as
well as the symbolic force of her given name, Asma'u. A friend
of Jean Boyd's, also called Asma'u, told her a story that sheds
light on the historical Asma'u's character. Upon graduating from
university, the contemporary Asma'u was required to register
with the National Youth Service Corps and serve for a year in a
part of Nigeria far from her home. She arrived in Sokoto where
she worked as directed alongside fellow ex-students but after
some months fell ill. She was admitted to hospital which she
found wanting in many respects, including cleanliness and the
availability of medicine. Her outspoken remarks were overheard
and she was asked her name. 'Asma'u', she replied, whereupon
an elderly woman who was lying in the same ward said: 'No
wonder she speaks out as she does – it's because she is called
Asma'u. That's why. Gidado's Asma'u was just the same, she
also spoke her mind.' (Personal communication, *ca.* 2001, from
Asma'u Joda, one of the founders of Women in Nigeria (WIN).)

Other attributes come from a story retold by a blind beggar in a place called Tambawal. This shows how luck played a part in rediscovering the elegy written for Asma'u. One day as the beggar's wife sang for alms in the marketplace she was heard reciting the poem by a well-known scholar who recognized that the song was an elegy about Nana, and one he had never heard before. He took the opportunity to write it down and bring it back to Sokoto. From it we have learned among other things that Asma'u had a highly personal nickname, '*Inji*', not mentioned in any other document. Waziri Junaidu pointed out that *Inji* is akin to the Arabic usage, *Injil* (for Evangel or Gospel), which indicates authority. He said it was used affectionately by close relatives.

Asma'u was a peacemaker and it is serendipitous that the elegy for her describes her in the same Hausa words as those used for the United Nations Organization: she 'stitched the world together' [H., *madùnkar duniya*]. However, according to the elegy, Asma'u's mediatory skills were discretely bestowed. She did not get involved in family quarrels; she had the wisdom to stand back and remain aloof when, for example, nephews and grandsons bickered and vied for public office. She reserved judgement, remained impartial and expressed an opinion only when asked by both sides to intervene. Asma'u's position was encapsulated in the title by which she was called, *uwargari*, Mother of the People. What is very clear in her role is the African concept of women's leadership, and the presence of a woman leader with direct access to the man identified as the ruler, be he chief, caliph, king, sarki or shaykh.[1]

---

1   In this context it is interesting that when the King of Morocco, Hassan II (r. 1961–99), on his accession, married Lalla Latifa, the daughter of a provincial governor (*The Guardian*, Obituary, 26th July 1999), she was called the 'mother of the king's children'. The expression implies protection, as does the Hausa title *uwardeji*, which also means 'mother of the king's children' in the Gobir region. The title *Inna*, also used in Gobir to refer to women leaders, carries very similar associations.

The composer of the elegy also expressed the sentiment that Asma'u was kind. He said: 'she benefited and helped the poor, the aged and the orphaned.' She redistributed any gifts brought to her by well-wishers and visiting dignitaries, and was entrusted with ensuring that the part of the booty captured in war that was intended for the poor was actually given to those most in need. Items included good quality clothes and slaves, many of the latter being allocated to work as labourers grinding corn, tending livestock, hauling water in struggling households where the main householder had fallen ill, been injured or killed. Female slaves were sent to help a sick widow or to care for children where the mother was incurably ill. Gidaɗo was himself described by Asma'u as constantly tending to the needs of the people. There is every reason to believe that husband and wife acted together, making it their business to find out who was in need, thereby anticipating people's requests.

In addition to her reputation as a mediator and just benefactor, Asma'u was known as a scholar of great intellect who put her gifts to practical use in the public arena. She sought rare books, some of antiquity, mostly imported from the East, which she then simplified and used to benefit her students. She wanted them to understand, and was infinitely patient in her teaching. Several of her works illustrate her skill as a teacher. Her work *Tibb al-Nabi* (*Medicine of the Prophet*), describes an Islamic healing system. Understanding it requires some knowledge of Hausa medicine, which is focused on the holistic concept of *lafiya,* wellness. *Lafiya* includes social and political well-being, as well as the state of health of mind and body, and extends to commonsense precautions, such as the protection of mothers during childbirth, and the preservation of grain stores against times of hunger.

Hausa herbalists had knowledge of the efficacious uses to which grasses, fruits, leaves and roots could be put. Anyone with broken bones, however, went to a bonesetter, a profession that, generally speaking, still has a very high reputation in the community. Many today prefer the bonesetter to a visit to the Accident and Emergency department of a hospital. People with unidentified malaises often went to barber-surgeons who did blood-cupping using a cow's horn with a small hole bored into it to allow for suction. This remedy was used to remove the 'dead' blood deemed responsible for feelings of lassitude. The procedure is still carried out in contemporary times at places like petrol stations, the sides of roads, and the periphery of markets, as well as in people's homes.

Not all conditions responded or respond to treatment by a bonesetter, barber-surgeon, herbalist or midwife – such as blindness (caused by, for example, glaucoma), incontinence, infertility, emotional complaints, complications in childbirth like internal fistulas, or dementia. People searched desperately for medicines to ameliorate their ailments. In Gobir and elsewhere they often turned to *bori*, the spirit possession cult, but the moral order of Islam pointed in the opposite direction, away from the practices of spirit possession to the Prophetic traditions dealing with medicine and related subjects. These traditions are presented, always in written form, as an integral part of the larger corpus of *hadith*s of the Prophet and therefore deemed authentic.

Bello had been very interested in curative medicines and wrote a treatise recommending medicinal herbs and minerals, recording their names in Hausa, Fulfulde and Tamachek. He addressed the problems of purgatives, eye diseases and piles and advised the Emir of Zaria about his kidney complaint. He had hoped Clapperton would send a doctor to his court and was delighted to welcome an Egyptian doctor-scholar in 1836.

Asma'u's document on the *Medicine of the Prophet* is dated 8 November 1839, almost exactly two years after Bello's death. She incorporated a poem of dedication to him as follows: 'I composed my book in the fortress of my Shaikh | The one called Bello, my bosom friend, my brother' (CW #17, vv. 1–2, p. 119). The work itself focused on the Qur'anic suras 44–108; the Arabic source material that was the basis for Asma'u's poem has yet to be identified. The poem opens after a short doxology:

In the name of Allah the munificent, the merciful. God bless and protect the noble Prophet and his Family, Companions and sincere supporters.

Asma'u, daughter of the Shehu, Commander of the Faithful, the light of the age. Uthman b. Fudi, (may God be pleased with him and pour blessings upon him), said: Now we proceed. This is a book which we have named 'Glad tidings to the Brethren on using the *suras* from the Qur'an of the generous Creator'.

(CW, #17, p. 102)

Medical conditions are named for, and thus paired with, specific Qur'anic suras, to be read or worn as an amulet. The ailments for which these prayers were prescribed included: sadness and depression, wounds, deafness, haemorrhoids, epilepsy, headaches and sickly babies. The poetic work fitted the Hausa concept of *lafiya*, wellness, prescribing for 'someone who is travelling at night', Sura 78; for boils, Sura 77; for 'protection against damage by insects', Sura 83; for 'a child at birth', Sura 90. These remedies would have been, and still are, administered in various ways. Any of the verses specified may have been recited aloud, possibly over the sick person, or written out in Arabic script onto a wooden writing board. In the latter case, when the vegetable-based ink had dried it was washed off and collected in a bowl. The inky water was then drunk or sniffed or washed over the affected part of the body. Qur'anic verses were also written on small pieces of paper which were then wrapped up and sewn into a soft brown leather cover worn dangling from a twisted leather necklace. Nearly all babies have one to this day. Other, bigger amulets were worn round the waist and sometimes hung prominently in a house. Knowing that the Qur'an itself was the source of the power being invoked gave relief to the believer and provided a perfect alternative to *bori*, which in this context was redundant.

126

Here is an example from Asma'u's work concerning Sura 90:

It was related by Ubayy ibn Ka'b (may God be pleased with him), regarding the Prophet (may God bless and protect him) that he said: 'Whoever reads *Surat al-Balad* will be granted protection from God's anger on Resurrection Day.' Its special property: if hung on a child at birth, the child will be protected from any evils and from colic pain. And if the child is made to sniff of its water, he will have sound nostrils, be free from colds and grow up in good health.

(CW #17, p. 113)

And of Sura 76:

Whoever reads it will have peace of mind and heart. And if he is unable to read it, he should have it copied, rub it off into water and drink it.

(CW, #17, p. 109)

Asma'u's work was written in Arabic because she intended it to be used by scholars who could best interpret the text for the benefit of ordinary people. The book, when circulated, carried with it the stamp of her authority authenticated by Bello, whose interest in medicine was well known.

Two other poems written at this time are remarkable for quite a different reason. They were the first that Asma'u composed directly in Hausa, intended specifically for her Hausa students, who spoke neither Arabic nor Fulfulde, for the *jaji*s and for other women of the community whose language was Hausa. This work, *In Praise of the Prophet*, was a contribution towards cultural Islamization through the introduction of Muslim themes and the adoption of the Prophet 'who excels all others in rank'. This was material that nurtured the religion of ordinary people in the marketplace, and demonstrated that Islam was no longer the preserve of an intellectual elite. These poems made a significant impact upon the common culture.

The words used in the poem are simple enough but contain information so compressed that every line has to be interpreted by a teacher. An example shows the layers of meaning that are being conveyed:

> Likewise the Qurayshi, when they were starving
> During the final battle in Mecca, for Ahmada.
> And the dried well of Hudaibiya
> Where the water appeared after arrows struck it,
>   for the sake of Ahmada.
>
> (CW, #19, vv. 38–9, p. 129)

Asma'u taught her students who the Quraysh were – kinfolk of the Prophet – and what the battle concerned. The significance of the dried well, paralleled the event at the place in the wilderness called Bulaici, where according to Asma'u in her poem about Caliph Muhammad Bello's last battle, he performed the miracle of finding water in a barren land. No one who had knowledge of Gawakuke would fail to see the link with the incident at Hudaybiyya or to understand what Asma'u was aiming at.

The second poem, *The Path of Truth*, also famous, was neatly organized for teaching purposes around lessons concerning religious obligations, rewards, and punishments. Its sections include commentary on religious duties; resurrection; sinners; salvation; and here, Paradise:

> For there is [in Paradise] no illness, no ageing, no poverty,
> No death: we remain for ever.
> Forever in enjoyment, relaxation and pleasant talk
> We walk in Paradise, we have seen Muhammada...
> The houses are made of gold, the clothes of silk
> We drink from fragrant rivers of Salsabil with Ahmada.
> The bodies of people are as beautiful as rubies or red coral,
> Their ornaments are jewels and topaz.
> They feel no sadness of heart and do not think sad thoughts
>   They are forever in Paradise together with Muhammada.
>
> (CW, #23 vv. 95–6, 98–100)

Asma'u's poem binds together local events and historical accounts, casting the Islamic reform movement of nineteenth century in the broader context of historical Islam, and drawing parallels between the Caliphate's struggles and those of the Prophet in the seventh century. She concludes the work with her own signature in v. 125, confirming her belief in the credibility of her account:

> If anyone asks who composed this song, say
> That it is Nana, daughter of the Shehu, who loves Muhammada.
> You should firmly resolve, friends, to follow her
> And thus you will follow exactly the Sunna of Muhammada.
> (CW, #23, vv. 125–6, p. 187)

In weaving her signature into the end of the poem, Asma'u followed classic Arabic poetic form, while also describing her role in the community. She was secure in her knowledge of her authority, and the rightness of what she advocated.

Asma'u remained a rock of integrity in times that were troubling when her kinsmen were involved in misdoings. For example, she vented her anger on one of her relatives, a regional governor called ɗan Yalli. She was disturbed by his ridiculous behaviour. This man was the son of the Fulani patriarch, Muhammad Moyijo who had offered a safe haven to the Shehu after the Community was forced to leave Gudu in 1803. Starving and weak, the Community was restored to health in Yabo, Moyijo's place, and the Shehu always held his benefactor in high esteem. In about 1830 ɗan Yalli succeeded his father and seems at first to have to have received plaudits, distinguishing himself in the Battle of Gawakuke, Bello's famous victory. During the reign of Bello's successor Atiku, who had the reputation of being very serious-minded, nothing was heard of ɗan Yalli. Change came with the reign of Caliph Aliyu, a man well known for bonhomie. Apparently ɗan Yalli felt free at last to enjoy the benefits high office could bring: gifts and tribute. What might have started as

generosity degenerated into extravagance and thence to buffoo-
nery, a state of affairs unacceptable to Asma'u. Many stories were
told about him – his notoriety was such that they live on. Two
tales are as follows – they are allegories in which the characters
and events stand for something else:

One day ɗan Yalli asked Ajia, a councillor, an asinine question:
what was it that made frogs so noisy. Ajia, who had a reputation for
being a wit, replied that it was because they felt so cold, whereupon the
chief had large bundles of clothes and food taken to the pond. The boys
who took the loads down to the pond stole the bundles and silenced the
frogs with stones. ɗan Yalli therefore praised Ajia's keen perception
and rejoiced to think of the frogs living in comfort. When they started
croaking again, ɗan Yalli asked Ajia Baro what it was they wanted now.
He replied they were simply voicing their thanks and saying, 'Hail to
the Chief!'

On another occasion when ɗan Yalli was on his way to the Caliph
in Wurno he met some men carrying bundles of cloth. He called them
to come to him but only three came. He told the three to throw their
bundles on the ground and dance on the cloth, which they did. He then
presented them with robes, horses and male and female slaves. So the
others cursed their own bad luck.[1]

Clearly, ɗan Yalli was not held in high esteem. The new caliph,
Ahmad Rufai ɗan Shehu, dismissed him forthwith and Asma'u
rounded on him in a withering attack on his conduct, opening her
poem (CW #49, vv. 1–2), without introductory lines:

Thanks be to God who empowered us to overthrow ɗan Yalli
    Who has caused so much trouble.
He behaved unlawfully, he did wanton harm
    And caused hardship to Muslims.

She then praised Caliph Ahmad for deposing him saying:

---

1   Personal communication to Jean Boyd from Sarkin Kebbi, in the company
     of Malam Attahiru and the Imam, at Yabo, 1980.

I swear he has extirpated evil and tyranny
    We can ourselves testify to the
Robberies and extortion in the markets, on the
    Highways and at the city gateways.

(CW, #49, vv. 9–10, p. 276)

Thus, in her writings Asma'u was unflinching in advocating the ethical and moral standards expected of Caliphate leaders. She expected actions to reflect those standards; no one's position exempted them, and she was unafraid of commenting publicly on these matters.

Indeed, the fact that civilizations in the Sahel have long had a tradition of reflective leaders like those in the community of Degel, made such transgressions the more egregious. The idea of the philosopher, theologian and writer was conscientiously nurtured and handed down through successive generations. In the case of the Shehu's community, women were integral to this ideal. Asma'u was part of the Sokoto Caliphate's intellectual elite and her interests led her to seek and enjoy close fellowship with the women she described as her beloved friends with fine reputations. Foremost among these was Asma'u's sister-in-law Aisha, the wife of Muhammad Bello. Aisha's father, Umaru al-Kammu, had been the closest of the Shehu's friends; the Shehu had been the first of Umaru's students and lived next to him at Degel where the little girls had played together, and later learned to read from their wooden writing boards at the school run by Hadija, Asma'u's older sister. When the Shehu was proclaimed leader at Gudu, Umaru was third after Abdullahi and Bello in pledging his allegiance to his friend, the Shehu, the new Imam. One of Umaru al-Kammu's sons married Asma'u's older full sister, Habsatu, and another son married Safiya, a half-sister; both women wrote poetry.

Umaru's daughter Aisha married Muhammad Bello at the same time that Asma'u married Gidado and when they moved to Sokoto the young brides lived in houses that were not more than five-minutes' walk away from each other. It was to Aisha that

Muhammad Bello entrusted the delivery of an acrostic poem he wrote for Asma'u on the occasion that enemy forces camped near Sokoto, the flickering lights of their fires visible from the city walls. Aisha is the only woman apart from Asma'u to be buried in a named tomb in the main precinct of the Hubbare. 'Oh, what a woman!', Asma'u wrote, in an elegy written in 1855 (CW, #36, vv. 3–13, pp. 225–6):

> The death of the beloved Aisha reminded me of those who have
>   passed away
>   from among wise and pious sisters.
> My sorrows, my loneliness, and my melancholy increase
> the flow of tears on my cheeks into torrents.
> At the loss of the noble Aisha.
> Oh, what a woman! She had all the virtues
> Of pious women, humble to their Lord;
> Of the women who have memorized the Qur'an by heart
>   and who do extra
> In prayers, alms-giving, then recitation of the Qur'an,
>   defending the unjustly treated, carrying the burdens of many
>   responsibilities.
> She was a guardian of orphans and widows,
>   a pillar of the community, ensuring harmony.
> I am desolate over losing her, for she was my bosom friend,
>   my confidante, from our earliest days.
> This is no surprise; the love we had for each other came to us
>   from our fathers before us; it was not short-lived.
> God in Heaven, judge her with pure forgiveness
>   and make room for a grave in perpetual light.
> On the Day of Judgement preserve her from all that is feared,
>   from everything terrifying on that day.
> And place her in Paradise with our Shaykh,
>   her father and her husband in the heavenly abodes.

Clearly, Aisha's friendship with Asma'u had much to do with their like minds, and shared interest in creative scholarship. Asma'u cultivated such friendships.

But not all Asma'u's scholarly friends lived in such close proximity as Aisha. For example, her sister Hadija, a woman of towering intellect, lived in a hamlet beyond Wurno, too far for frequent visits. Evidence that exists of Asma'u's communications with scholars across the Maghreb indicates that it is likely that these formidable women scholars also wrote to each other and exchanged the poetry they created. (See CW, #54, p. 282; #55 pp. 284–7.) Hadija was described by her son Abdulkadir, born at Degel, as 'affectionate, merciful and tender' to him. She wrote a commentary in Fulfulde on the *Mukhtasar* of Khalil and composed a long work about Fulfulde grammar. More accessible works are her poems on the coming of the Mahdi, the presager of the end of the world, and a prayer for patience in adversity. (From the collection of Waziri Junaidu in Jean Boyd's personal archives.)

Another relative and half-sister to Asma'u was Fadima, a full sister of Muhammad Bello. Fadima was born at Degel. She married the Commander-in-Chief, Aliyu Jedo, and was pious and scrupulous about her religion; she fasted a lot and went into religious retreats (H., *halwa*; Ar. *khalwa)*, balancing this aspect of her life with her support for the Muslim kinship. Asma'u described her:

> She succoured the Community with her many acts of charity;
> feeding people,
> Relatives and strangers alike, she showed no discrimination.
> She produced provisions when an expedition was mounted
> and had many responsibilities.
> She sorted problems and urged people to live peacefully,
> and forbade quarrelling.
> She had studied a great deal and she had a deep understanding
> of what she had read.
>
> (Waziri Junaidu mss.)

Two poems by Fadima have been discovered, the first concerns the physical changes which portend death like greying hair and decaying teeth. The second lists the merits of extra invocations, *dhikr*, recited with the help of prayer beads.

Much as she respected intellectual productivity, Asma'u did not measure the affection she felt for her friends by the number of poems they produced. She valued most highly their contribution to the Community, speaking warmly of their work, including good neighbourliness and quiet commonsense. For Asma'u, a person's character was the most important part of their being; this perspective is reflected in her works. An example of her concern with character is the elegy she wrote for a frail youth, thought to be her adopted nephew Habsatu's son, Umaru, who cared for her ceaselessly. When he was killed by a bolting horse, she was overcome with emotion and gave a rare glimpse of her personal circumstances: '...[He] cheered the loneliness I have felt since my parents | And siblings died, and never made me anxious. | Whether it was a message to be taken or a job to be done, he did it, | And was always there to assist me. | He was especially helpful as far as family matters were concerned' (CW, #32, vv. 6–8, p. 211). She delighted in the willing giver, the cheerful helper, the volunteer. She praised Zaharatu, a person about whom nothing is known other than what is given here:

> My friends, with this song I sympathize with you
> > over the death of Zaharatu.
> She was a fine person who benefited the Muslim Community
> She gave religious instruction to the ignorant and helped
> > everyone in their daily affairs.
> Whenever called upon to help she came, responding
> To lay out the dead without hesitation.
> With the same willingness she attended women in childbirth.
> All kinds of good works were performed by Zaharatu.
> She was pious and most persevering: she delighted in giving
> > and was patient and forbearing.
> I grieve for her in this song: I weep because unhappiness
> > fuels my aching heart.

And I am sorrowful because the world is
   being depleted by the deaths of my beloved women friends.
                                   (CW #41, vv. 5–12, pp. 250–1)

The fascinating thing about Asma'u's personality is that it combined an ability to speak directly to rulers and scholars, with a determination to educate illiterate rural women at the bottom of the social scale, the very poor women without connections to the elite, who could not write their names or recite the *Fatiha*, the opening verses of the Qur'an. For these women Asma'u wrote works in Hausa, their first language, and since she could not visit them, scattered as they were among hundreds of villages and hamlets, she devised the plan of the 'Yan Taru to bring them to her. This is the kind of poem she wrote for them:

And trust in Muhammad [God's] Messenger,
Then you will be an upright Muslim.
Do not innovate. Keep strictly to the *Sunna*
For the *Sunna* will suffice you until you reach Heaven
                                  (CW, #39, vv. 6–7, p. 243)

Listen to my warnings, brethren,
And heed them: admonition is good for you
Let us repent because repentance
Is the gateway to God the Merciful
Give the alms you must and those you wish, and pray…
Say your prayer-beads in the mornings
And in the evenings, and say extra prayers in the night.
                               (CW, #39, vv. 14–17, pp. 244–5)

Women, a warning. Leave not your homes without good reason
You may go out to get food or seek education.
In Islam, it is a religious duty to seek knowledge
Women may leave their homes freely for this.
Repent and behave like respectable married women.
You must obey your husband's lawful demands.
You must dress modestly and be God-fearing…

I have written this poem of admonition
For you to put to good use in the Community.

(CW, #39, vv. 20–3, 25, pp. 245–6)

For Asma'u everyone was equally deserving of attention, equally capable of learning, and equally responsible for using what they learned for the betterment of society at large.

Death of Asma'u and the elegy on her passing

Asma'u died in 1280 (1864-5) at the age of 73. Her body was carried to the Hubbare and laid to rest next to the Shehu's tomb; to echo her own words about Aisha: 'Oh what a woman!'

The elegy for Asma'u, believed to have been written by her youngest brother, Isa, is unpublished. It particularly celebrates her peace-making, kindness to whoever sought her help, and charity: 'Everyone who came could depend on Nana... She gave robes, trousers, hats to men | And clothes of good quality to women'.

Fig 10 Traditional male attire: robe, turban, slippers
(Photo: Jean Boyd, 1960)

POETIC WORKS

*Fig. 11 Hausa woman wearing Sokoto hand-woven robes
(Photo: Jean Boyd, 1997)*

Alhaji Muhammadu Magaji heard the elegy for Asma'u being sung by 'Yarbuga, wife of Sarkin Makahin Tambawal 'Danwuronange in Tambawal in 1978, and wrote it down:

At the end of the year 1280 Nana left us
    Having received the call of the Lord of Truth.
When I went to the open space in front of Gidado's house
    I found it too crowded to pass through
Men were crying, everyone without exception
    Even animals uttered cries of grief they say,
Men and women alike asked dan Ardo [household servant] for news.
    My song is of Nana; you know who I am
Out of obedience and respect to Inji I have ceased to weep
    Lest people say I failed to do what she said.
All of us, the children of the Shehu, followed the leadership of Inji.
    I held love and respect for her in my heart.
Let them write their elegies; I will write mine.
    Although the gesture will be inadequate.

Our lamp has been taken away; it was as brilliant as lightning.
May God preserve the rest of them[1]
She benefited the aged Muslims
Nana's charity was a thousand fold
She helped the poor, men and women alike
Everyone who came could depend on Nana.
She helped orphaned boys and girls
She gave robes, trousers, hats to men
And clothes of good quality to women
To some she gave female slaves to others male ones.
Oh God of Grace no one has power to act except You
Who alone has authority, the one Only God
Lets us fling aside the useless deceptive world
    We will not abide in it for ever; we must die
The benevolent one, Nana was a peacemaker
She healed almost all hurts

---

1   That is, her surviving siblings, Maryam and Isa. There were others, including Ahmadu Rufa'i, who was caliph 1867–73.

She did not get involved in arguments or quarrels
    She stopped family rifts when she heard of them
Whenever Caliph Bello's children visited her
    She showed she loved them, their aunt, the saintly Nana.

***

Greetings to you Caliph, the watchful, on account of the loss
    Of your Aunt, your father's younger sister, whom she helped.
And I greet the children of Sufura'u's (wife) son
    None is discriminated against in extending condolences to them,
    None is left out.
Greetings to you Dije (Asma'u's slave) the Gobir woman
    And to you Siddiq's mother and Alhajiya (co-wives)
I greet all of you, our visitors who have come to condole us
On the calamity that has befallen me, causing me to weep.
Greetings to you Bawa now in Zaria
    O Tower of Strength who supports the needy
May God be pleased with Nana and may He dispel the darkness
    Of the grave and the terrors
    Of the questioners in the after life .... (unfinished)

That Asma'u's elegy was preserved for over a hundred years in the oral form in the absence of its publication is testimony to the vitality of her legend. Anyone in Sokoto – or anywhere throughout most of northern Nigeria (with a twenty-first century population of over fifty million) – knows who Nana Asma'u was, and what she stands for in contemporary times.

Continuing Asma'u's example: her sister, Maryam

The Shehu had a daughter, Maryam, whose mother was a slave girl called Mariya. Nothing has yet been discovered about Mariya's background; all that is known for sure is that she was captured at the beginning of the Jihad, and that she was the Shehu's only concubine. Her name, Mariya, was significant because in the time of the Prophet Muhammad a Christian slave girl was sent to

139

him by the Coptic governor of Egypt Muqawqis and her name was Mariya. Alone among the women of the Prophet's house she bore him a child, the longed-for son, Ibrahim, who died. Likewise the son Ibrahim born to the Shehu's concubine also died. In all, she had seven children of whom two lived to adulthood, Maryam and Isa. Maryam was brought up in her mother's room inside the Shehu's compound where it was his custom to sleep with each wife for one night in turn.[1]

Maryam and all other women were encouraged to follow the traditions of Asma'u because Muslim women were actively encouraged to become educated, regardless of their social background. When she was twelve Maryam was married to Adde, a son of Gidado by his first wife. Maryam bore Adde two children, a girl called Ta Modi, and a boy, both of whom were adopted by Gidado's brother who lived in close proximity to the Waziri.[2] The first of the dynastic connections between the metropolis of Kano and Sokoto had begun when Maryam was a girl, with the marriage between the Emir of Kano, Suliman, and Maryam's niece, Muhammad Bello's daughter.[3] In about 1828 Maryam, by

---

1   It happened that the Shehu was in Hauwa's room when he died, and, fol-
     lowing the custom, he was buried there. Hauwa moved to a new apart-
     ment nearby. After the Shehu's death the wives stayed on in the home
     compound which later became known as the Hubbare. Therefore today, in
     the twenty-first century, the rooms of the Shehu's wives are still cared for
     by direct women descendants who, through the years, have continued to
     teach women and girls. Maryam, Hadija, and Fadima were, respectively,
     in Kano, Salame, and Binji as married women, but their rooms in the
     Hubbare have been preserved.

2   Cf. Clapperton, vol. 1, p. 107: 'the practice of adopting children is very
     prevalent among the Fulani though they have sons and daughters of their
     own.'

3   The Kano palace was called Gidan Rumfa, named after the prosperous
     fifteenth-century ruler Muhammad Rumfa, who had attracted famous
     scholars from the Maghreb of North Africa. It is generally agreed that
     it was one of them, Shaykh Muhammad al-Maghili, who advised Rumfa
     when rebuilding the palace to follow the style typical of those of the

then a twenty-year-old widow, was married to the Emir of Kano Ibrahim Dabo (r. 1819–46). Little is known about Maryam's life in Kano other than that she had no more children and she made good friends with the Emir's senior wife, Shekara, who had five sons, all of whom esteemed Maryam as much as they respected their own mother. Three became emir.

Prior to the Emir's death in 1846 there had been plans afoot to strengthen Sokoto–Kano relationships by marrying three of his daughters to Sokoto notables. The first Sokoto figure was Isa, Maryam's full brother and the last born of the Shehu's children. The second husband was to be the reigning Caliph, Aliyu, and the third Abdulkadir, Gidado and Asma'u's son.

When Kano Emir Dabo died it was decided to go ahead with the planned weddings because the preparations had been made. So in due course the young brides from Kano were accompanied to Sokoto by his wife Maryam who had decided to return home, and other adult women companions. The bonds between Sokoto and Kano were thus further strengthened by the trio of young brides who travelled together from Kano to Sokoto, accompanied by sensible senior ladies to supervise their behaviour as they grew up. They gave instructions about hygiene, for example, and ensured the young girls said their prayers correctly. Each bride also travelled with a group of young slave-girls who acted first as their playmates, then as their servants, and finally as concubines of the bridegrooms, Isa, Caliph Aliyu, and Abdulkadir. Isa's bride Hussaina made particularly strong bonds with her aunt Maryam, who was 37 then, and did not remarry. Instead, she made a new

Maghreb. There was an outer wall as the first line of defence within which there was ample space for imposing buildings, all adobe structures. These were regularly re-covered with a kind of plaster which served to protect the walls and render them a handsome brown in colour. To this day Gidan Rumfa, the Kano palace, looks much as it always has. At the turn of the millennium it was refurbished with extensive painting and tile-paving in public areas, but the structure itself remains largely true to the original.

life for herself and lived in her mother's house within the confines of the Sokoto Hubbare for the remaining forty years of her life.

Maryam had in her possession a very special copy of the Qur'an which her husband, the Emir of Kano Ibrahim Dabo, had given her. It had been written, some say, by the Emir himself. The writing out of a Qur'an was a great responsibility because the task had to be done in a strictly prescribed manner. The writer had to be someone known to have paid close attention to what he or she was doing and understood the meaning of every word. The writing had to be clear and easily read by all, not just the very able. Each letter had to be distinct and all necessary words correctly placed so that the copy would be of maximum advantage to the reader. The ink had to be of good quality which would not rot the paper nor fade with age.

This copy of the Qur'an brought from Kano has been bequeathed through four generations of Malam Isa's family, as one of the descendants named *Modibo* Hajara told Jean Boyd.

This Qur'an was originally owned by the Shehu's daughter, Maryam. In due course she gave it to a descendant of Isa, the Shehu's son who had been married to Hussaina, one of the three brides. Hajara explained to Jean Boyd: 'A long time ago I, Hajara, left my marital home because of a dispute I had with a co-wife, and I then trekked to my mother's house. My mother persuaded me to return to my husband and she gave me the precious Qur'an with the instruction *"Kada ki yi wargi da shi."* Do not misuse it.'[1] In 1983 when Boyd was in Hajara's home, Hajara brought the copy of the heirloom Qur'an from its place of honour. It had a leather cover, *bango*, which was hard and shiny with age and usage. The cover was held tightly closed by a leather strap wound round it and the end of which was a cowrie shell. A soft nest in the *bango* was the spot where the shell had been tucked into

---

1   Personal communication to Jean Boyd from *Modibo* Hajara (1983).

place every time it was put away over the course of the past 150 years. Her Qur'an had been damaged by water long ago, but the most badly affected part, perhaps one tenth of the whole, had been replaced. Hajara said it was the most precious thing she owned.[1]

Maryam was 'unworldly, saintly and a scholar of the Qur'an', according to Waziri Junaidu. 'she warned against doing evil and urged people to do good. She was virtuous and innocent.' She followed in Asma'u's footsteps and became a principal voice in the Hubbare and a leader of the 'Yan Taru, but she appears to have written only two poems. The first, undated, concerned the categories of people eligible to be appointed imams or disciples of the Prophet. Among those excluded from leading prayer were: the paralysed, a person with suppurating sores, the adulterer, the slave, the incontinent, the unknown stranger, the emasculated, the uncircumcised. Those properly fitted to lead prayers include one who knows the *hadith*, the learned, the God-fearing, pure in spirit, one who wears clean clothes, with washed hands and feet, a family man with many relations, the virtuous and local ruler ... (from the Waziri Junaidu collection). As these qualifications were already common knowledge, perhaps the list was made for an occasion when Maryam was involved in sorting out a problem.

The second of Maryam's poems, also undated, was directed against the guerrilla activities of the long-lived Sarkin Gobir

---

1   In a file called 'The Preservation of Antiquities' in Sokoto Jean Boyd saw a document that showed that, while making a survey of Arabic documents in 1958, at Aliero, in Kebbi State, Dr. Bivar found part of Yunfa's Qur'an. This information proves conclusively that Islam was of great significance in Gobir at the end of the eighteenth century. In addition, in the same file, listed under the category, 'Autograph and Official Documents' there appeared the title 'Letter from Yaya of the household of the Emir of Bauci to Asma daughter of Shaikh Usuman dan Fodio.' This was shown to Bivar by the Waziri, who was with Kadi Haliru Binji. (Jean Boyd: field notes on 'Yan Taru centres, 1958.)

Bawa. In it Maryam makes fun of Bawa in a style reminiscent of Muhammad Bello's mocking tone in some of his poetry. She wrote:

Sarkin Gobir was dismayed when he saw the spears, he turned and fled. He spent the day running until he was exhausted because the Shehu's descendants were out like lions after game. Bawa rode off without a saddle on his horse, leaving behind his turban, amulets, shoes and his belt. He forgot about his cloak, prayer beads, pillow and water bottle. He left behind the camels carrying his belongings. He lived like an owl coming out only at night, his appearance was so bedraggled.

(Waziri Junaidu mss.)

In spite of the absence of proof that letters were frequently exchanged, there is no doubt that Maryam sustained an interest in life at Gidan Rumfa in Kano, and proved to be an astute and patient negotiator. Dynastic marriages continued as a regular practice, though few of the names of the Kano brides were recorded. A notable exception to this was Zainab, who was married to Caliph Abubakar Bello na Raɓa. Zainab's grandson became the famous statesman and politician Alhaji Sir Ahmadu Bello Sardauna, who led Northern Nigeria to self-rule in 1959.

A pilgrim who, having left Sokoto turned up in Southern Tunisia in 1894 where he was picked up, interviewed and then released by French agents, is reported to have said: 'In her family *Uwar Deji* Maryam was consulted on all major matters. Nothing was done without her advice.'[1] Records in Kano and Sokoto prove that this claim was not exaggerated. Maryam was involved in sorting out problems, the first of which concerned Emir Abdullahi. A conspiracy was hatched in court circles which caused letters to be sent to the Caliph complaining of Abdullahi's misrule. The

---

1   A. S. Kanya-Forstner and Paul Lovejoy, *Pilgrims, Interpreters and Agents. French Reconnaissance Report on the Sokoto Caliphate and Bornu 1891–1895* (Madison, WI: University of Wisconsin Press, 1997), p. 65.

letters bore the forged signature of one of the Emir's sons and were intended to damage his reputation. At this point Abdullahi paid a visit to Sokoto where, on account of the letters, he was given a cool reception. The Caliph Muazu felt inclined to depose Emir Abdullahi but before he acted he turned to Maryam for her advice. She was in no doubt: 'Ignore the letters and back the Emir,' she said. After Abdullahi's death there was no obvious successor and another crisis loomed. The Waziri of Sokoto favoured Muhammad Bello, one of the late Emir's sons, but Caliph Muazu was against him. The deadlock was resolved by Maryam who, on being asked for advice, recommended Muhammad Bello because he was the most experienced administrator. Thus, as a result of her intervention, he was appointed.

During the reign of the new Emir of Kano, Muhammad Bello, there was a popular uprising in the locality of the Nilotic Sudan concerning the widely held belief in a Guided Deliverer, the Mahdi. In 1877 Charles George Gordon had been appointed administrator of the Sudan by the Turkish government in Egypt and in 1881 the Mahdi of the Sudan, Muhammad Ahmad proclaimed a jihad against the Turco-Egyptian government. At much the same time French colonial forces were advancing towards Timbuktu, the great centre of scholarship on the Niger. Reports coming from both directions caused the Emir of Kano, Muhammad Bello, to send a letter to Maryam about the then current wave of emigrants.

The reason that Maryam's input was sought on this occasion was that she had information handed down to her by the Shehu, her father, which was pertinent to the coming of the Mahdi. She advised a man called Hayat, one of the grandsons of Caliph Muhammad Bello, a representative of the Sudanese Mahdi in Bornu. Hayat, though he might draw adherents to himself as a lieutenant of the Mahdi, could not succeed so long as the Caliph and the surrounding emirs ignored his call to join the jihad. To preempt any possible moves by Hayat, Maryam *Uwar Deji* wrote the following letter, which revealed vital information entrusted to her by the Shehu and Caliph Muhammad Bello:

I received your important letter and have noted, with thanks, your kind greetings. May God bless you. You described in your letter how Hausa people from many different places are passing through Kano and are describing to you certain phenomena, even saying that it is time to evacuate the region. You therefore wish to know whether what they are saying is true. No, it is not! They are acting in ignorance and what they are saying is untrue. No matter how difficult the situation is at present the time is not yet ripe for departure. My father, Shehu ɗan Fodio certainly prophesied the evacuation of Hausaland and he even described the route which is as follows: [The names are omitted here because the list is so long.] At this place there are 99 peaks, I don't know all their names ... from Fandatal it is only two days to the River Nile. I wish to make it clear that the Shehu did not say when the exodus would take place. However, when the time comes it will be clear to everyone, just as a fire on top of a hill is clear to everyone. Among the signs are the following: prolonged drought leading to a complete lack of water even in wells sunk in the river bed. Another clear indication that it is time to leave Hausaland will be great upheavals in the lands to the west of us which will lead to their people coming in to Hausaland, but by the time they arrive our people will have left. I received these prophesies from the Shehu and [his son] Muhammad Bello. The present drought and the fighting taking place between ourselves and the unbelievers are not the fearful signs of the exodus. God will relieve us of these burdens and we shall conquer the unbelievers' cities until in time there will be no more unbelievers. But if you receive reports of drought and troubled times and the movement of people eastwards then these are the signs foretold. Let me give you notice as from a father to his son, fear God in private and in public, this is the most important thing. I beseech you to enact the reforms brought by the Shehu. Never let doubt enter your mind. And always follow the advice of the majority of the community. Don't rely on your own opinion. I am grateful for your letter. I give thanks to God for a praiseworthy son. May God bless you.

(Waziri Junaidu mss.)

In addition to adjudicating disputes and advising political figures, Maryam received annual tribute from subordinate emirs just as the Caliph himself did. It was her bounden duty to redistribute the articles – clothes, horses, boots, elaborately woven blankets, honey and slaves – to those in need, the valorous or the bereaved for example. Thus, in her many capacities in the Caliphate, Maryam continued the role that Asma'u had played. She was a respected senior member of the Community whose wisdom was sought, and whose advice was valued. She exemplified the ethical code by which Asma'u had lived, and the values that Asma'u taught in her writings, her teachings, and her actions.

A poem about Maryam which came to light in 1984 had lain forgotten for decades in a pile of manuscripts in one of *Modibo* Hajara's cupboards. Written by one of the Shehu's descendants a hundred years ago, the author praised Maryam and prayed for her as she lay very ill:

> Oh Lord, preserve the life of Maryam.
> > She is compassionate to the Muslim Community, peasants,
> > and her relations; she does not discriminate against anyone.
> Restore her to health – let everyone say Amen and rejoice
> She is a pillar of strength to us, to Islam, to theology and
> > the Path of the Prophet.
> She distributed robes to men and wrappers to women – all
> > fit to please them.
> She was generous to scholars and jihadi warriors
> > and gave them good horses, O God preserve her!
> As for women she constantly tutored and encouraged them.
> Maryam followed the Path of the Prophet, the one followed
> > by the Shehu.[1]

The great lady Maryam, *Uwar Deji*, carrier of Asma'u's flame, died in the reign of Caliph Umaru on a date unknown but proba-

---

1   From papers in the collection of the successor to the late *Modibo* Hajara.

bly about 1885. No elegy for her has yet been discovered, but she was featured at the heart of a poem written by Waziri Buhari, Asma'u's grandson, who had known her well. The poem is a reflection on the past when the moral and political certainties of Islam were not threatened. He wrote:

> Community, it is to you I speak, you hear me, O men of my time.
> Old men, youths and boys,
> To you I speak, to those who are far away and to my neighbours.
> I feel a great fear my brethren about the things that I see. This has
>   grieved me.
> If you seek to enquire what troubles me
> The ways of yesterday which today are different, terrify me.
> Heedlessness because of evil men has entered all but a few.
> This is what I hear and see in everyone,
>   that which was among us has declined.
> Formerly I knew it not; a saintly woman has made it clear to me.
> This fear Maryam saw and gave heed.
> Thank you, Maryam, you reminded me and I pondered,
>   at first because I was among the forgetful.
> I failed to understand.
>
> (Waziri Junaidu mss.)

After Nana Asma'u's death, Maryam *Uwar Deji* was the leader of the 'Yan Taru at the Hubbare. She appropriated the title used by the *Inna* of Gobir. Maryam's grave lies within the precincts of the Hubbare.

Aisha, Hauwa, Hadija and Shatura were all widows of the Shehu; their descendants have continued to live in the Hubbare to this day. As for this accounting (shown in the table on the facing page), it is the best that is available, and the authors are respectfully appreciative of having been entrusted with this information.

	father	*mother*
Maryam *Uwar Deji* married (1) Malam Adde, son of Gidado; (2) Emir of Kano Dabo	The Shehu	Mariya
List of her descendants who inherited her room		
Maryam, known as Ta Modi, married Caliph Ahmadu Atiku. She was alive in the late 1890s	Malam Adde	Maryam *Uwar Deji*
Safiya known as Nahi	Isa dan Shehu	
Amiru	Isa dan Shehu	
Modibo Hajara	Marafa, brother of Ta Modi	
Modibo Dikko	Malam Bayero, son (possibly grandson) of Isa	
Modibo Habsatu (in 1997)	Malam Bayero	

5

CALIPHATE CULTURE UNDER COLONIAL RULE

A brief account of the advance of colonialism in
West Africa and the defeat of the Caliphate in 1903

> Whatever happens we have got
> The Maxim gun and they have not.
> —Hilaire Belloc

Asma'u's childhood corresponded to significant events in world history that were to have a bearing on life in Sokoto. The 1815 Congress of Vienna marked the close of the Napoleonic wars, and the ensuing peace allowed European powers to seek new areas of conquest. European cooperation against Barbary piracy led the British, Dutch, the Habsburgs (in both Austria and Spain), and the French to turn toward North Africa. Algiers was overwhelmed in 1830. European interest in the region began in earnest at this time and continued into colonization of the Maghreb by the end of the century. Meanwhile, North African traders continued their centuries-old trans-Saharan trade with merchants in cities of the African interior like Timbuktu, Kano and Sokoto. Merchandise was essential to the economy of the Sahel, and Islamic scholars kept in touch through these overland routes. The traders were acutely aware of political trends and did not lack for reliable information about constraints affecting these routes. Leaders in Sokoto were aware that threats to the balance of power were afoot, if not aware of the magnitude of the changes to come.

150

Around this time, European powers began to make their presence felt in Africa. Tunisia fell under the control of France and the ruling elite there adopted European dress, manners and way of life: in 1845 lavish receptions were held in honour of two sons of King Louis-Philippe of France. In 1850 General Faidherbe started inland forts on the Senegal River and by 1862 St Louis was a full-fledged French colonial capital. In 1854 an expedition on the Niger river led by Dr. William Balfour Baikie used quinine that proved an effective prophylactic against fevers. An important consequence of this discovery was the establishment of a trading settlement at the confluence of the Niger and Benue rivers, less than 400 miles from Sokoto. In 1861 Lagos Colony was ceded to Britain, which was eager to advance its trading interests. Asma'u died in 1863.

In 1867 the Suez Canal was opened; two years later a performance of the opera Aïda, commissioned by the Khedive of Egypt, was staged in Cairo. In 1877 Charles George Gordon was appointed by the Turkish government in Egypt as administrator of the Sudan. In 1881 the Mahdi of the Sudan was proclaimed. Meanwhile, the 'chartered' Royal Niger Company (RNC) was busy exchanging treaties with a wide range of local rulers and giving out handsome subsidies for permissions to buy and sell. However, the RNC was not just a trading company; the British government had decided it had the right – throughout the world – to impose customs and excise duties, execute its laws, and maintain armed men under British army commissioned officers. By the 1880s 'intelligence agents' were employed by British and French authorities to inform them about the northern regions bordering on the Sahara. Inevitably there were misunderstandings: the RNC looked on the northern emirates as potential markets, while the Caliph regarded the treaty he received as a simple compact of friendship. When the RNC attacked Nupeland, a vassal of Sokoto, the Caliph annulled the treaty and when at last he yielded to pressure, he insisted that no part of his territory, the Caliphate, would ever be handed over to the RNC. Meanwhile, French colonization was proceeding apace: in 1899 in Mali, Timbuktu, the great centre of Islamic scholarship, came under French control.

In 1900 Britain's knowledge and experience of Northern Nigeria was remarkably slight. For example, Frederick Lugard (soon to be appointed High Commissioner for Northern Nigeria), addressed Caliph Abdurrahman, who had reigned since 1891, as 'Abdullahi'. He remarked: 'I still find it impossible to get in touch with Sokoto. The question of translating letters forms one of the greatest difficulties.' When the date for the transfer of power from the RNC to the Colonial Office in London was decided, Lugard drew up the proclamation which was approved by the Secretary of State. Over 2,000 words long, it began – 'Be it known to all men that by order of Her Most Gracious Majesty, the Queen of Great Britain and Ireland, Empress of India the administration of the Protectorate of Northern Nigeria hitherto known...' Lugard had great difficulty getting the text translated into Hausa by the professor of Hausa at Cambridge, at a fee not nominal in amount. The document was promulgated on the first day of 1900, though it did not reach Sokoto until October or November. It is doubtful if it was ever understood. Lugard married Flora Shaw in Madeira on 11th June 1902. Together they reached his headquarters at the end of July. Caliph Abdurrahman died in October 1902. The new Caliph, Attahiru, had 125 days to reign.

In late January of 1903 the Emir of Kano, Aliyu, paid his respects to the new Caliph Attahiru. A deeper bond was established in the subsequent arrangement of a marriage between Attahiru's daughter and Aliyu.[1] His joy was not to last, but that is another story. The serious business presently facing the Caliph was the advance of the British. Some of his advisers said Sokoto

---

1   The Caliph presented the Emir with twelve Asben, desert-bred mares, on
      this occasion.

should reach an agreement with the invaders; others believed that they should fight; and yet more said they should depart on hijra to the east and never return.

In February 1903, Colonel (later Lt.-General) Morland, who was in charge of a force of mounted infantry, wrote as follows:

We are coming to Sokoto and from this time and for ever a white man and soldiers will sit down in the Sokoto country. We have prepared for war because the Sultan Abdu [who was dead] said there was nothing between us but war. But we do not want war unless you yourself seek war. If you receive us in peace we will not enter your house nor harm you or any of your people... My present to you is five pieces of brocade.
(T. L. N. Morland, *Annual Reports Northern Nigeria*, p. 160)[1]

The Caliph had disregarded those who counseled surrender. Instead, he prepared to evacuate the city and leave for good. To this end mules, donkeys, and camels were accumulated, shoes and riding boots stockpiled, and dried food prepared in large quantities. The day of departure was set but when scouts galloped to the palace with news that the British had been spotted, there was no alternative but to stand and fight. Two days later the city erupted with noise as trumpets and drums warned of the imminent arrival of the enemy.

The day of the battle, 15th March 1903, thousands of horsemen stretched in battle array for a good mile; most had spears and swords and were supported by bowmen on foot. A few had guns but they were ineffective. At the centre of the massed cavalry was the Caliph on his horse in the shade of a palm tree, a *giginya*, his hand on the tree trunk. The British artillery opened up and the shelling started – one shell which failed to explode was later hammered open and was found to contain 200 shrapnel balls. Then the maxims began firing and pandemonium ensued.

---

1   Copies of these reports were placed in each Resident's office. The copy bequeathed to Jean Boyd contains no publication information.

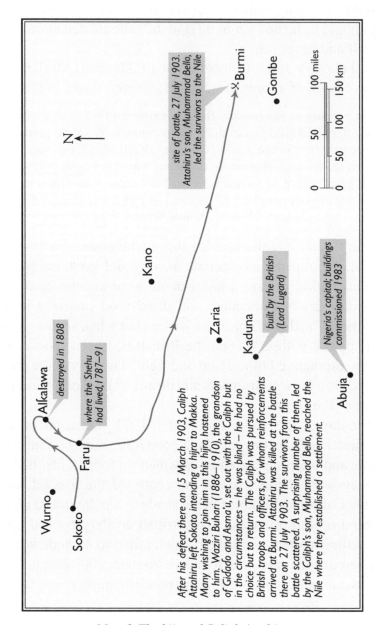

The map contains the following labels and text:

Burmi — site of battle, 27 July 1903. Attahiru's son, Muhammad Bello, led the survivors to the Nile

Gombe

N ←

100 miles
50   100   150 km
0   50   100

Kano

Zaria

Kaduna — built by the British (Lord Lugard)

Abuja — Nigeria's capital; buildings commissioned 1983

Alkalawa — destroyed in 1808

Faru — where the Shehu had lived, 1787–91

Wurno

Sokoto

After his defeat there on 15 March 1903, Caliph Attahiru left Sokoto intending a hijra to Makka. Many wishing to join him in this hijra hastened to him. Waziri Buhari (1886–1910), the grandson of Gidado and Asma'u, set out with the Caliph but in the circumstances – he was blind – he had no choice but to return. The Caliph was pursued by British troops and officers, for whom reinforcements arrived at Burmi. Attahiru was killed at the battle there on 27 July 1903. The survivors from this battle scattered. A surprising number of them, led by the Caliph's son, Muhammad Bello, reached the Nile where they established a settlement.

Map 6. The hijra of Caliph Attahiru

154

'Bullets were falling like rain,' one observer noted. Horses wallowing in blood screamed as they plunged and reared; there was bedlam. The square of disciplined soldiers quickly dispersed the cavalry. The rest of the inhabitants of the city fled in panic; women and girls, young boys and the elderly looked for hiding places in irrigation channels, groves of vegetation, and vacated frail reed huts. It was on that day that Hauwa, the wife of a great-grandson of the Shehu, gave birth to a son. She ran in her terror, carrying the baby on a bed of cotton wool placed in a calabash. Her woman servant accompanied her as they trekked out of danger. Hauwa's son, Abubakar, born on that day in 1903 when Sokoto fell to the British, was to become Sultan of Sokoto in 1938. He ruled for fifty years.

Meanwhile Caliph Attahiru and a huge, growing host of followers journeyed eastwards believing in the knowledge of the Shehu's prophecy made clear by Maryam, of events which, he said, needed no sign in the sky. They would be obvious. High Commissioner Lugard arrived in Sokoto four days after the Caliph's departure. This is part of his first address 'to the Waziri and Headmen of Sokoto':

> I am very glad to see you, very glad that you have come back. You made war on us; we beat you and drove you away. Now the war is over and there is peace. It is not our custom to catch the people who fight us or to kill them. Therefore all those who have run away must come back to their houses.
>
> There will be no interference with your religion nor with the position of the Sultan as head of your religion. The British government in London never interferes with religion. Taxes, law and order, punishment of crime, these are matters for the Government, but not religion.
>
> (*Colonial Annual Reports*, no. 346, 1900–11, p.160)

Lugard appointed a new Sultan who, confusingly, was also called Attahiru. He and the blind Waziri Buhari were then faced with the statement that law and order was now a matter for the

Colonial Government. The huge revolution inaugurated on 20th March 1903 continued to resonate throughout the twentieth century.

Four months later, on 27th July 1903, at a walled town called Burmi, well east of Kano, the British caught up with the fugitives. Under his command the senior British officer had two political officers, eighteen military officers, three NCOs, two medical officers, 449 rank-and-file infantry, 60 mounted infantry, four maxims, and one 75 mm gun with artillery personnel.

Attahiru made his way on foot to the far side of the town. He stood leaning against a wall on his right hand one son and on his left another. His people lined up ... the hour of the great battle drew near.[1]

Attahiru died a martyr's death, surrounded by the corpses of ninety of his followers. Many others were killed, all of whom were buried in mass graves, ten bodies to a hole. The thousands of survivors dispersed – some to return to Sokoto, others to seek safety elsewhere. A sizeable number traversed Africa to reach the Nile where one of Attahiru's sons, Muhammad Bello, founded the town of Shehu Talah. The new Caliph was accompanied by Usman Mai Rugga, a great-grandson of Gidado and Asma'u, and a brother of Waziri Junaidu, who at a later date received a photograph of Muhammad Bello alongside Mai Rugga.[2]

What transpired after 1903 is to a large extent only known these days through the eyes of the colonialists. The ulema put themselves out of the reach of the British by practising a policy of peaceful non-co-operation. They maintained a resentment which was never aimed at rousing popular opinion but served as

---

1   David J. M. Muffett, *Concerning Brave Captains, being a history of the British occupation of Kano and Sokoto and of the last stand of the Fulani forces, with a foreword by Alhaji Sir Ahmadu Bello* (London: Andre Deutsch, 1964), p. 198.
2   Ibrahim Junaidu, *Rayuwar Wazirin Sakkwato* (a biography of Waziri Junaidu), p. 5.

a constant reminder to the Caliph, now renamed Sultan, of their disapproval of the new regime. The absence of full, reasoned and expository documents supported by confirmatory reports and letters written by the Sultans, their chief advisers and the emirs is a great loss. A few snippets of information have started to emerge and it is possible that more will be revealed, but for the most part it must be accepted that what they really thought is impossible to judge. What went on behind closed doors at the Sultan's palace is not known. No records were kept, no minutes taken, and what was discussed was not relayed to outsiders, the keeping of privacy being viewed as a most serious matter.

No understanding of the struggle to preserve the Shehu's legacy can be achieved without understanding the nature of the invasion. At a stroke the Caliph lost his authority and the Caliphate its infrastructure. A completely new system of government was introduced, at the head of which was King Edward VII, a man no one knew anything about, and a parliamentary system that was absolutely foreign. The rules of procedure were unknowable because they were written in English, and lines of communication through military and civil hierarchies impossible to work out. The *Northern Nigerian Gazette*, the official journal listing appointments and other public notices, replaced the output from the Caliphate chancellery in Sokoto. The *Gazettes* published by the British on the last working day of each month were prescribed reading because they listed new regulations and proclamations to do with, for example, the abolition of slavery, statute laws, new coinage, traders' licences and land revenue, which affected all the inhabitants of the northern region of Nigeria, which came to be known as simply 'the North'. Neither the Sultan nor any of the Caliphate title-holders were consulted on any of these matters. Control had been removed from them by the new government, which alone had knowledge and, therefore, power. Perhaps nothing more clearly illustrates the dislocation of culture than the inclusion in a *Gazette* of 1907 of an Order in

Council signed at Buckingham Palace on 11th February 1907 'relating to the United States Extradition Treaty' and a Post Office notice about parcel post to New Zealand in respect of packages exceeding 'four feet in length and girth'.

Thus the beginning of the colonial era was one of confusion. Caliph Attahiru had been killed by conquerors who brought an entirely different system of government, into which the Caliphate had to fit without understanding what it was about. The Caliphate was not a 'protected state' like the Bugandan kingdom of East Africa: it was completely subordinate. What was described as 'the personal and official adviser' to the Sultan (i.e. the Shehu's successor), was the British Resident. The first to be appointed in Sokoto was Major J. A. Burdon, the son of Christian missionaries to China, a soldier who had joined the Royal Niger Constabulary and become its commander.

In 1918 the work of the Resident was summed up as follows by C. L. Temple, Lieutenant Governor 1914–17:

A resident's life and work are almost of unparalleled interest, and fortunate was the group of young men who were lucky enough to be placed in such a position of such responsibility and power. It is true that… as technical departments, forestry, public works etc. have extended their tentacles and as these work to a certain extent independent of the resident, his pinnacle is not quite so high above that of every other man, white or black, in the neighbourhood, as it was. Still it is high enough to permit him to flap his wings and boast in *corum publicum* (in public) to a highly gratifying extent.

(Speech made at a private club in London in 1918)[1]

For those who were not there and never experienced what it was like to live in Northern Nigeria before independence it should be made plain that the Resident of a province ran the place like a fief and he had the means to enforce his will. No expatriate had the right to visit an emir without first seeking the

---

1   From the private papers, shown to Jean Boyd, of a retired British officer.

permission of the Resident, who was the conduit through which all interviews and correspondence with any native administration were channeled. All colonial officers – medical, public or whatever – were answerable to him and all government officials, employees of trading companies, missionaries, as visitors to the Province, had, as a matter of protocol, to sign the book left at the guard-house to the Residency. Control was everything.

From the beginning, the British were nervous about Islam, and what Sir Richmond Palmer, a one-time acting Lieutenant Governor, called 'the general tide of Islamic Mahdist Revivalism'. It was Palmer who said in a letter to the Resident Sokoto in 1922 that the descendants of Caliph Muhammad Bello,

remained more or less passively hostile to the British administration and were more inclined to adopt Mahdism or other revolutionary doctrines on any suitable opportunity or pretext than others.[1]

The British never understood the ulema, who in turn never wanted to have anything to do with the British. There were very few meetings of minds in the shaded courtyards near the great mosques, or in the *shigifa*s (meeting rooms) of the imams and the *mallamai* (as the ulema were locally known), who were heirs to the Shehu's legacy. The colleges they ran were away from the main thoroughfares, behind high walls and were not open to inspection. Students went to these colleges to study subjects such as *hadith*, law, grammar, philosophy, poetry and mathematics. They read books as fundamental to Islam as Shakespeare is to English literature, and were familiar with all the important classical commentaries. The colleges were not organized in European style with furniture and blackboards, but according to the well-established traditions of Arabic study: students sat on the floor on mats or sheepskins, cross-legged, while the teacher read out the text in Arabic and explained it. Each student had a copy of the

---

1   See previous note.

text and when he had completed his portion went out to a nearby room to go over the text again, each making progress at his own pace. Some colleges had a rolling programme of activity which started at dawn and continued until about eleven at night. The students travelled hundreds of miles to study with a teacher they thought would meet their needs. If he did not, they left and went elsewhere.

These activities continue to this day, but in the past teachers and students were even more integrated into the community than is the case now. They resided in the same environment, ate the same kind of food, and lived in the same type of housing. The economy that sustained the society as a whole was the one that sustained the school and its scholars, who supported themselves through trading, agriculture, sewing clothes, selling products such as grass for fodder, and working as labourers. Scholarship and learning in these schools was considered part of worship. In these schools and colleges in addition to all the other books, the works of the Shehu, Abdullahi, Bello, Asma'u and others were, and it has to be said, still are in the twenty-first century, studied, copied and discussed. The traditions and sayings of the Shehu were handed down; this is an activity that has been going on since the Shehu's time and is still to this day being implemented. It is important to emphasize that the Shehu's life, achievements and literary legacy have never been forgotten or devalued.

However, one great blow had been struck against Islamic scholarship, of which, at the beginning of the twentieth century the ulema had no knowledge. It happened one night in Jebba on the River Niger in the year 1900. Lugard's military forces were preparing to advance north and were camped at what was then the government headquarters. They were joined by the missionary Dr. Miller. He had set out from England with great hope of evangelizing the Hausa people. This is how he described the evening in his autobiography:

The talk after dinner at Jebba camp turned upon what might seem to many a very trivial matter but which to me was vital. It was this: in the educational programme which H. E. [Lugard] was already thinking out, what was to be the orthography? Should we retain the Arabic script already in use throughout the whole of the Northern Provinces, the script for Muslim literature, the Koran and the traditions, or the Roman character which would one day make the youth of Northern Nigeria heirs to the literature of Greece and Rome and Judea and the whole of the civilized world?[1]

The Arabic script for official usage was soon discarded, and when books were prepared for government-sponsored school use they were printed in Roman script. The products of 'Western' schools were deemed to be literate and the rest, of the Arabic tradition, were not included in government statistics. So the then Governor's wife, Lady Sharwood-Smith, was able to write in 1948 of places like Sokoto, where literacy was highly valued and scholars venerated, that 'compared with other Regions, the North was extremely backward'.[2] Suddenly, instead of being acknowledged as the most literate territory in the nineteenth century, it became the most 'illiterate', as a result of the spectacular cultural upheaval that had taken place:

[I]n 1962 so eminent a historian as Professor Trevor-Roper could pronounce the much quoted verdict from his august chair at Oxford that 'Perhaps in the future there will be some African history to teach. But at the present there is none: there is only the history of the Europeans in Africa. The rest is darkness... and darkness is not the subject of History.'[3]

---

1   Walter Miller, *An Autobiography* (Zaria, Nigeria, n. d.). Files in the G3/A9/0 series. (CMS Archives, Heslop Room, University of Birmingham, Private Papers, ACC 237.)
2   Joan Sharwood-Smith, *Diary of a Colonial Wife* (London, 1992), p. 85.
3   Michael Crowder, *West Africa under Colonial Rule* (London: Hutchinson, 1968), p. 10.

Another British woman was also outspoken about the course of history in Northern Nigeria. Flora Shaw was the daughter of General Shaw and of his aristocratic French wife. They lived in Woolwich, England, where she had use of an excellent nearby library and began writing for *The Manchester Guardian*. With her undoubted ability she eventually became editor of the colonial column of *The Times*. In about 1898 she met Frederick Lugard and wrote to him as follows:

I look upon it as part of my personal work to endeavour to bring all the influences which I believe to be working for good in Africa into harmony with each other.[1]

Flora Shaw married Lugard in Madeira 1902. They embarked for Nigeria with forty-six trunks and cases and lived in Zungeru. She was bored and disliked the isolation of her home life, rarely seeing her husband except at meal times. To the Colonial Secretary in London she wrote:

Sir Frederick has nearly killed himself – and a fair proportion of his staff too – with over work. Yet they like it. After all they are working for an idea and that is more than most men can say. It is a great idea too and fills one more and more as one thinks of it. This conception of an Empire which is to secure the ruling of the world by the finest race – the best plan for the exercise of justice and liberty and individual effort which the world has seen.[2]

Loneliness and isolation made her ill; after only five months Lady Lugard went home, never to return. Nevertheless, in 1903 she wrote out, at astonishing speed, her book, *A Tropical Dependency*.[3] Whether her husband who took seven months

1   Cited in Marjorie Perham, *Lugard: the Years of Authority 1898–1945* (London: Collins, 1956–60), vol. 2, p. 64.
2   *Ibid.*, p. 87.
3   The book's full title is *A Tropical Dependency: An Outline of the Ancient History of the Western Soudan with an account of the Modern Settlement of Northern Nigeria* (Oxford University Press, 1905). It has recently

leave in London helped with assembling the work is not known. Lugard's biographer wrote:

It was a volume with 50 chapters, 500 pages, a majestic sweep of history from the first Arab conquests in Africa to those of Goldie and Lugard. It is a book in the grand manner and is somewhat of a pioneer work in the use of Arab chronicles and other sources. Its chief demerit is the lack of reference to her authorities and of a bibliography.[1]

A specially bound copy of the book was sent to the King, and other copies were dispatched to a clutch of influential politicians.

The grandiloquent prose of Lady Lugard's book was not entirely in keeping with the facts. Her chief source for the short chapter on Caliph Bello appears to have been a Fulani scholar called al-Hajj Sa'id who stayed in Sokoto from the mid-1830s to 1850 whereupon he departed for his home in the area of Timbuktu. A text of the chronology he wrote was acquired by the French administration and a French version published in Paris in 1899. Lady Lugard wanted to leave the reader with the impression that she was familiar with the works of Bello – for instance she described as 'purely essays' what he had written and the comments he had made 'upon the poems of his father which were composed in the Soudanese language' (Shaw, *A Tropical Dependency*, p. 398). She concluded that (p. 239):

Bello maintained himself in his early life entirely by his own exertions refusing to live on the public treasury, but it is more probable that after his accession he yielded like his father to the pressure of necessity and made use of public funds.

The book closes with the author's triumphant words (p. 500) about 'the genius for administration and the adventurousness in

---

(2010) been reissued by Cambridge University Press as a paperback in the series 'Cambridge Library Collection – Women's Writing'.

1   Perham, *Lugard*, vol. 2, p. 235.

trade which have always characterized the British people', a combination which

gave us India, it gave us Canada and ... there is reasonable ground for hope that the chapter of Imperial History which has been opened in the interior of West Africa will not prove unworthy of the rest.

Dedicated to 'My Husband' the book was an unbroken paean to Sir Frederick Lugard. Lugard himself wrote of that period:

By the end of March 1903 the Resident, Major Burdon, was able to report that everything was settling down peacefully, the fugitives were returning, Sokoto and surrounding villages were filling up. Traders were beginning to come in and the market was gradually regaining its normal position.[1]

The amiable and learned Waziri Buhari ensured in this time of turmoil that Asma'u's classes founded by her ninety years previously began to function again and the women teachers at the Hubbare, the *Modibos*, progressively returned to their activities. There is no evidence that the 'Yan Taru ever ceased to visit Sokoto once things quietened down: the unbroken lineage of the leaders is known. Had Lugard's wife, Flora Shaw, known about the activities and intellects of Asma'u and Maryam, about how they had organized an educational system for women, and if she had seen for herself how they had always been honoured, she might have persuaded her husband to look again, and in so doing changed the course of history.

Twentieth-century changes in education

In Sokoto early marriage for girls had always been the norm; sometimes girls were as young as nine. By puberty, all girls were ensconced in their married homes where, in all well-run

---

1   *Annual Report Sokoto Province 1903* (Sokoto: Archive History Bureau), p. 174.

households the education of young wives continued uninterrupted under the supervision of their husbands. As far as is known the British showed no interest in the education of women until the early 1930s when Resident Carrow let it be known that the Sultan was most anxious that his own children and the children of important office-holders would be the first to receive instruction at a school to be built in Sokoto. This was an astonishing proposal. The Resident's Annual Report for 1933 glows with optimism:

Female education started in 1933 has already proved successful and the girls' school needs no longer be regarded as experimental. The rapid progress made, and the ease with which difficulties have been smoothed away is, in my opinion, remarkable. The question of starting a Northern Provinces Women's Teachers College which the Sultan has asked should be established at Sokoto is under consideration by the Education Department.[1]

When this is read alongside the letter written by Commander Carrow forty years later on 27th February 1973, a very different picture emerges:

What I am trying to emphasize is the unplanned way in which female education started in Nigeria. There was no demand for this education; in fact it was against the whole African opinion, Emirs, District Heads, Village Heads and the people.[2]

It is obvious that any moves towards female education by the government were made by the British, and that the Sultan neither demanded girls' schools with much 'zeal', nor clamored for girls' schools 'desperately'. The Sultan did what he could to reassure the ulema and in view of the 1973 letter it seems that his hand was

---

1   Letter from Jean Trevor, cited in Helen Calloway, *Gender, Culture and Empire* (Urbana, IL: University of Illinois Press, 1987), p. 113.
2   Letter to Malama Rabi Bada cited in a B.Ed. dissertation, Exeter University, seen by Jean Boyd. The university no longer retains copies of B.Ed. dissertations.

forced on the issue. He agreed on condition that an undertaking was given that the girls would be allowed to leave school to be married at puberty, having regard to the role of women in society. In 1935 Commander Carrow was right when he said: 'The education of women must, in the years to come, have an important effect on the future development of these Muhammadan Emirates.'[1]

Unfortunately no one in the colonial government devised a way of introducing Western education in an acceptable manner to Muslim girls in the North. They were taught in English by expatriate teachers using books produced by the government. Neither girls nor their mothers liked their being at these schools, for obvious reasons. The exceptions were few in number and no effort was made to put things right.

In 1936 Commander Carrow married a lady described as '… petite and dainty. She liked long necklaces and jangly bangles' (Joan Sharwood-Smith, *Diary of a Colonial Wife*, p. 66). She encouraged the Resident's interest in the education of girls and in women's issues. Carrow arranged for the posting of an expatriate nursing officer to Sokoto, a most timely appointment, and planned the construction of a woman's hospital. He wrote: 'When this is complete it is optimistically felt that unlimited good will be done for the women and children of the Province.' In the same Report (1936) he said that young girls had been admitted to some of the existing elementary schools and that he believed that this first step towards co-education was 'genuinely welcomed by the girls and their parents'. The lack of trained 'native women' teachers, as they were termed, was obviously a grave handicap to progress: so a Women's Teachers College for the training of Muslim women of Northern Nigeria was planned for Sokoto, at the urgent request of the Sultan, according to the Resident. In October 1939 the establishment was opened by His Honour the Chief Commissioner of the Northern

---

1   Jean Trevor, Rhodes House, Oxford. MSS 79A.

Provinces. Known as the Women's Training Centre, it was a college for girls who had been through the local elementary school and wished to take up teaching. Twenty-five young women from seven of the Northern provinces were to be trained as vernacular teachers for classes one and two of the primary schools. But it was hardly an ideal situation. In those days the roads were untarred and mostly corrugated; bridges were often only planks spanning ravines. The girls, who travelled hundreds of miles to Sokoto from places as far away as Adamawa and Bornu to the east and Kontagora to the south, were exposed to risks from untoward events such as traffic accidents, storms, and illnesses of all kinds; they were always lonely, missing their families and homes.

The first headmistress, Miss Booker, *mai zafin rai* (hot-tempered) but also *mai son mutane* (who made friends easily), demanded better conditions for her school and her pupils. She said: 'Walls fell down, pupils did not arrive and nobody seemed to help or care.'[1] She became frustrated and impatient and wrote impassioned letters to the Resident and even the Secretary of the Northern Provinces. The Resident said that her letters were not in accord with the tone of official correspondence as stated in General Orders and her behaviour was not appropriate for an English lady: he advised her to go on leave.

The Centre was protected by a wall nine feet high, built at the insistence of Miss Booker, and had a model compound where domestic science was taught. At least one student had a baby whilst at the Centre. A cot and mosquito net were provided for the infant and the baby was kept in the cot as much as possible to avoid any possible risk of suffocation if it slept with the mother. The European teachers taught the girls that it was wrong to carry babies on their backs 'because this could cause curvature of the spine', an example of the inappropriateness of some of the training given.

---

1   Jean Trevor cited in Calloway, *Gender, Culture and Empire*, p. 113.

Parents could see no point in their daughters learning things which did not conform to the cultural values of their society and they encouraged them to be naughty so that they would be expelled. A prominent educationist, Aisha Lemu, said in 1983:

I saw girls go through the schooling in the sense that they were physically present but with the firm belief installed in them that their western education was a bad thing. Naturally their progress was almost nil. They would fail all subjects every year and draw hardly any further knowledge from all their years in school.[1]

This was precisely the same experience Jean Boyd had in the 1950s. The girls were unhappy and the parents resented that their daughters were forced to attend a boarding school and to be educated in a foreign language by foreigners. It goes without saying that the same teachers knew nothing about the history of Sokoto or the scholarly Nana Asma'u. Yet among one of the pioneer girls in the period 1939–42, was Hadija, daughter of an early student of the Women's Training College, Sokoto. In 1944 Hadija married Kashim Ibrahim, later Sir Kashim, Waziri of Bornu and Governor of the Northern Region. She was the first woman elementary school teacher in Maiduguri, the capital of Bornu Province. In 1990 she was honoured by the International Women's Club of Nigeria for her contribution to raising the status of women.

In the newly established Provincial Girls' Schools of the mid-1950s the curriculum was patterned on the British model, but there was only a very limited range of equipment. In September 1957 for example, there were only three maps on the premises of one Provincial Girls' School, one of the world, one of the continent of Africa and one of the British Isles – there were no maps of Sokoto Province, none of Nigeria. Most of the girls did not want to be there and continued to show this by open acts of defiance such as

---

1   Aisha Lemu, *A Degree Above Them: Observations on the Condition of Northern Nigerian Women* (Zaria, Nigeria: Gaskiya Corporation, 1983).

banging desk lids in unison when a teacher entered a classroom and refusing to stop. The headmistress was a kind person and the girls showed their respect for her even though they went on believing that they had been very unlucky to land up where they were. The two senior matrons in the compound probably acted as marriage brokers. On one occasion in 1958 there was *bori* spirit possession cult dancing in the school. Adult women danced to the drums, became 'possessed' and demonstrated the spine-jarring falls which are a feature of the cult. News of this happening would have reached the ears of at least some townspeople and served to further lower the esteem in which the school was held by many.

In spite of all the school's weaknesses and shortcomings, two girls were selected to attend the first government secondary school for girls in the North, the Queen Elizabeth School, Ilorin. One of them, Hajiya Ta'Allah Aliyu, the first woman engineer in Northern Nigeria, wrote to Jean Boyd on 12th September 1965 after her brilliant results in the West African School Certificate:

I am indeed aware of the difficulties involved in my pursuit of education. It was a battle before I was able to return and as you are well aware, people are talking. They talk too much. The only thing I do is turn a deaf ear and go on doing what I believe is right, with God's assistance. Our classes are now in full swing. From the beginning the science section was combined with that of the PSS. [Provincial Secondary School, for boys] and some of the subjects are taught there while others are taught here. I am taking Physics. Pure Maths and Applied Maths. Since I did not take Chemistry for School Certificate I am trying to see whether at the end of my two years I can take it at [GCE] Ordinary Level. However, the work is tedious because there is not even a Chemistry teacher at the school to help me, and I might have to give in after all. Anyway I hope not. I will try my best to see that I take it and see if I can get to help my fellow women.

(Personal communication to Jean Boyd, 1965)

THE LEGACY OF NANA ASMA'U

In the early 1970s the massive expansion in oil production and revenues which increased by 250 per cent in one year led to a rush to perform development miracles. If the people involved had been experienced administrators of the highest integrity all might have been well. However, the start of the great tide of oil money was followed by the fragmentation of Nigeria into twelve states, each of which had to establish its own government. From Northern Nigeria, six states were created. Instead of one bureaucracy in the North with one Ministry of Health for example, there were now six needed. A newly recruited inspector with no experience of school work and virtually no knowledge of the country landed the position of Chief Inspector in one state. A man noted for his drunkenness became Finance Officer in another and eventually used to sign contracts and calculate estimates in the beer parlour round the corner from the Ministry in which he was supposed to be working. Other deployed officers were well qualified, experienced and honest, but in all ministries there was friction and a reduced level of efficiency.

This led to another complicating factor. Since, in the newly created states in the North, none of the bureaucracies had anything like the doctors, nurses, engineers, accountants, agronomists and communications experts needed to work the systems that were necessary, recruitment drives were conducted world-wide. Many British officers had chosen to leave Nigeria on independence in 1960, others left during the civil war 1969–1970. They were replaced by men and women from the Indian subcontinent, Egypt, Sudan, the Philippines and Europe, including countries inside the then Communist bloc. These were supplemented by American Peace Corps members and young graduates from the British Voluntary Service Overseas organization. Many had perfectly adequate qualifications but most found it difficult to work well in the situation as they found it. However, the blame for what went wrong and for what Shehu Shagari, later the first Executive President of the country, called 'the stupendous corruption', should be placed on the shoulders of those who looted the nation's wealth.[1]

In the 1970s it became the vogue for girl students at the School of Nursing and Government Girls College Sokoto to be required to act as waitresses at Government House evening drinks parties where the majority of those invited were men. There were even bolder moves. The Principal of Government Girls College Sokoto was asked to provide a team of girls to play football against a team of male civil servants in what was termed a novelty match and invitations were sent out marked 'RSVP Chief of Protocol Military Governor's Office' (Invitation card to event). The venue was to be the Giginya Memorial Stadium, so called in memory of Sultan Attahiru I. The date was set for 30th September 1971. The Principal, Mrs. Aisha Lemu, and the Advisory Board stipulated that the fathers of the girls involved must give their permission in writing. In the absence of rural postal services the chances of the letters reaching their destination was not high. The possibilities of replies reaching the Principal before the date of the match were zero, so the whole thing was called off.

Politicians wanted girls to be released to assist in various activities. One principal resigned; another, in a letter dated 28th December 1975, wrote to the Permanent Secretary complaining of the 'continual frustration and indiscipline which arises from the interference of outside authority in the internal matters of the school' (Personal communication to Jean Boyd). Referring to the compilation of National Census statistics, which involved counting secluded women living in rooms inaccessible to male enumerators, she said:

I was compelled to release all the female students without using my discretion or being asked my opinion as to their suitability or disciplinary records. There were many serious consequences. The schoolgirls were

---

1   Shehu Shagari, *Beckoned to Serve* (Ibadan, Nigeria: Heinemann, 2001).

seen at public social functions at night time and were driven around in cars at all hours of the evening. Census supervisors on this occasion took over the school authority and seemed to have the right to do so.

(Personal communication to Jean Boyd)

By the 1980s schools were in a distressing state. Sheikh Ahmed Lemu, an educationist who became Grand Kadi of Niger State, put it eloquently in a speech he gave *ca*. 1980 on 'The Role of Muslim Youth in Africa: the New Nigerian'.

With the colonialization of Africa, Western education gradually became the key to general success and means of political power. The respect for Islamic culture is strongest among Muslim traditionalists and proprietors of Qur'anic schools but unfortunately they have very little or no knowledge of modern Western education and are out of touch with the realities of anti-Islamic forces which are working in post primary and tertiary institutions. However, there has been a mysterious Islamic awakening among the Muslim youth all over the continent of Africa.

The sense of disquiet at the many alarming, even sensational, happenings at girls' schools throughout the North led to the emergence of very radical protesters able to stir the teenage girls themselves into action. In (*ca.* April) 1981, for example, under the headline, 'Sokoto police investigates violence in School' a newspaper report said that the violence had emanated from the refusal by certain female students of the College to recite either the National Pledge or sing the National Anthem, which they said went against the teaching of Islam.

The Principal of the Federal Government College said that of the 700 students only 120 were Muslim. What is more, he said the Muslim boys were not a problem – only the girls. Of those girls, 15 were arrested and taken to the Divisional Police Office, which was then besieged for four hours by some hundreds of students seeking the release of their colleagues. Nearly two weeks later, the religious stir had still not abated, despite the arrest of the

172

man suspected of being the instigator, a dismissed student from Ahmadu Bello University, a religious fanatic who had written a number of religious books now in circulation. More students joined in the protest and there were further arrests.

These happenings were all the more disturbing because well -mannered girls were among those involved and the incidents sent a shiver down the spine of the establishment. Sweet and proper fifteen-year-olds stood up in court and repudiated their parents. Such untoward occurrences, and the public utterance of deeply wounding statements affected the thinking of all those in authority at the time when modern 'Western-educated' Northern women began to ponder the issues and make their views known.

For example, the Commissioner for Health in Sokoto State, a woman, said in her speech at the Sokoto State Students' Association Week on 14th May 1984:

The National Secretary of WIN [Women in Nigeria] rightfully cited in *The Democrat* of 22 April 1984: Women cannot be emancipated if the whole of society is not emancipated. Equally society cannot be said to develop freely if half the population is subordinated by the other half. Underdeveloped 11-year-old girls continue to produce babies: women still continue to neglect their health and that of children and worst of all, a lot of women are nothing more than part of the furniture in a man's house.

It is safe to say that much of the outspokenness on the part of women came from their awareness of a long tradition of women standing up for their rights. Although Asma'u's works had not yet been published, her example was legendary in the region. Nana Asma'u had been an inspiration to the women of the 'Yan Taru and she was by far the most prolific woman writer and influential lady to emerge in the western Sudan in the nineteenth century. The populace at large respected and honoured her and knew some of her poems by heart. The ulema were well informed and performed the absolutely essential task of preserving and transmitting her works. The 'Yan Taru practised discipleship, modeling their lives on the pattern she had set them. They exercised influence for good at a rural level. All the claims can be substantiated, but none appeared in the textbooks published in English in the post-Independence era. Here are excerpts from three books containing comments about Nana Asma'u:

[1960] This Asma'u is the authoress of an Arabic ballad
(Hogben and Kirk-Greene, *The Emirates of Northern Nigeria* [London: Oxford University Press, 1960], p. 390.

[1967] Shehu's daughter Nana, who incidentally was the outstanding woman of her day, had been given to Gidaɗo in marriage
(H. A. S. Johnston, *The Fulani Empire of Sokoto* [London: Oxford University Press, 1966] , p. 113.
[1982] These were the daughters of aristocratic homes who had slaves and servants to free them from the need to expend their labour on household chores and concentrate on education.
(Saleh Abubakar, Birnin Shehu, *The City of Sokoto, A Social and Economic History*, 1809–1903, PhD. thesis, Zaria, 1982)

Although the West was ignorant of the region's past, the tradition of women's scholarship was no surprise to those who had grown up there. Asma'u was indeed extraordinary in her prolific poetic output and activism, but she was not an exception. In fact, she was typical of her time and place with regard to the degree to which women pursued knowledge. That she and her father, the Shehu, were both educated by their mothers and grandmothers indicates that women's scholarship was not unusual in Asma'u's world. Generations of women before Asma'u pursued scholarly endeavours in the same way that she and subsequent generations did so, up to the present. It is crucial to understand that although Asma'u as an individual was exceptional, she was by no means an exception as a scholar in a Muslim community. She was one in a long tradition of women scholars that continues unbroken to the present; the proof of this is in annotated family genealogies. This

174

pattern of women's scholarship in the Maghreb has persisted, even in the face of interference like that imposed by colonialism. Evidence of this exists in the example of genealogies that trace eight generations of female scholars both before and after Nana Asma'u's lifetime, spanning the period from the early eighteenth century to the present, and interviews with women who trace their lineage as teachers back to Nana Asma'u.[1]

The works they studied are not as easily identified, but it is by no means impossible to do so. Through attention to the works the Shehu studied and wrote,[2] Asma'u's collected works,[3] and poetry of contemporary women in the region,[4] we can begin to understand the ways in which a canon of classical pieces formed the basis for the education of both women and men in this community over several generations. Furthermore, the Shehu's clearly acknowledged devotion to the *Sunna*, which guided his life and actions, is the hallmark of a devotional community.[5] It is logical that the Fodio family would have held in its library classical works from prior eras of Islamic scholarship. Those works remain in the Hubbare, the family compound in Sokoto, and can be documented by other scholars.

Genealogies

The women of these genealogies were 'the others', that is, women of the Fodio clan who were the exemplars as Asma'u

---

1 This information is from Jean Boyd's field notes from her period of residence in Sokoto, from1957–1984.
2 Many of these are being translated by Shaykh Muhammad Sharif and posted on line: http://www.siiasi.org/
3 Boyd and Mack (*Collected Works of Nana Asma'u*) cite especially Sufi women, based on al-Jawzi (twelfth century) based on al-Sulami (tenth century).
4 Beverly Mack, *Muslim Women Sing: Hausa Popular Song* (Bloomington, IN: Indiana University Press, 2004).
5 This is clearly evident in several of the works by Nana Asma'u, and also in biographies of the Shehu.

was growing up. Later, the women were Asma'u's 'beloveds'. It is logical that in a family that reveres the pursuit of knowledge, women, as well as men, should be encouraged to learn.

Fig. 12 A walima *to celebrate the reading of the Qur'an*
(Photo: Jean Boyd, 1979)

Shehu Usman dan Fodio's family tree leaves no doubt about the high levels of literacy and religious education that predate his birth. The genealogy confirms that education, literacy, and spirituality were the foundational goals of the extended family for many generations, but also that women's status in these pursuits was equal to that of men. The numbers given here indicate a running tally of women scholars, counting from the period of the Shehu's grandparents (eighteenth century) through Asma'u's children, in the nineteenth century, four generations.

Grandparents' generation. On his paternal side, the Shehu Usman dan Fodio's grandparents were Usman and [1] *Maryam.*[1] Their distant relatives were among those Fulani who had migrated eastward from Futa Toro in Northern Senegal and settled in the Kwanni area north of Sokoto. They lived as a religious community, sharing chores, living on what they grew and what they accepted as gifts, like books, garments, grain, and other foodstuff donated by those who came to them to receive instruction. This couple had three children whose names are known: Adamu, who married a woman named [2] *Hassantu*; Muhammad Haji, who married [3] *Inna Kabo*, and Muhammad Fodio, who was the Shehu's father. Muhammad Fodio married a woman named [4] *Hauwa of Marnona.*[2] Hauwa was the Shehu's first teacher. Her brothers, the Shehu's uncles, were Muhammad, Muhammad Sa'ad, Kawurul, and Ade. The Shehu's maternal grandparents, and his mother Hauwa's parents, were Muhammad and [5] *Rukaya*, the latter of whom was also one of the Shehu's first teachers. Rukaya's brothers were Hussain, Abdullahi, and Adam.

Parents' generation. The Shehu's father, Muhammad Fodio, and his mother, Hauwa, were both literate, educated, Qadiriyya Sufis, which indicates that they pursued learning as a means of increasing spirituality. They passed this devotion to learning on to their children. So it is no surprise that the Shehu himself was one of a whole generation of educated women and men. On his maternal side, his cousin [6] *Habiba* (uncle Muhammad's daughter) was a

---

1   The names of these women are shown in italic and numbered, to facilitate an appreciation of the number in this one family alone who were involved in education in the region at this time.

2   Marnona is located southwest of Wurno at 5°30 E, 13°40 N.

teacher of women. Her younger sisters, also the Shehu's cousins, were among his students. They are: [7] *Ja'ibatu* (Kawurul's daughter), [8] *Amina Lubal*, [9] *Amina* (Ade's daughter), and [10] *Yahina*. The Shehu's wives Hauwa (his paternal cousin, daughter of uncle Adamu and Hassanatu), and [11] *Aisha* (maternal cousin, daughter of Muhammad Sa'ad) were both Sufis. The Shehu's first wife [12] *Maimuna*, the mother of Asma'u was also his cousin – a daughter of his paternal aunt Inna Kabo and Muhammad Haji. The honorific 'Haji' indicates that this Muhammad had made the pilgrimage to Makka and/or achieved a level of religious education sufficient to make him worthy of such a title of respect. Pilgrimages to Makka were not unusual – for example, among others, Jibrillu, the Shehu's teacher at Tafadek near Agadez, went to Makka.

Considering that [13] *Nana Asma'u* grew up in a family in which she was taught by her mother and grandmother, and had eight aunts (some on both sides) who were teachers, students and Sufis, it is no surprise that the women of her generation were, as a normal part of their lives, immersed in teaching, learning and producing scholarly works. It was quite simply the expected way in which to spend one's life as a member of the 'Fodio' or 'learned' family. Asma'u had sisters, female cousins, and nieces who also wrote, and were married to men whose scholarly inclinations endorsed such activities. Among her learned sisters were: [14] *Hadija*, married to the scholar, Mustafa; [15] *Habsatu* (Asma'u's only full sister), married first to the scholar Demba Hamal, and then to Muhammad Atan Ji'do ɗan Umaru Alƙamu, with whom she had a son, Umaru, who was raised by Asma'u;[1] [16] *Faɗima* was married to Sarkin Yaƙi, a jihad battle commander named Aliyu Jeɗo; their daughter was [17] *Maryam*. Another student, [18] *Safiya*, was married, but her husband's name is not known. *Maryam* [17] was married first to Ade ɗan Giɗaɗo, with whom she had a daughter [19] *Matar Modi*, and later to Ibrahim Dabo, Emir of Kano. Asma'u's cousin

---

1   Umaru was killed by a runaway horse in his adulthood.

who wrote was [20] *Aisha*, daughter of Abdullahi ɗan Fodio. Her niece who wrote was [21] *Faɗima*, daughter of Muhammad Bello.

Nana Asma'u married Giɗaɗo, and they had a son Ahmadu, who in turn married [22] *Ha'ija ·yar Bello*, and [23] *Aisha ·yar Buhari ɗan Shehu*. Ahmadu and Aisha's son was Buhari, who was the Waziri at the time of the British invasion of Nigeria, at the beginning of the twentieth century. Buhari's son, Waziri Junaidu, worked with Jean Boyd on the Nana Asma'u manuscripts, his great-grandmother's writings.

Thus, in just four generations of the Fodio family, from the early eighteenth century to the mid-nineteenth century, we can account for more than twenty women who identified themselves and were identified by others as scholars and teachers:

Inna Kabo
Rukaya (the Shehu's maternal grandmother)
Hauwa of Marnona (the Shehu's mother)
Hauwa, the Shehu's wife
Habiba (cousin)
Ja'ibatu (cousin)
Aisha (wife)
Juwaida (cousin)
Amina Lubal (cousin)
Amina ·yar Ade (cousin)
Yahinu
Aisha
Maimuna
Nana Asma'u
Hadija
Habsatu
Faɗima
Maryam
Safiya
Maryam
Matar Modi
Aisha

Faɗima
Ha'ija ·yar Bello
Aisha ·yar Buhari ɗan Shehu

The men these women married were themselves accomplished scholars, and therefore unlikely to marry a woman who was not their equal in intellect and inclination. Indeed, in contemporary times, men of comparable scholarly accomplishment in comparable Islamic communities attest to the importance of spouses working together on 'the (Sufi) path'. In Islam, marriage is valued as 'half the religion'; it is a religion whose opening revelation was the command to read and recite.

Asma'u's great-grandson, Waziri Junaidu himself composed an Arabic manuscript *Arfuraihani*, in which he detailed the lives of nine sons and four daughters of Shehu Usman ɗan Fodio. The information that follows is from Junaidu's account. He says:

Hadija was born in 1782 in Degel to the Shehu and his second wife, Aisha. She was the Shehu's first daughter, following two sons. As expected for a scholarly family, Hadija grew up to be pious, ascetic, and extremely learned. She married Malam Mustafa, probably a cousin, who was descended from the same line as the Shehu. Their son, Abdulkadir, was described by a nineteenth century German traveller [Barth] as the 'greatest living scholar' of his age. It was this Hadija, Asma'u's elder sister, who was Asma'u's first teacher. It is known that she produced several written works, among them the following:

1. Explanation of the Mahdi
2. Elegy for her husband Musdafa
3. Translation of Bello's prayer on Wurno
4. Poem on *fikihu* (jurisprudence)
5. About obedience to parents
6. Poem about grammar

7. Commentary in Fulfulde on *Mukhtasar*[1]
8. '... and others too numerous to mention ...'

(Waziri Junaidu, Arfuraihani)

Hadija's son Abdulkadir, who was born on the eve of the family's hijra, which marked the beginning of the Sokoto Jihad, eventually wrote the elegy on his mother when she died many years later. Hadija and Musdafa and their family lived at Salame beginning in about 1825. Fadima was born in Degel in 1787 to the Shehu and his wife Hauwa, who was also the mother of Muhammad Bello. She was regarded as saintly, with a gracious manner, and received from her father the Shehu special secrets, probably Sufi visions. At maturity she married Aliyu Jeɗo (Sarkin Yaƙi), and they settled at Binji. She is described in Asma'u's *Sufi Women*. Fadima wrote a Fulfulde poem about growing old, and another about the merits of Sufi invocations (*dhikr*). Her daughter Maryam married Abdulkadir ɗan Gidaɗo.

Women scholars in Sokoto in the twentieth century

It was at the end of one of the regular visits that Jean Boyd paid to Waziri Junaidu in 1981 that he asked her what she knew about the *jaji*s of the time. Had she noticed them as they walked in procession to the Hubbare? The Waziri did not pose questions without requiring answers so Boyd turned to the manuscript he had allowed her to have copied, along with many others, several years previously. It was a list of Asma'u's students, written down shortly after her death. The unspoken implication was that the places needed to be seen; women needed to be asked about the 'Yan Taru.

To trace these associations, first of all the villages had to be located; as it happened they were to the southwest of Sokoto,

---

1   This is the famous epitome of Maliki fiqh by Khalil b. Ishaq al-Jundi (d. *ca.* 1365).

scattered in an area of farmland which could be reached only by a four-wheel-drive vehicle. Most were deep in rural areas beyond signposts. Boyd travelled 1,245 kilometres in the cold season of 1981–82 primarily to find out whether the names of Asma'u's students in the list were remembered and to see how the *jajis* and 'Yan Taru had fared in the last one hundred years. She found herself in a different world where Asma'u was talked about as if still alive. Asma'u was a reality to the women Boyd met.

All the eighteen *jajis* that Boyd interviewed were different – some lived in large villages, some in hamlets, some were very old, others were bustling matrons, yet they had many things in common. Most had inherited their titles from the best candidates in the family descended from the *jajis* appointed by Asma'u. All had been given their *malfas*, straw hats, at the Hubbare, and were responsible for the good behaviour of each of the participants. All took alms to the Hubbare – grain, cloth, money, butter – for the sick poor and elderly. According to their abilities some *jajis* helped women in childbirth, or washed the bodies of dead women. Some swept the village mosques. All taught women and girls and sang famous songs for them. One *jaji* summed up Asma'u's life work as 'she was the teacher of women'. Another said: 'Nana told us to always keep calm, avoid arguments and live in peace.' Yet another: 'Nana said: Any alms that you take to the Hubbare must have been lawfully acquired, otherwise your prayers will have been made in vain.'

As for the names of Asma'u's students, Boyd was surprised at the number of *jajis* who firmly knew their genealogy, though not all knew the full list of names leading back to Asma'u. This legacy lives on in the collective memory of the 'Yan Taru women just as their meritorious works live on.

By talking with women in the region, Jean Boyd was able to collect information on women scholars since Asma'u's time, and trace the continuous traditions of the 'Yan Taru through to the present. The women who were remembered as significant scholars were:

Malama Hauwwa'u Mamangi. She was a Fulfulde scholar, the elder sister and a distinguished aide of Malam Abubakar Bube, the most senior of the scholars advising the Waziris of the day. As a young man Junaidu (later the Waziri, 1947–97) studied with her books in translation (Fulfulde) like *Kurtaba* by Malam Yahaya Alkurtabi and *al-Akhdari* by Abu Zaydi Abdurrahman ɗan Saghiri. He went on to study Fulfulde poetry with her and under her instruction his pronunciation improved as did his understanding and his ability to interpret difficult texts. On occasion Malama Hauwwa'u would seek her brother's help with certain verses and thereafter discuss the matter with Junaidu. (Ibrahim Junaidu, *Rayuwar Wazirin Sakkwato*, pp.10, 13)

Modibo Kilo. She was the mother of the wife of Sambo Junaidu, the Professor of Arabic at Sokoto's Usman ɗan Fodio University. She died in Makka.

Modibo Suma of Dogondaj. She taught Alhaji Ibrahim Dasuki, later the Sultan of Sokoto, 1988–96.

Inna Wuro, a daughter of Caliph Ahmadu Rufai (r. 1867—73). She died in 1961, the last of the Shehu's grandchildren. Professor Sambo Junaidu said in conversation: 'I visited her several times as a boy. She was fair in complexion, plump and of average height. She was in the house of Mariya, Isa Mai Kware's mother. I used to drink from a vessel believed to be that of Shehu Usumanu.' Presumably he was sent with greetings (*gaisuwa*) from the Waziri, a means of paying his respects.

Lamido Kilo, a daughter of Caliph Ahmadu Rufai, a teacher at Shuni, several miles from Sokoto.

Modibo Mowa and *Modibo* Audi, daughters of *Modibo* Mairamu of Kware, teachers of Sultan Hassan's wives during the 1920s and 1930s.

Modibo Jima of Assada Felete (informant Malam Sidi Sayuydi, Ubandoman Sokoto, *ca.* 1979).

Modibo Amo at Kware.

The 'Yan Taru influence extends beyond the region, as far as Kano, with which emirate the historical connection has been well established for generations. Hajiya Rabi Wali reported in the 1980s that 'the jihadists' religious ideas were still circulating among Kano women in the mid-twentieth century'. She said:

Women have been teachers for a long, long time. Even I have my mother's books with me, which she used to write. And they were forming discussion groups because they have prayers. Even in the palace...my mother's group...always gathered together. They discuss books and kasidas, you know, poems written by malams, or Shehu Usman's poems. They have people from Sokoto, women who used to visit the palace ...and all those people who like learning, they will come and stay the day with them discussing all those things like the Shehu was telling people. And most of them live in the Hubbare, that is where the Shehu's tomb is. They were reading them like the writing of people like Nana [Asma'u]...So there have been teachers, women teachers, all along. Women from Sokoto visit the palace in Kano and stay with my grandmother for three months or even six and all those people [the palace women] who liked learning came and spent the day with [them] discussing all those things the Shehu told people. Most of them lived in the Hubbare where the Shehu's tomb is. They read the works of people like Nana Asma'u and Isa Mai Kware. So there have been women teachers all along.[1]

Women from Kano make their own pilgrimages to Sokoto for the purpose of education. That the 'Yan Taru continued to function at the end of the twentieth century is evident in the Mai Hubbare's observation (in a personal communication to Jean Boyd) in February of 1997:

---

1   Balaraba B. M. Sule and Priscilla Starratt, 'Islamic Leadership Positions for Women in Contemporary Kano Society' in Catherine Coles and Beverly Mack (eds.) *Hausa Women in the Twentieth Century* (Madison, WI: University of Wisconsin Press, 1991), pp.29–49, at 39.

Seven car loads of pilgrims arrived from Kano today.[1] Sometimes there are as many as one hundred cars in one day. Pilgrims come from as far afield as Senegal, but generally speaking those from outside Nigeria find travel difficult because of immigration controls. They come because the Shehu lived his life for the sake of God, not for power or wealth or anything else. He was totally committed, an ascetic and a selfless human being. The women's organization, the 'Yan Taru, are from Sokoto. They come endlessly, their organization is as strong as ever.

Further evidence of the respect given to these ladies in the Hubbare is found in the remarks made by *Modibo* Auta, the last surviving child of Sultan Muhammadu Mai Turare, who, in 2003, was in charge as the Mai 'Daki of 'Dakin Hauwa. She told Boyd that at the last Eid, because of ill health, she was unable to go to the palace to greet the Sultan, Maccido. He had noted her absence, in spite of the thousands visiting him at the time and sent messages to her which had obviously given her solace and comfort.

Hauwa, the *Jagaba* (super *jaji*) of Yabo said (in a personal communication to Jean Boyd) in 1983:

The pilgrims at the Hubbare go to each room and give alms. In each room there is a bed and a *buta* [water jug for ceremonial ablutions] and a container to drink from. They promise in their hearts to pay a fixed sum, even a penny or a shilling, if their prayers are answered. Each woman tells the Mai 'Daki what her desires are. Adults drink from the water container (*shantali*) taking three gulps each. Two very old ladies once described how their heads had been stroked by Ta Modi eighty years previously. They leave hoping that their urgent desires for a child, for the recovery from ill health or for a loving husband [may be realized]. The Mai 'Dakis have set times at which *tafsir* [Qur'anic commentary] is given – in the case of Mai 'Daki Aisha for example, she has students of *tafsir* on Thursdays.

---

1   This included carloads of both men and women, travelling in separate groups.

Western scholarship values what is written on paper. Muslims like the Qadiriyya Sufi Fodios valued instead that which is written on the heart. Among them, the pursuit of knowledge is a devotional act; to study and learn is a way of being spiritual. Since this activity is not quantifiable, it is too easily discounted by those who take account only of tangible evidence of scholarly activity. Examination of the number of women scholars who trained one another across generations deepens and enriches contemporary understanding of the value of learning in a Muslim African context. Research and reflection on the canon of materials they studied can indicate to contemporary scholars the nature of this community's spiritual and philosophical life, and link their interests to a larger canon of materials known in wider Islamic circles. This information and these materials will change profoundly historians' assumptions about women in Islam and women's roles in Islamic African cultures.

6

MUSLIM WOMEN SCHOLARS IN THE TWENTIETH
AND TWENTY-FIRST CENTURIES

As Asma'u's Sokoto-based 'Yan Taru movement continued
operating into the late twentieth century, women throughout
Nigeria were coalescing in other organizations that reflected the
spirit of the 'Yan Taru. Their aim was women's education and
activism for their own betterment and that of their communities.
These movements included an organization which began in the
early 1980s called Women in Nigeria (WIN) and another, a subsequent outgrowth, called the Federation of Muslim Women's
Associations in Nigeria (FOMWAN).

Independence from British colonial rule on 1st October, 1960
brought political turmoil, followed by the rise of multinational oil
investments that poured wealth into unscrupulous hands in the
1970s, and then the eventual breakdown of public services. In the
1970s the educated elite at post-independence universities started
to criticize the state of public services. Dr Ibraheem Sulaiman
said:

There are many things the people need: sound education... adequate and
indeed free health facilities devoid of the fraud that goes on in hospitals
these days; work for those who can work, adequate compensation for
the work they do and care for those who cannot fend for themselves;
free access to justice and the implementation of a just system of law;

and freedom from exploitation of manipulation... The fact is that our people are being wasted and misused.[1]

His remarks included criticisms of the way in which women were regarded. He spoke emphatically in favour of the education of women and the need for Muslim men and women to work together to reconstruct society: '...justice to women entails... that their right to education must never be curtailed or abrogated.'[2]

Beginning in the 1970s, criticism of inequities and inadequacies in the educational system came from many corners. Much of it focused on the equitable example of the Caliphate. In 1971, Waziri Junaidu, great-grandson of Gidado and Asma'u, gave a speech at Ahmadu Bello University which created something of a sensation. Titled *The Relevance of the University to Our Society*, it was circulated throughout the country in Arabic, the language in which it had been delivered, as well as in Hausa and English. In it he praised the highly cultured society of Timbuktu, which he used as metaphor for Sokoto, because 'it was in Timbuktu that Shehu dan Fodio could easily have been seen'. Sokoto, he said, was a place

...concerned with self-discipline, piety and the love of learning, justice and truth. Above all it was concerned with the maintenance of the spirit of the community, so that those who were born and raised in it recognized, accepted and perpetuated the high moral ideas and codes of conduct on which the community depended for its peace and harmony. The remarkable thing was its sense of self-possession and its belief in the virtue of the Sudanic ways, despite its acceptance of many new ideas which permeated to the area via caravan routes. I shall be frank with you; in matters such as this, one must resist shyness. I must state

---

1   Ibraheem Sulaiman, 'The Agony of a Complacent Nation', *Radiance* (1983; published by Muslim Students Society)

2   Anon., 'A Place for Women', Radiance 1984, at the launch of the Muslim Ladies Movement at Kano State Institute for Higher Studies, later Bayero University.

that your university like all others in Nigeria is a cultural transplant whose roots lie in another tradition.[1]

In 1976 the University of Nigeria at Nsukka conferred an honorary degree on the Sultan of Sokoto, Sultan Abubakar III, great-grandson of Caliph Muhammad Bello. At the ceremony the Sultan took the unusual step of levelling criticism in public against Western-educated intellectuals who made the serious mistake of adopting foreign mores without stopping to think what they were doing:

Since the arrival of the Europeans a medley of divergent and conflicting ideas has been preached as intrinsically and exclusively properties of something modern. Cars or tractors have [mechanical] advantages over the horse or the hoe, but they have no moral or intellectual superiority. Nigerians must remember their own native creative genius.[2]

This rising tide of critiques freed increasing numbers of individuals to speak out. Over the next decade, by the early 1980s, there was a need to reduce staple food prices and ensure equitable distribution of essential goods. Ordinary people were affected and their unease increased as they listened to daily stories of victimization and rancorous politics together with rumours of very serious corruption. Well-educated, influential men and women began to speak out in public addresses and through the media. In 1981 the Governor of Sokoto State gave an interview which was widely reported. In it he walked a fine line between acknowledging a consensus on misogyny and appearing to offer tentative support for active roles for women:

Sokoto is a place where I can say 80% of husbands including myself would like their women to be in the house, and also 99% of men would

---

1   Waziri Junaidu, *The Relevance of the University to Our Society* (Ahmadu Bello University Press, 1972).
2   This speech was widely published in a variety of newspapers at the time.

like to be in total control of the women. She is supposed to be in the house looking after the children; they are not even expected to come out. My wives don't go out; they are always in the house. Husbands would not welcome the idea of having their wives act as Commissioners; because of the exigencies of the office she would go out and come in at any time. ...I would very much like to have a woman in my Cabinet because I believe in women's liberation in the sense that they have the right to exist and pursue certain goals. My society at the moment finds itself in a certain position. First of all, I think we have only four graduate women in the whole of Sokoto, three of them are school principals and one is an engineer, so with that kind of limitation you can see how narrow the field is. Then, of course, I told you about our system where the husbands are very particular about what their wives do. I am not saying we are not going to do anything about it, we are still looking and I am still trying to persuade even one among this number to come so we can have some kind of representation. Having a woman in the Executive Council will help us understand what the aspirations of the women are.

(New Times, 26th April 1981)

In the far North at this time, men and women did not seem inclined to work together to reconstruct society. Reflecting on these circumstances decades later, Hajiya Aisha Lemu explained that, at the end of the 1970s,

The North and South of the country were not the same. In the southern States there were already numerous women's Islamic organizations, many of them attached to mosques and engaged in various charitable and educational activities. In the North where the practice of seclusion was widespread especially in urban areas, women's Islamic groups, if they existed, were not known about, an example being the 'Yan Taru in Sokoto. There were as well a few branches of the Muslim Sisters Organization (MSO), an offshoot of the Muslim Students Society (MSS), mainly in the universities. For example intellectual women contributed papers to a seminar on Law and Social Reform held in Kano, and others on the Rights of Women to Education.

(Aisha Lemu's speech, 10th FOMWAN conference, Abuja, 1995).

In the late 1970s women in the North began to organize in order to speak out about their circumstances; by the beginning of the next decade women were a visible presence in Nigeria.

Women in Nigeria: 'WIN Will Win'

In May, 1982 the First Annual Women in Nigeria Conference was held in northern Nigeria. It was organized by a group of activist women at Ahmadu Bello University in Zaria, Nigeria, who met in a seminar to discuss the situation of women in the country. The title of the organization that grew from this meeting is indicative of their hope for the future: Women in Nigeria, or WIN. Their pink tee-shirts expressed a healthy tongue-in-cheek perception of the struggle they had assumed: superimposed on an outline of Nigeria, a raised fist clutched a pestle. On the back, green letters stated simply 'W.I.N. Will Win', a subtle reminder to the man whose gaze might linger as the shirt passed by. The group's preamble stated:

We believe
That the majority of women, like the majority of men, suffer from
    the exploitative and oppressive character of Nigerian society.
That, however, women suffer additional forms of oppression and
    exploitation.
Women, therefore, suffer double oppression and exploitation – as
    members of subordinate classes and as women.[1]

---

1   The second part of these aims and objectives stated: 'Our organization will engage in research, policy-making, and action, aimed at improving the conditions of women.' The third: "The organization will act: 1) To promote the study of the condition of women in Nigeria – in the family, in the work-place, and in the wider society; 2) To defend the rights of women under the constitution; 3) To provide non-sexist alternatives to government and institutional policies; 4) To combat sexist practices; 5) To fight against the harassment and sexual abuse of women in the family

The organizers of WIN sought to address and initiate improvement in social conditions in areas as diverse as medical care, education, the arts, and legal issues. Reporting on the first WIN conference, Bilkisu Yusuf emphasized that participants cited ubiquitous patriarchal oppression in Nigeria: 'Hausa, Igbo, and Yoruba societies and many other ethnic groups are patriarchal and in Igbo society women do not inherit' (*The Sunday Triumph*, 13 June 1982, p. 8). In addition to attitudinal barriers to equality, it was acknowledged that urban/rural situations appeared to cut across ethnic lines, with rural women having considerably less access to the education, health, and technical opportunities that could significantly improve their lives.

WIN's two-day inaugural conference (27–28 May 1982) included individuals from all over the country, presenting 28 papers in eight panels.[1] Sessions ranged from general discussions of women's roles in contemporary life to more specific concerns, like the roles of women in production, history, and politics. Lively debate concerned issues such as the double oppression suffered by women in agrarian cultures which allowed only for male ownership of land, the legendary warrior queens of the Hausa, and the long hiatus in political involvement suffered by Nigerian women since before the colonial period. Even more significant than what was said, was the fact of Nigerian women creating for themselves a forum for the re-evaluation of their situation.

and elsewhere; 6) To provide a forum for women to express themselves; 7) To ensure for women equal access to education; 8) To promote an equitable distribution of domestic work; 9) To combat sexist stereotypes in literature and the media; 10) To form links with other women's groups; and 11) To form links and work with other organizations fighting gender and class oppression.' This and other citations and information, unless otherwise attributed, are from Beverly Mack's notes and materials from the first and second conferences, which she attended.

1   Theoretical Framework for Understanding Women's Position in Society; Contemporary Experiences of Women in Nigeria I–IV; Women in Nigerian History; Women and Production; and What Is To Be Done?

These women were their own toughest critics, willing to evaluate their positions with severe honesty and to share with one another concerns that overshadowed any potential ethnic divisions.

The second WIN conference was held over three days, 20–22nd April 1983, and included 30 papers given in nine panels.[1] Its theme, 'Women and the Family', provided a forum in which one of the most enthusiastically discussed issues was that of forced early marriage, its physical, psychological and social consequences. Yusuf commented:

In most cases these girls are too immature to deliver children, labour in childbirth is often prolonged and obstructed, leading to internal ruptures of the bladder and rectum... As a result, these girls are divorced by their husbands and become social outcasts in their communities and are often forced to turn to prostitution to stay alive.

(The Sunday Triumph, 29th May 1983)

The third WIN conference (1984), whose focus was 'Women and Education', reflected Nigerian women's growing awareness of education as critical to the improved quality of their lives. Since the colonial period, Nigerian men had realized that achievement in Western education was the primary means by which they could compete in the public work force. While this was the goal of some women, others strove to become literate so that they could run their own businesses from the seclusion of their homes, to assist their children with their school work, or to know first-hand the political developments discussed in the newspapers. Several southern Nigerian women had become authors of critical acclaim. Buchi Emecheta has more than seven novels to her credit, and Flora Nwapa has long been acknowledged as a chronicler of Igbo women's traditional life. Women from southern Nigeria have since the 1920s been attending higher education

---

1   General; Family, Society and Development I and II; Literature, Media Culture; Women in Rural Areas; Law, Religion; Double Workload; Medical; What Is To Be Done?

courses overseas and, at the end of the twentieth century, made up a considerable portion of the university-level student bodies and professional schools in Nigeria because Western education had been introduced to southern Nigeria far more readily than in the North. Indeed the disproportionate access to Western education caused social inequality and strife between northern and southern Nigeria throughout the second half of the twentieth century, following independence in 1960.

In the North, where women often cite Nana Asma'u as exemplary of women's scholarship, education has long been revered as a means to greater religious edification. Education in Asma'u's Islamic context included substantial social welfare work and *da'wa*, teaching about Islam. As early as the 1930s and 1940s a major political figure, Mallam Aminu Kano, advocated education of women for the betterment of the nation. In the 1970s Kano State instituted urban and rural centres for adult education, including extensive women's education programmes with both day and night classes in literacy, numeracy, and religious instruction, which made it possible for Muslim women whose schooling had been interrupted by early marriage to finish their primary and secondary education. In the twentieth century Hausa–Fulani North, the nineteenth-century Caliphate precedent for such a programme of grassroots education was so self-evident as to be nearly unspoken. Whenever the issue was raised, Nana Asma'u's example was cited.

Thus, it is not surprising that the establishment of WIN, taking place as it did in the Hausa–Fulani North, included reference to Asma'u and her aims. The consensus among its founders was that realizing improvement for women involved remedial social action for all:

The founding group believed... that the liberation of women cannot be fully achieved outside the context of the liberation of the oppressed and poor majority of the people of Nigeria....Therefore women must organize and fight for their full social and economic rights in the family, in the workplace and in society in general as a necessary part of the continuing struggle to create and develop a just society for all.[1]

It was clear that this organization, with its overwhelming majority of women, reflected a communal confidence in their ability to change the social order. The name of Nana Asma'u was mentioned more than once, almost as a talisman for the movement. That indigenous women had long been in control of the social order and should be activist in improving their own society in their own way was clearly the sentiment of these meetings, as this assessment indicates:

Indeed, there are fore-running women's organizations in Nigeria just as there are traditions of resistance and activism which go back to pre-colonial times. It needs to be stressed that there were indigenous 'feminisms' prior to our contact with Europe just as there were indigenous modes of rebellion and resistance in the mythified African past. Therefore 'feminism' or the fight for women's rights and women's interests is not the result of 'contamination' by the West or a simple imitation as divisive opponents like to charge. One of the most recurrent charges made to and about Third World women is that of being blind copy-cats of Western European feminists. Many Third World feminists, in awareness of the 'divide-and-rule' tactics of their accusers, have replied perceptively that the accusers' play is consciously conceived and maintained to confuse women, to bind to them their respective men and male systems and to prevent a dangerous comparing of notes and a potentially dangerous unity. WIN follows in the long tradition of organized women's associations and movements. Previously, we have had associations of women, social political activists and plain strugglers who in their daily living have tried to raise the status of women in the society and the home through various ways... [2]

---

1   Altine Mohammed and Bene Madunagu, 'WIN: A Militant Approach to the Mobilization of Women', *Review of African Political Economy*, 37 ('Oil Debts and Democracy in Nigeria': Taylor & Francis Ltd., Dec. 1986), pp. 103–05, at 103.
2   *Ibid.*, pp. 103–04.

Although Asma'u's works had not yet been published in translation at the time of the WIN conferences, her reputation in the region was well established, and her example was significant in Nigeria's pre-colonial history. WIN's motivation was avowedly political, as had been Asma'u's aim to resocialize war refugees, through which the fabric of society was repaired for the betterment of all.

During each of these three WIN conferences, women from a wide range of backgrounds spoke adamantly about the need to establish better opportunities for women in education, health care, entrepreneurship, the media and the law. Speakers critiqued the ways in which women's contributions to social order and development were being ignored and uncompensated. Women involved with WIN were especially concerned to accomplish this in ways that were well suited to Nigerian conditions, and to avoid imitation of Western feminist practices. The proceedings of this and a subsequent WIN conference were published and served to strengthen the women's activism that was to follow.[1]

FOMWAN:
Federation of Muslim Women's Associations in Nigeria

In 1984 Jean Boyd's article, 'An Account of the Life of Nana Asma'u, Daughter of Shehu Usman ɗan Fodio', was translated into Hausa and published in the Hausa newspaper *Gaskiya Ta Fi Kwabo*, with the encouragement of activists of the Muslim Sisters Organization (MSO) at Bayero University in Kano. The following month the English version was published in the Nigerian newspaper *The Sunday Triumph*. Meanwhile, Muslim women who had participated in the development of the WIN

---

1   Ayesha Imam edited these three volumes: *The WIN Document: the Conditions of Women in Nigeria,* and *Policy Recommendations to 2,000 AD* (Zaria: WIN, 1985); *Women in Nigeria Today* (London: Zed Books, 1985).

organization hearkened increasingly to Asma'u's example, and felt moved to act in the Islamic context of education for the purpose of social welfare reform, and for personal development. Bilkisu Yusuf's discussion of the difficulties of engaging in *da'wa* in a secular context outlines the origins of a new Nigerian women's organization that aimed to educate and engage in social development. In it she cites Asma'u's tradition of scholarship and teaching, and laments that it has been followed by too few Muslim families in contemporary times:

Muslim women in Nigeria have long been among the victims of the general ignorance of Islam among the population, and of the refusal of all but a few Islamic scholars and leaders to speak out about the true role and status of the Muslim woman. The greatest and most honorable exception was Sheikh Usman ɗan Fodio, the great 19th century scholar, reformer and jihadist, who spoke out most forcefully against the local way of treating women like chattels and failing to educate them… By educating all his daughters to the highest standard, he showed a shining example of the Islamic way, and left as a legacy his daughter, Nana Asma'u, who, herself, became a famous scholar, writer, poet, teacher, leader and *da'wa* worker among women.[1]

The formation of the Muslim Student Society and Muslim Sisters Organizations in the North allowed students to become actively engaged in educational programmes without conversion to Christianity (which had been increasingly the pressure in the South), as well as providing them with a platform for the social welfare work in which they felt obliged to participate. But beyond student life, and in the face of a plethora of women's organizations, there existed no organization of Muslim women working toward the educational needs and socio-religious rights of other Muslim women. WIN was useful, but some of its members realized the

1 Bilkisu Yusuf, '*Da'wa* and Contemporary Challenges Facing Muslim Women in Secular States – A Nigerian Case Study' in Nur Alkali *et al.* (eds.), *Islam in Africa: Proceedings of the Islam in Africa Conference* (Ibadan: Spectrum Books, 1989), pp. 276–95, at 282.

need for an organization that operated within the tenets of Islam in striving to assert the rights of Muslim women throughout the country. The next step was the establishment of a national Islamic organization by and for women:

With all these needs in mind, the women concerned met in April 1985 in Kano and agreed to call a conference to establish the organization, which was done in October 1985 in Minna. Thus was born the Federation of Muslim Women's Associations in Nigeria (FOMWAN).[1]

FOMWAN's first national Amira, Aisha Lemu, wrote:

The arrival day in Minna coincided with the last storm of the season. It was so violent that the little plane bringing delegates from Lagos was tossed around like a leaf and had to be diverted from Minna. The most traumatic experience came later when sisters travelling by road had a breakdown and as they stood by their car a police vehicle ran into them at speed. One of the sisters and the driver were fatally injured. None of the sisters gathered for the meeting slept that night. Those not at the hospital spent the night in prayer and anxious consultation as to whether the meeting should be cancelled. The consensus was that since they had died in an Islamic cause, we should not go back without achieving what we had gathered to do and render their sacrifice in vain. So, while some of the sisters accompanied the dead back to Zaria for burial, the rest stayed on. Over the weekend they hammered out the basic structure of FOMWAN as a Federation of affiliates, and a simple constitution with which to get the organization started and incorporated by the Federal Government.

How did FOMWAN then proceed? We established a National Executive and appointed a number of State Amirahs with the responsibility of getting FOMWAN established in their respective states. Over the following months they contacted other interested women, set up their state committees and launched state chapters of FOMWAN.

Many of the members of the newly created state branches did not know what to do at first, but they read or heard the reports of other

---

1   *Ibid.*, p. 284.

states, picked up ideas and developed their own operations, staging events like:

> printing posters to encourage Islamic culture;
> teaching women how to make saleable items like pomade and soap;
> participating in UNICEF guinea-worm eradication programme;
> providing sunset meals for the needy men and women found near the mosques in Ramadan;
> establishing orphanages;
> assisting in hospitals;
> holding classes where women were educated; and
> donating Qur'ans to women prisoners.[1]

One of the most important factors was the ability of the state committees to pay regular visits to get the support of the Chairmen of Local Government Areas, of emirs and local dignitaries. In the North, some husbands and Islamic teachers opposed the whole idea of women having an Islamic association, or indeed any kind of association. As Aisha Lemu remarked: 'such men forbid women going out to attend meetings; they are the diehard traditionalists who think their women exist only to serve the menfolk.' The Amira Sa'adiya and her colleagues in Sokoto who met with local dignitaries were not surprised to find that many of them were reluctant to give their support to FOMWAN. These men already knew that Nana Asma'u had been a scholar, poet, teacher, wife and partner of Gidado, known as 'the reconciler'. She wanted to persuade them that Asma'u's work as an exemplar was not finished, but could continue to inspire and motivate women in the future as she had in the past.

Thus the best educated women in Nigeria banded together of their own volition to address the issues facing them, without direction from government, or from even the most supportive,

---

1   'FOMWAN History and Experience. A Case Study'. Presented by B. Aisha Lemu at FOMWAN tenth anniversary international conference, Abuja, 16–20th August 1995.

sympathetic of men. The FOMWAN organization and others like it (WIN and MSO) were home-grown institutions working their own solutions to their own problems. Some of the women at the heart of these movements knew about Nana Asma'u, having grown up hearing stories about her, and her poetry. Asma'u was a living legend and role model. Even toddlers chant short rhymes beginning, 'Oh Nana, Shehu's daughter, Mother of all ...' (*Nanuwa, 'Yar Shehu, Uwar gida*).

Fig 13. Women buying books at the tenth anniversary of FOMWAN, Abuja 1995 (Photo: Jean Boyd, 1995)

At the first FOMWAN National Conference in 1986 the committee decided to approach Professor Jibril Aminu of the Federal Military Government concerning the kind of school uniform currently worn by Muslim girls in Federal Government Colleges. The Professor, who met with the committee at Queen's College, set up a committee to examine the matter of the uniform and within a few months it was ordained that FGC girls would have two options; one, as before, a dress and hat, the other a tunic, trousers and a draped head covering. This was the first example of what could be accomplished through a united front.

The ceremony of FOMWAN's tenth anniversary conference was held at the National Mosque Conference Hall in Abuja on 17th August 1995. Abuja Mosque Hall is a very well appointed building and on the day of the Conference it was full of ambassadors, delegates from abroad, imams, government ministers, and national officers of FOMWAN. The chairman was the Grand Kadi of Abuja, the national capital. The distinguished guest speaker, Usman Bugaje, the Secretary-General of the Islamic Africa Movement, said, 'For the first time since the Sokoto Caliphate, women have pooled their talents, resources and energies together for the advancement of the cause of Islam'. At the ceremony the National Amira, Sa'adiya Omar said:

After the 19th century Jihad of Shehu ɗan Fodio Muslim women in the Caliphate were mobilized. Now another movement, FOMWAN, has emerged which aims to rally and organize Muslim women in Nigeria so that they will achieve betterment in every way. I must also say that it is sad to note that Muslim women are being exploited and are being brought up in accordance with teaching and ideas which are totally different from Islamic objectives. They are denied a proper place in the education system of the country while in the civil service their socio-religious norms and values are steadily eroded. What a pathetic situation!

God in his infinite mercy has made a miracle out of FOMWAN. It is the most united and most effective women's organization in the

201

country. Over 600 women's organizations are now under the leadership of FOMWAN. It has erected both large and small education, health and welfare centres in various States. It is in direct touch with ordinary people, offering services to those in need. Members visit hospitals, distribute food and assist in times of disaster. Importantly too FOMWAN holds courses on many aspects of the faith – the hajj and Ramadan for example.
(Sa'adiya Omar Bello, National Amirah of FOMWAN, tenth anniversary and international conference, Abuja, 1995)

Nothing could detract from the exuberance of all the women and their good humour in the hall as they moved to join their colleagues – a thousand in number – in the afternoon session held at the National Youth Service Corps camp about thirty minutes' drive from Abuja. The hall, the size of an aircraft hangar had a tin roof, no ceiling; there were window frames but no windows; and in the surrounding grass-swards millions of mosquitos ready to come out after dark. Still, the enthusiasm of the women knew no bounds. Bank executives, university lecturers, doctors, school principals, business women and two granddaughters of the Sultan of Sokoto, all assembled together in the camp with the delegates who had arrived by lorry, balancing their mattresses on their heads as they trekked to the dormitories allocated to them. There was a great sense of sisterhood throughout the next three days.

A decade into the twenty-first century, FOMWAN continues as a vibrant women's organization dedicated to educational and social welfare work throughout Nigeria.[1] Like the 'Yan Taru,

1   Its website explains: 'The Federation of Muslim Women's Associations in Nigeria (FOMWAN) was established in October 1985 and registered with the Corporate Affairs Commission the same year. With a consultative status with the United Nations, FOMWAN is a non-profit and non-governmental civil society umbrella body for Muslim women associations in Nigeria. Today FOMWAN is in 34 States of the federation and has over 500 affiliate groups. FOMWAN national headquarters, Utako Abuja, is under construction. The multi-million naira project includes an administrative building, a hostel block, conference hall and a mosque. FOMWAN

FOMWAN serves women's and families' needs by educating holistically, with attention to economic welfare as well as health, literacy, and spirituality. Its mission statement includes dedication to education and social welfare activities, especially with regard to women's and children's lives.[1] FOMWAN is organized by a Body of Trustees (BOT) who work together to plan its projects. The BOT members meet once a year, to 'chart direction, agree on strategy, formulate policies and oversee performance.'[2]

is a network of Muslim Women organizations nationally. It is emerging and growing as a national faith-based non-governmental organization with emphasis on promoting and protecting the interest, welfare and aspirations of its members in line with Islamic injunctions. The impetus for the establishment and existence of FOMWAN is the provision of social service especially to its members and the desire to contribute to national development. In particular, FOMWAN seeks to contribute to the overall health, literacy and economic empowerment of its members and promotion of positive social behaviour of Muslim girls for responsible living and adulthood in Nigeria. Recently, FOMWAN reviewed and adopted a new strategic plan redefining its vision, mission, value statements, goal and strategic objectives.' http://www.fomwan.org/index.php

1   'Our mission is to propagate the religion of Islam in Nigeria through da'wa, establishment of educational institutions and other outreach activities. And to improve the socio-economic status of the populace, especially women, youth and children, through training, provision of qualitative education, health and humanitarian services, microenterprise scheme and advocacy. The vision of FOMWAN is a world where women are totally empowered to be role models in making positive impacts in religious and secular matters.' http://www.fomwan.org/index.php

2   The National Executive Council (NEC) consists of national officers led by the Amira (the President). Other members are the Naibat al-Amira (Deputy President), national secretary-general and assistant national secretary-general, national financial secretary, treasurer, public relations officer/organizing secretary, da'wa officer, assistant da'wa officer, legal adviser, national auditor, ex officio members, chairpersons of standing national committees and FOMWAN State Chapter Amiras. The duties of the body include but are not limited to the day-to-day running of the Federation and laying down its broad, basic policy and programme in accordance with its aims and objectives. The national committees perform

203

FOMWAN operates nation-wide, keeping transparent funds, which are audited on a regular basis. It receives its operating expenses from a variety of sources, including local, regional, and international donors.[1] Just as Nana Asma'u oversaw multiple *jajis* who led numerous 'Yan Taru groups, FOMWAN is managed by an Amira, the National President (who oversees operations, volunteers, and the few recent paid staffers), national executive (volunteer) officers who are chairpersons of boards of education, health, publications, finance, welfare and disciplinary and international relations, and another tier of zonal coordinators for the North East, North West, North Central, South West and South East.[2] Together they operate the organization to engage in literacy education, entrepreneurial training, and social welfare work for women throughout Nigeria.

'Yan Taru: The Film

In the 1960s when Jean Boyd and her husband taught in Sokoto it appeared that no one in the colonial service showed the slightest interest in the history of the illustrious people who had

specialized functions and some oversight functions as defined by the constitution and reviewed and updated from time to time by the BOT or NEC as appropriate. The NEC members are the asset of the organization as they constitute the core of volunteers that spearhead the design and implementation of all FOMWAN programmes and activities. http://www.fomwan.org/index.php

1   These include: 'membership [affiliate and individual] dues, sales of publications, donations, Zakat and grants from donor agencies [like the following]:USAID, Compass AGSP, the British High Commission, Youth Rehabilitation Centre, UNICEF, Save Our Children – England, NACA (National Action Committee on AIDS)/SACA, Federal/State Governments, OSIWA- Rights of Muslim Women under the Shari'ah, Pathfinder International, Packard Foundation, DFID. http://www.fomwan.org/fomwan.php?id=6

2   http://www.fomwan.org/fomwan.php?id=5

lived there. A book referred to as 'Batten',[1] had been prepared on the instructions of the Director of Education and was in use until the 1960s. Astonishingly biased against the Caliphate and all it stood for, the book remained the only source of history available apart from a handbook containing potted biographies of people like David Livingstone, Bishop Crowther, and Florence Nightingale. The history textbook used in secondary schools was the very same book that her husband had been taught from in his school in the 1940s (*The House of History, Greeks and Romans*). The question was did people in her home region still know about Nana Asma'u and her achievements? It was too big a task to even think of attempting to assess this until a surprising turn of events made it possible.

Fast-forward to 2002, when an organization called Islam and Citizenship (Islam en Burgerschap), was established in the Netherlands to aid the integration of the Muslim community into Dutch society, with emphasis on shared values. At that time, two years after the publication of Mack and Boyd's *One Woman's Jihad*, an essay competition was arranged in Rotterdam for young people, with the support of the Dutch Ministry of Justice. It was decided that a best-essay prize would be awarded in the name of Nana Asma'u. The competition organizers liked the book featuring Nana Asma'u because it focused on Asma'u as a scholar in the Islamic tradition and described her dedication to women's participation in the community. Muslims recognize two different kinds of jihad; the 'greater jihad' is the Sufi fight against self; the 'lesser' is the external battle enjoined as a religious duty by the recognized head of the community or state. Asma'u was involved in both, the former because she was a Sufi, the latter because she lived when a jihad was fought.

Three days before the competition was due to take place the influential Dutch newspaper *Trouw* published a major article

---

1   T. R. Batten, *A Handbook on the Teaching of the Elementary History and Geography Syllabus in Nigeria* (Lagos: CMS Bookshop, 1934).

condemning the use of Nana Asma'u's name because she was what they described as a 'war mongering jihadist'. The event co-ordinator, Mirjam Lammers and Jean Boyd wrote to *Trouw* refuting the misleading and badly informed article's conclusions; the letter was not published. As a result of the appalling publicity the use of Nana Asma'u's name was withdrawn by the essay organizers. Mack and Boyd met with the author of the article but to no avail. The prize-giving went ahead although many fewer people than expected attended; fortunately there was wide TV and radio coverage. Officials working for a Dutch broadcasting organization heard and read of the controversy surrounding the Nana Asma'u prize giving in Rotterdam and met with Mirjam Lammers and Jean Boyd in The Hague in August 2002. It was decided to investigate by making a TV documentary in Sokoto to explore attitudes to Nana.

In pre-mobile phone days it was difficult to make telephone calls with Nigeria, internally or overseas, mail was unreliable, even couriers occasionally failed to deliver important letters. In spite of the communication problems a letter containing a draft agreement of possibilities reached Sokoto on 9th January 2003 and we heard that the Sultan had given permission to make the film. His Eminence Alhaji Muhammadu Maccido wrote about 'the great scholar and poet whose works were worthy of emulation' and he promised every help in visiting the historic places linked with Asma'u's name. The rest unfolded day by day, as visa difficulties multiplied and news broke about rioting in Kaduna making colleagues nervous. On 13th February 2003 a party consisting of Jean Boyd, with a manager and a technician flew to Nigeria; a camera man followed a week later. The team had only a few days at their disposal but within that time they interviewed and filmed the Sultan, the Waziri, the Principal of Government Girls College, a *Modibo* at the Hubbare, a group of 'Yan Taru in a village and six members of FOMWAN including the Amira. Interviews were held as follows:

2nd March 2003: 1) the *Modibo* at Aisha's room in the Hubbare; 2) Sultan Muhammad Maccido at the palace.

3rd March 2003: 3) Six highly educated FOMWAN women at Sokoto FOMWAN headquarters. 4) 'Yan Taru women with their *jaji* at Birnin Ruwa village west of Kilgori;

4th March 2003: 5) Principal and some girls at Government Girls' College. 6) Waziri Usman and seventeen members of the family at the house of Gidaɗo and Asma'u.

On the evening of her arrival in Sokoto Jean Boyd walked alone, a matter of five minutes, from the Sultan's palace, where she was staying, to see Waziri Usman at the house built nearly two hundred years earlier in the time of Gidaɗo and Asma'u.

Fig. 14 Waziri Usman, direct descendant of Waziri Gidaɗo and Asma'u
(Source: Jean Boyd, 2003)

207

The Waziri greeted her warmly and fixed a time to interview members of the family. When the day came she was astonished to see how many senior and highly educated members of the family had gathered. Waziri Usman, commenting on the gathering of descendants of Nana Asma'u, said nothing like this had ever happened before. There were seventeen men, six women and twenty-three students present. Included were the ninety-two year-old doyen of the family, Dr. Bello, a retired judge, two professors, a Commissioner for Education, a consultant veterinarian, teachers, engineers and accountants and a woman post-graduate student in microbiology. As someone remarked: 'the genes still run strong'.

On the day he was interviewed Waziri Usman wore what he always wears on formal occasions – long robes, a cloak and a turban, he also donned a large hat, a *malfa*, exactly like the one given to Gidaɗo by the Shehu when he sent him in 1804 to deliver the flags of authority to the chosen leaders living in Hausaland. Waziri said that before the Shehu handed over the *malfa* he first prayed, then placed it on Gidaɗo's head saying, 'I beg that God will bring you back safely'. It was a dangerous mission because the roads led through remote and difficult regions but he did return safely. Listening to the Waziri as he related the history of his ancestors put some of the audience in the right mood for making known their own views about Asma'u, her scholarship and her devotion to the welfare of the people. Muhammad ɗan Junaidu, Professor of Education at Usman ɗan Fodio University, said (at the Waziri's house, 4th March 2003):

Nana's greatest contribution was her innovative approach to education – her ability to fashion an outreach system through which she touched the lives of rural women who had no adequate access to education. She could have lived a quiet life in seclusion; she was the Caliph's sister, the Shehu's daughter and the wife of the Waziri, who was the second in command, in modern parlance the Prime Minister. Instead she decided to address the plight of rural women and educate them.

This was her great contribution and there is a lot to learn from that system. There was no way she could have had all the women coming to her house. Instead she identified women in different areas and appointed the *jaji*s as ambassadors, her own representatives, who were made responsible for the 'Yan Taru and ensured that they passed on to others what they had learned from Asma'u. The most important factor was her commitment to the cause of women's right to education.

What fascinated me was her ability to devise methods which proved to be very effective. We have a lot to learn from her.

From the men's part of Gidado's house the film crew was astonished when the Waziri led them through into the women's part where they filmed in the very school that Asma'u founded and in which she taught until her death. Waziri Usman said:

This school was Asma'u's and it is still run today as it was when she was alive. People came from far and wide to be taught by her. When they returned home they used their knowledge to teach others. Since that time this school has been here, an unbroken tradition with pupils coming from many places. There are children who learn the Qur'an and adult women who study from textbooks, about the law for example. The pattern set by Asma'u has not changed.

The school room was full. There were adult women in one section who were there to study and another division for small boys and girls, each with a writing board. Waziri introduced his eldest sister saying:

Hajiya Laddo, a descendant of Asma'u and eldest daughter of Waziri Junaidu, teaches all the children as you see. And this lady Hajiya Safiyatu [indicating another person] also belongs to the family. She teaches law and religion to women. There have been women teachers in this room since Asma'u's time.

As a young student read from the law book, the old judge, standing erect, his only aid the stick he held, listened intently, nodding his head in appreciation at her fluency. Meanwhile, with her own copy of the book in front of her, the teacher followed the student's progress.

Near to the classroom was Nana Asma'u's personal room, the one built when she came to live in Sokoto in 1807, and a room which bears the imprint of the Shehu's hands. It was last occupied by Rukaya, daughter of Sultan Abubakar III and wife of the late Alhaji Dr. Junaidu Waziri of Sokoto. It was fitting that, from Asma'u's room, the last place to be visited was the library in which the manuscripts had been housed since the days of Gidado. The traditional soft goatskins, each full of documents, together with the heavy books, are all vulnerable – in the dry semi-desert climate, paper easily crumbles. For this reason manuscripts are copied when they become too fragile to handle. Examples of handwriting dating back to the beginning of the 19th century are rare; nevertheless the film crew were shown a letter in the handwriting of Muhammad Bello who died in 1837. From the house of Waziri Usman the crew went to the Government Girls' College where they met Hajiya Nana, the Principal, whose father, Sarkin Baura, is the Sultan's cousin. At the Provincial Girls School, where Jean Boyd had been a teacher forty-six years previously, there had been only two hundred very unwilling primary school girls. Now, there are 1720 students, who seemed to be happy with their schoolwork. Then the girls wore wrappers and head ties; now they wear tunics, trousers and white hijabs.

The old 'Booker Wall' built in the late 1930s to safeguard the girls (about 20 in number), when Miss Booker was Headmistress, was still there, and even some of the old classroom. New buildings included dormitories and a mosque. The Principal, Hajiya Nana Asma'u, said:

I am named after Nana Asma'u because our people admire and appreciate her. That is why many parents decide to give their daughters this name. We have over 1700 students. About half of them are indigenes of this state the others come from different parts of the Federation. The focus of the curriculum at the senior level is on Physics, Chemistry, Biology and Health Science. We also continue with Hausa and Islamic Religious Knowledge. The latter is not an option; it is compulsory. Every evening there are religious classes which the girls have to attend. Girls make good progress and are expected to reach the standard known as *sauka kur'ani*.

(Hajiya Nana Asma'u, at Government Girls' College, Sokoto,
4th March 2003)

One senior girl explained how she had come to know about Asma'u before she ever set foot in the college:

It was my grandfather who told me that Nana was the most eminent of Sokoto women. He showed me many of the poems that she had written and even gave me one. Grandfather and Shehu ɗan Fodio were related.

(Schoolgirl aged about fifteen at Government Girls' College, Sokoto, 4th
March 2003)

In 1951 the then Resident A. J. Weatherhead spoke of girls regarding school life as 'purgatory before the heaven of matrimony'. Now the older girls seemed composed and very pleasant as they talked about their futures while the little ones pirouetted and clapped their hands with excitement at seeing the camera crew.

On the morning the film crew arrived in Sokoto they spotted a group of 'Yan Taru at the palace. The 'Yan Taru moved purposefully, led by their *jaji* wearing her *malfa* hat until they found a place to sit and await the Sultan. They were very anxious to spend a little time with him and hear him as he prayed for them. Meanwhile, the young girls in the group fidgeted. At last he emerged and there was a collective sigh of relief. To them this was the most important day of the year and he lingered, speaking with kindness although this for him was an almost daily occasion.

211

It was because of the encounter with those women that the crew decided to visit them in their village, Birnin Ruwa, which stands at the end of a long, rough track. The silencer of their old banger of a car fell off when they hit the path, and without a hope of getting it repaired and with the silencer in the boot they limped on until they reached a small hill where the car refused to go any further. With a lot of help from young boys, they did eventually arrive at the village, where there was neither electricity, nor running water, nor a sewage system. The people were hard-working farmers and there was fish in the nearby pond, but the cluster of cracked and broken-down houses spoke of poverty and neglect. This is one of the villages from which women descendants of the students educated by Asma'u travel annually to the Hubbare in Sokoto.

The visitors asked the 'Yan Taru to re-enact for filming how they set out for Sokoto, the *jaji* in their midst, wearing her *malfa*. As they started, they sang songs about the Hubbare, another about the famous twelfth-century Sufi 'Abd al-Qadir al-Jilani, and then one by Nana. In a discussion the senior ladies, led by the very elderly *jaji*, described how the *malfa* hat had been formally handed over to her many years ago at the Hubbare. They said that the 'Yan Taru make their customary pilgrimage to the place every year. This journey represents a considerable effort especially as they have to walk ten kilometres in order to reach a tarmac road to find a lorry to take them to Sokoto. However, none of them made any complaint, despite their badly calloused feet, legs pitted with scars of healed ulcers, and their skin in need of oil. These were the kind of rural women that Asma'u set out to teach.

On the next day the crew visited the well-swept, unpaved, unadorned Hubbare that has at its centre the mausoleum which contains the grave of Shehu dan Fodio, one of the most famous persons to have lived in West Africa. First we met the custodian of the Hubbare, who conducted us through the main courtyard where we saw the Shehu's burial place and Asma'u's adjacent tomb. Hassan, Asma'u's twin brother is close by. Moving to a line of ten graves delineated in the open ground we saw where Aisha, Muhammad Bello's wife and Asma'u's life-long friend was buried. Gidado's grave is to the west of the mausoleum. Close to Asma'u's grave a narrow path leads through a gate to a cemetery where generations of the Shehu's women descendants lie buried; among them, clearly marked, is the site of Maryam *Uwar Deji's* burial place. There Jean Boyd met with one of the *Modibos* who today represent the Shehu's wives who once lived there. On a very hot and windy day Boyd entered a small room where she met *Modibo* Maimuna. She skirted the neatly stacked ancient calabashes that had once formed someone's dowry and joined the *Modibo* on the mat proffered. The *Modibo* said:

We who live here inherit the position. The first in this room was Aisha, the Shehu's senior wife. When she died she was buried over there [indicating a place in the nearby burial ground]. Aisha's daughter, who inherited the place, was Hadija, a scholar; she died in this room and is buried nearby, just beyond the door. Successive generations of women scholars followed on. Then, as the eldest, I too succeeded to the position of *Modibo* and after me it will be her turn [indicating another lady in the room]. And so it will continue. The line of the Shehu will never fail, it will go on and on. The descendants of Asma'u's 'Yan Taru come here from very many villages in the area. Thousands also come from elsewhere.

(Modibo Maimuna, at the Hubbare, 2 March 2003)

The *Modibo* and her assistant demonstrated how they teach, sitting on mats facing each other. One played the part of the student, using the text of one of Asma'u's poems. The 'teacher' read ten lines, and then the 'student' recited them from memory with the 'teacher' correcting errors. Memorizing is an important element of the methodology used and Boyd was told that the rate of progress varies with some memorizing five lines a day, others twenty.

Students come here from a desire for education and receive the blessing of the blessed. When a woman returns home she teaches others. We do not summon women; they come of their own volition. You see, it is about education. There is no need to call people; the motivation is in their hearts. Very large numbers of people attend *tafsir* classes on Thursday evenings. The place is absolutely full of women who come to learn and be educated. Nothing has changed. What Asma'u did, we do.

(Ibid.)

In addition to filming the heritage sites where Nana Asma'u had lived and women associated with the contemporary forms of 'Yan Taru work, Jean Boyd also interviewed a group of six senior FOMWAN members at the Sokoto headquarters. Sitting outside, under the shade of a rather spindly tree, the six women were: Sa'adiya, Director of the Centre for Hausa studies at Usman dan Fodio University; her daughter Fadima; Sutura, Head of Processing Division University Library; Hajiya Ta'Allah Aliyu, the first woman engineer in Northern Nigeria, Permanent Secretary Kebbi Urban Development Agency, Kebbi State; Karima, Resident Doctor, Department of Obstetrics and Gynaecology, Usman dan Fodio University; and Asabe, Lecturer Usman dan Fodio University. Boyd had special reasons for looking forward to meeting them again, not least because she had taught three of them: Ta Allah, Karima and Asabe. All are highly educated and articulate with perspectives about society, health, economics and development which are completely beyond the comprehension of the 'Yan Taru of Birnin Ruwa. These fine women are determined to improve the lot of the underprivileged and see Asma'u as an exemplar. Ta'Allah said: "'Nana Asma'u was not just a teacher – she directed social and economic development which demonstrates to me that everyone has to be involved in these matters.' Karima (who had been up all night attending a woman with an obstructed delivery) added: 'Nana combined motherhood with humanitarian work and we can do the same using modern technology.' Asabe (a teacher herself) underlined the educational role of Asma'u, and Sutura talked of the legacy of her poetry. Sa'adiya as chairman summed up the views of everyone:

The aim of FOMWAN is to upgrade the status of Muslim women through religious awareness and education. These are exactly the things that Nana Asma'u did. She mobilized women and brought them together for something good, and by that I mean she taught, educated and reformed them, making them better members of society. In brief, that is what we try to do and our motivation comes from Nana. She is our model. Esteemed daughter of the Shehu, a highly educated scholar, she was inspired to give of her learning to society. This is what we are doing.

Whatever we achieve is indigenous. The idea did not come from the United States or UK or Arabia. It did not come from elsewhere. We are so proud, you know. We may learn from other societies, we may learn from other people but the genesis, our initial upbringing, our development is through her. We believe in what she did. She motivated me and all the others that are here to acquire education.

(Hajiya Sa'adiya Omar Bello, at FOMWAN Sokoto headquarters, 3rd March 2003)

His Eminence Sultan Alhaji Muhammadu Maccido was a direct descendant of Shehu ɗan Fodio. He was the nineteenth Sultan of Sokoto and President-General of the Nigerian Supreme Council for Islamic Affairs. His support for the venture was of the utmost importance. The Sultan wanted it to succeed and willed people to overcome any misgivings they might have had, more especially because we were to film in the Hubbare itself, there being no place more sensitive than that. His words to the film-makers (at the Sokoto palace, 2nd March 2003) were:

I have been encouraging people to emulate Nana Asma'u's example; by this I mean how she cared for womenfolk, children and the general population too, since her education was not just for women. Yes, she was restricted to helping women in the first instance, for she was limited to that, but everybody could benefit from her knowledge. Educate a woman, as the saying goes, and you educate the world.

When the forty-five minute video was ready, Jean Boyd flew alone at the end of January 2004 to deliver the film. At Abuja airport she was met by one of the Sultan's guards in full regalia of red and green robe with a yellow turban. He travelled with her because there had been strong rumours of armed bandits on the road.

In accordance with protocol it was arranged for the Sultanate Council to judge whether or not they wished to release the film for public view. They gathered at the palace on 4th February: the Sultan, Waziri Usman, Sarkin Malamai Ibrahim Gusau, Magajin Rafi Usman, Magajin Gari Hassan and Turaki Shehu Shagari. Jean Boyd had been invited to be present and heard the Sultan pronounce his approval, words echoed by Waziri Usman. The next day an invited audience of about a hundred people assembled to see the video. They included those who had taken part in the interviews, all the District Heads of areas close to Sokoto, several TV and radio crews, the acting Vice Chancellor of the university and retired grandees including Dr. Karima's father. All the videos Boyd had taken were distributed and that night the film about Nana Asma'u was shown on Sokoto TV. Sa'adiya wrote this letter to Jean Boyd in 2008, some years later:

As you are aware our FOMWAN conference this year took place in Sokoto and we thought it wise to link the past with the present by involving the 'Yan Taru of Nana Asma'u in the programme. Their *jaji* with her *malfa* led them on the stage and they performed wonderfully. They sang the songs to acknowledge the contribution of Shehu. Their presentation was nostalgic to hundreds of the audience who converged for the event. Since we had the attendance of FOMWAN delegates from 28 states of the Federation the 'Yan Taru arrangement created much awareness about the person of Asma'u and her contribution to Islam and her society. Many delegates became inquisitive, asking questions about her life and her role in history. On our part, Sokoto FOMWAN, it created an avenue for us to establish good rapport and excellent relations with them. We have realized that many of them only sing the songs of Asma'u and other jihad leaders and visit the historic places in Sokoto without being as knowledgeable as people were in Nana's time. We will try to see if we can improve their standards educationally, socially, religiously and otherwise.

(Hajiya Sa'adiya Omar Bello, 23rd October 2008)

The connection between FOMWAN and the model established by Nana Asma'u's 'Yan Taru is evident in a 2008 article on allafrica.com, whose title makes clear the extent to which Asma'u's organization is at the heart of FOMWAN: 'Nigeria: FOMWAN – Lessons from the Sokoto Caliphate'.[1] As was true for the 'Yan Taru, FOMWAN aims to be inclusive, to teach women in the languages they know, and to provide assistance when and however it is needed.

Twenty-first century American 'Yan Taru

More than a century, a continent, and a language away, Muslim American women established their own 'Yan Taru groups for the same educational purposes that had inspired Nana Asma'u, but they discovered her via a circuitous route. The history of African-American Muslims in the Americas is extensive and well

---

1   The article, by Bilkisu Yusuf, reads: 'The Federation of Muslim Women's Associations in Nigeria (FOMWAN) held its 23rd Annual National Conference from August 21–24 2008 in Sokoto, the seat of the Caliphate. The conference was attended by over 1,000 delegates from all the states of the federation. Since it was established in 1985 the federation has been organizing these conferences and workshops which rotate between the Northern and Southern parts of the country. The event is a grassroots affair with delegates drawn from various States and local governments. The conference papers, although delivered in English, are always translated into Hausa and Yoruba. All the members of the South East branches speak English which eased the task of translating into Igbo for the conference organisers. The activities began on Thursday with a spiritual and social night that featured a Qur'anic recitation competition in which award winning female reciters participated.' http://allafrica.com/stories/200808280883.html

documented.[1] The Nation of Islam was founded in 1930 by Elijah Muhammad in the context of African-American concerns about racism; initially it was not consistent with Sunni Islam as practised in the rest of the world. Malcolm X's conversion from the Nation of Islam to Sunni Islam was directly connected to the pilgrimage he made to Makka and his travels in West Africa after his hajj. Disillusioned with the Nation of Islam, Malcolm X established the Muslim Mosque Inc. (M.M.I.) in New York in 1964, along with a School of Islamic and Arab Studies. Then, in April of the same year he departed for Makka on hajj, where he became El-Hajj Malek El-Shabazz. In July 1964 he travelled to Cairo to study Sunni Islam intensively for four months, and then to Makka to complete the '*umra* (the lesser pilgrimage). Before returning home he made several stops in West Africa, including a visit to scholars in Sokoto, Nigeria, where he learned of the Fodio family, talked with scholars there, examined written documents, and decided that the Sunni interpretation of Islam was the one to which he should dedicate his energies. He was photographed wearing the traditional turban and long white robes favoured by Qadiriyya Sufis there. During the months between his disassociation from the Nation of Islam and his assassination (February 21, 1965), El-Shabazz promoted Sunni Islam to serve the needs of African-American Muslims, who shared his interest in this West African-derived Qadiriyya affiliation. The M.M.I. subsequently became known as the Mosque of Islamic Brotherhood (M.I.B.) in 1967.

---

1   See for example: Michael A. Gomez, *Black Crescent: The Experience and Legacy of African-American Muslims in the Americas* (New York: Cambridge University Press, 2005); Amir Nashi Ali Muhammad, *Muslims in America: Seven Centuries of History 1312–2000* (Beltsville, MD: Amana, 2001); Manning Marable and Hishaam D. Aidi (eds.), *Black Routes to Islam* (New York: PalgraveMacmillan, 2009); and Edward E. Curtis IV, *Islam in Black America: Identity, Liberation, and Difference in African Thought* (Albany, NY: State University of New York Press, 2002).

By the late twentieth century, an African-American majority Muslim community in Pittsburgh PA, which favoured the precepts of the M.I.B., was also deeply attached to the Sokoto Fodio family legacy, studying the works of Shehu Usman d̶an Fodio, and adhering to Qadiriyya brotherhood prayer and custom in the style of the Fodio family. Several of their members had spent time studying Islam in West Africa and in the Sudan. Seeking the cultural roots that had been cut generations earlier in the trans-Atlantic slave trade, and taking their cue from El-Shabazz's interest in the Sokoto Qadiriyya community, they became affiliated with a *shaykh* of the Qadiriyya community and began to establish an Islamic Sufi community like that of the Fodios, engaged in study and social welfare efforts. The Sankore Institute was established in Timbuktu as an organization to facilitate restoration of cultural ties between African-Americans and Africans. While the physical home of the Sankore Institute was originally in Sudan, and is now in Mali, scholars affiliated with it returned to the United States and continued their work translating the Shehu's writings into English, and promoting the values of the Sokoto Qadiriyya community. The web-site for this Institute explains its origins in 1985 as an institution to promote Islamic African heritage.[1]

---

1   The Sankore Institute of Islamic-African Studies International (SIIASI) is a non-profit, non-political educational institution founded [in 1985] for the sole purpose of researching into the educational, political, cultural and religious heritage of Islamic Africa. The primary area of concern is that part of Black Africa traditionally known as the Biladu s-Sudan (The Lands of the Blacks). These lands include all the regions located south of the Sahara desert and north of the tropical jungles, between the Atlantic Ocean and the Red Sea. The purpose of the SIIASI is to elucidate and evidence the Islamic traditions which were born out of African nations such as Takrur, Songhay, Mali, Ghana, Kanem-Bornu, Wodai, Fur, Funj, Sokoto, Segu, Massina and the Mahdist kingdom of the Nile valley. http://www.siiasi.org/

The men of the community in Pittsburgh favour attire that symbolizes their cultural and religious affiliation: white robes and turbans of the Qadiriyya brotherhood. They regularly use the Islamic rosary, the *tasbih*, for prayer. The women of this community also have adopted modified forms of West African dress, wearing *hijab* (instead of head ties), long skirts and long sleeves. Thus, at the end of the twentieth century, a community of African-American Muslims in Pittsburgh has modeled itself in action and appearance on an African Muslim community they believe to represent their heritage. But it is not ethnically exclusive; in keeping with Islamic precepts of equality, it also welcomes anyone who adheres to the Qadiriyya Sunni Sufi precepts of the Fodio family. The membership of Latino converts/reverts[1] is significant in Pittsburgh and other chapters throughout the U.S.

Education is a central focus of this twentieth-century North American community, as it had been for the nineteenth-century Sokoto community. In the nineteenth century the Shehu's reputation was widespread in the region, and his written works were not only housed in his Sokoto family compound, but also distributed throughout the Maghreb, as far away as Timbuktu and the Sudan, having been disseminated by other scholars. At the end of the twentieth century, several African-American Muslims from the Pittsburgh community spent time studying Arabic and translating Fodio family manuscripts with scholars in the Sudan. When they returned to the U.S., one of their aims was the preservation of these tomes by the Shehu. Their website explains the formal partnership established between West African scholars and their students in the U.S.[2]

---

1   Muslims believe that every person is born a Muslim, but then perhaps raised as a believer in another faith. Thus, when someone converts to Islam, they are considered to be reverting to their original faith. This is the reason they are called reverts instead of converts.

2   'The Sankore Institute of Islamic-African Studies International was

Meanwhile, Jean Boyd's biography of Asma'u had been published in 1989,[1] so the women of this contemporary Pittsburgh *umma* knew something about Asma'u's role in the community. With the publication of Asma'u's poetry in 1997, followed by a volume explaining more about the 'Yan Taru organization in 2000, they had available to them both material that they could use in the same way that it had originally been implemented, and a model for women's involvement in education and community development.[2] With this in mind, they procured permission to post Asma'u's works on a website for their own 'Yan Taru organization. In 2005 the American 'Yan Taru organization, a part of the Qadiriyya-affiliated *umma* in Pittsburgh, launched an electronic newsletter (called 'Yan Taru); new issues appeared every two months.

---

first conceived December 15, 1985, in the Republic of Sudan as the result of conversations between the present Sultan of Maiurno al-Hajj Abu Bakr ibn Muhammad ibn Bello Maiurno ibn Attahiru ibn Ahmad Zuruku ibn Abu Bakr Atiku ibn Shehu Uthman dan Fodio, our *shaykh*, Imam Muhammad al-Amin ibn Adam Karagh, Ahmad Abideen Hassan, and the founding director, Muhammad Shareef. The Sultan gave written authorization and commissioned SIIASI to collect the Arabic and Ajami manuscripts of the Sokoto Caliphate from Northern Nigeria and convey them to the town of Maiurno in order to be edited and republished to provide capital for the public amenities and the general welfare of the people. As a result, trips were made to Chad, Northern Nigeria, Mali to collect and copy old manuscripts relevant to the Islamic heritage of Biladu s-Sudan. Later the *Sultan* al-Hajj Abu Bakr and the *Imam* Muhammad al-Amin gave written authorization for S.I.I.A.S.I. to translate these works into English and disseminate these works among the Muslims of the United States.' http://www.siiasi.org/digitalpreservation.html. 'Collection' of manuscripts referred to was digital; none was removed from its place of origin. See the Sankore Institute of Islamic-African Studies International for images of the mss and their translations in the 'library' section. They are freely available, and are still being translated and added to the site.

1   Boyd, *The Caliph's Sister* (London: Frank Cass, 1989).
2   Boyd and Mack, *The Collected Works*, 1997; and Mack and Boyd, *One Woman's Jihad* (Bloomington, IN: Indiana University Press, 2000).

Yan Taru

NEWSLETTER
August/September 2005

Our Mission...

"To provide services to women and children through establishing an organization that facilitates Education, Entrepreneurship, Social Welfare and Community Outreach in accordance with the Koran, the Sunnah, and the methodology of Shaykh Uthman ibn Fuduye (1754-1817 CE)."

Fig. 15 Newsletter of the Pittsburgh Yan Taru 2005: Banner

The organization's mission statement explained that, by highlighting Asma'u's materials and methods, they aimed 'to provide services to women and children through establishing an organization that facilitates Education, Entrepreneurship, Social Welfare and Community Outreach in accordance with the Koran, the Sunnah, and the methodology of Shaykh Uthman ɗan Fuduye (1754–1817 CE).'[1] The website included commentary on the organization itself, notices about local fundraising events, a column on health issues, business advice, recipes, childcare, religious education lessons, community service announcements focused on orphans, and outreach to minority ethnic groups. One of its prominent columns was the poetry corner, in which Nana Asma'u's works were featured as educational tools.[2] Asma'u's poem 'So Verily' was deployed to recommend perseverance in the face of misfortune; her poem 'The Qur'an' was used, in keeping with its original purpose, as a means of memorizing the names of all 114 suras of the Qur'an. The web-site's structure reflected the concerns of the organization: women were inspired by Asma'u's example as much as by her poetry, but the poems were valued for underscoring her ethical perspective, which they shared. The organization and its site were created around the image

1 Owing to variations in transliteration from the Fulfulde in Ajami (i.e. Fulfulde language in Arabic script), the family name Fodio is spelled variously: Fodio, Fodiyo, Fuduye. All are equally acceptable.
2 The organizers contacted Boyd and Mack for permission to post translations of Asma'u's works from the *Collected Works* volume.

YAN TARU OFFICIALS

Yan Taru Foundation

- Umm Maryam Rukayat – Director
- Umm Talha Alymah – President
- Umm Asiyah Aminah – Secretary
- Umm Aminah Yasmeen – Trustee
- Umm Suja' Nahaya – Treasurer

Majis Ash-Shura (Advisory Council)

- Umm Maryam Rukayat
- Umm Asiyah Aminah
- Umm Talha Alymah
- Umm Suja' Nahaya

THIS MONTH'S FEATURES:

For more information: Visit www.yantaru.org or
Send Email to: info@yantaru.org

Fig. 16 Newsletter of the Pittsburgh 'Yan Taru 2005: Contents

of Nana Asma'u as a teacher and social activist, and both operated as resources for women learning in and working for the entire community. These contemporary 'Yan Taru found in Nana Asma'u a role model who provided a means of helping Muslim women to benefit themselves and their communities 'without compromising our religion or dignity'. The Pittsburgh 'Yan Taru organization was a women's organization, but its activities benefited everyone in the community.

This web-site's connection to its local community – a natural outgrowth of Asma'u's intentions for the 'Yan Taru – was also impressive. One issue summarized the group's social welfare accomplishments, which included delivering clothing, shoes and bedding to Somali refugees in nearby towns, partnering with refugee families, participating in the distribution of clothing at the Muslim Community Centre of Greater Pittsburgh, and developing a method of providing for the food pantry and for anonymous assistance for needy families in Northside Pittsburgh. These are exactly the kinds of social welfare efforts that Asma'u's works encouraged among rural women students in the nineteenth century – her poems were all about teaching ethics and right behaviour toward others. Thus, the 2005 inaugural issues of the 'Yan Taru website presented a chronicle of contemporary women's activities based on Asma'u's example.

The Pittsburgh congregation, however, was not allowed to flourish. It was subject to United States governmental scrutiny, and in 2005 it was already under surveillance. In the next few years it was disrupted by an FBI raid that led to the dispersal of many of its families.[1] Although the reason for the raid was never clarified, it is likely that FBI surveillance of Muslim communities in America is part of the fallout of the 9/11 tragedy. So the women who began the American 'Yan Taru movement in Pittsburgh did not stay in one place. As families moved away to ensure their safety, the irony of technology's fragility became evident: although it took only

---

1   For an account of this, see the DVD 'New Muslim Cool' (Specific Pictures), narrated by Hamza Perez.

one person to make materials available to thousands via a website, conversely, the absence of that one web-master left a vibrant 'Yan Taru website moribund.

Meanwhile, the idea of an American 'Yan Taru organization had spread wherever affiliation to the West African Sokoto Fodio community had taken hold. Interest in and affiliation with the Qadiriyya Fodio order spread, and with it, sister organizations appeared in Hartford CT, Atlanta GA, Houston TX, and Oakland and San Diego CA.[1] These were small groups, comprised of the women of each local *umma*. In San Diego the Latina membership was significant; Qur'anic classes are increasingly held in Spanish. An on-line In Focus article (3rd March 2007) ran the headline: 'Traditional Islam for the Hip-Hop Generation' (by Zaid Shakur, staff writer):

SAN DIEGO — In the heart of San Diego's inner-city, just blocks away from 'the Four Corners of Death' (an intersection so nick-named by locals in the 1980s because of its notoriety for gang violence), nestled unceremoniously between a martial arts dojo and a neighbor-hood grocery store is the Logan Islamic Community Center (LICC). Situated in a working-class neighborhood that is overwhelmingly Latino, LICC serves a Muslim congregation that is small yet incredibly diverse. Within its 27 founding members there are Filipinos, Africans, African-Americans, Caucasians and, of course, Latinos. The most striking characteristics of this up-and-coming community is the fact that it is made up entirely of reverts to Islam—and though some regular attendees are anywhere from 40 years of age well into their 70s, the average age of LICC's members is a tender 26 years old. It is precisely this youthful energy that one feels pulsating through the masjid and fuelling its impressive list of programs, activities, and services. Presently the sisters sponsor each other to attend 'Deen intensives' around the country and hold classes for the other sisters when they come home. The women of LICC also perform charitable work for the

---

1   In September 2010 Beverly Mack visited the 'Yan Taru group in Hartford CT, whose membership is drawn from a wide area of the state. The group was small, about ten, and included a Latina who was a new Muslima.

community, recently holding a community sponsored rummage sale with the proceeds going to buy food vouchers that were given to the needy.

Inspired by Nana Asma'u's accomplishments and activism, the 'Yan Taru in San Diego worked to resolve problems unique to their community in the manner demonstrated by Nana Asma'u, that is, through thoughtful attention to problems, and positive action.

Wherever the 'Yan Taru meet, they establish study groups and organize community charity projects whose benefits extend beyond the Muslim community. As was true in the nineteenth century, twenty-first century 'Yan Taru are not solely focused on one aspect of education. It may appear that the nineteenth century 'Yan Taru were solely about the oral transmission of poems, while twenty-first century American 'Yan Taru are all about literacy; neither literacy nor morality is the sole point. The focus of 'Yan Taru groups is instruction by whatever means is suitable to the audience. A *hadith* notes that the Prophet advised that one should teach at the level of the student; for the nineteenth-century woman in rural West Africa, this meant oral transmission of information, while for the contemporary North American Muslima, this means material transmitted electronically, through the written word. But despite the difference in the means of transmission; the information conveyed is the same, offering an ethical foundation based on Islamic values of service to the family and the community, in addition to Qur'anic instruction. When we discuss the original students of the 'Yan Taru, the focus on Asma'u's poetry should not blind us to the point of the poem's messages: the point of each work is its content, not its literary style. Thus, what the contemporary website emphasizes – community service, health care, childcare – are issues that would have been major topics of instruction in the course of discussing Asma'u's poems 150 years ago. The delivery may be different, but the product is the same.

As in nineteenth-century Africa, the role of the local American twenty-first-century *jaji* is to orchestrate women's efforts; as was also true for the nineteenth century; contemporary women are hard-pressed to balance their domestic and childcare obligations with their spiritual interests. More often, in the twenty-first century, these women have the additional economic burden of needing to work outside the home. This leaves little discretionary time for 'Yan Taru work. Nevertheless, these women are inspired in contemporary North America by their nineteenth-century West African mentor. It may be that Asma'u's most useful contribution to them is as a model of respectability: she was a woman whose intellect and contribution to the betterment of society were revered and appreciated, and because of that model, contemporary American Muslim women are confident that this can also be their role.

In 2010, when a new web site for the Sankore Institute was established, the 'Yan Taru Women's Educational and Charitable Foundation link was featured on its home page. This new 'Yan Taru site picked up where the earlier one left off, featuring: discussions of health as understood in the Shehu's writings, environmental concerns as discussed in the Qur'an, a library section with a brief piece, 'The Essential Nana Asma'u' by Jean Boyd (2005); a synopsis of the 'Yan Taru origins in the 'About Us' section, and a business section that was being developed. It is expected that the site will develop, reflecting the features of previous 'Yan Taru sites: an outline of the organization's history, examples of the services the modern 'Yan Taru provide for communities, advice on childcare, health issues, and charity work, and guidance on scholarly and religious activities. The earliest 'Yan Taru website focused on a particular local community, so it was able to include weekly notices about charitable projects and calls for assistance for families in particular neighbourhoods. How a new website will unite 'Yan Taru groups across America remains to be seen. The religious scholarship, leadership, and activism of these organizations and the extent to which they are youth-focused suggests that the voices of the young Muslimas who comprise contemporary 'Yan Taru communities will have significant impact on the evolution of American Islam in the twenty-first century.

In 2010, Dylia bint Hamadi Camara, a Malian raised in Houston TX, was named the national *jaji* of U.S. 'Yan Taru groups. She trains and oversees *jaji*s and their 'Yan Taru in a handful of urban centres, including Los Angeles CA, Hartford CT, Springfield MA and Pittsburgh PA. She recruits and helps in the formation of new 'Yan Taru groups, such as those beginning to be active in Oakland, Sacramento, and San Diego CA. The training programmes she has developed for both *jaji*s and 'Yan Taru are rigorous. The *jaji* training programme includes eight core texts and areas of study, including Arabic language and grammar; Asma'u's works; Qur'anic recitation; and media training. The 'Yan Taru programme is more complex, involving three levels of education: Level I: seven parts, 25 texts; Level II five parts, 26 texts; and Level III nine parts, 31 texts. Most texts are classical Arabic works in translation, Arabic texts as part of the language/grammar curriculum, and the Qur'an in Arabic. *Jaji* Dylia travels extensively, conferring with and training the women in the regional centres. At the same time, she is planning recruitment internationally, in South Africa, Senegal, and other African countries.

The American 'Yan Taru organization is a work in progress. The 'Yan Taru model may operate organically, spreading geographically through universal electronic access to materials on the website and then to expand the site as local examples of activities and new study documents are fed back into it. But that possibility rests in large part on the extent to which the African-American Muslim community embraces the model, and integrates it into their own local communities throughout North America. Such action may or may not involve dependence on electronic media.

This raises another interesting issue, that of racial-ethnic affiliations among Muslims in America. African-American Muslims have struggled through successive generations of change – from African-American-affiliated Nation of Islam origins in the philosophy of Noble Drew Ali and then Elijah Muhammad, to Warith Deen Muhammad's dissolution of the Nation of Islam and affiliation with mainstream universal Sunni Islam on the one hand, and Louis Farrakhan's reinstitution of the Nation of Islam on the other. In addition, since the mid-twentieth century, a wave of Muslim immigrants into the United States has resulted in wide variety in North American Islamic communities. Added to these, are the vast numbers of converts/reverts who affiliate with Islamic communities depending on their denominational preferences. Thus far, 'Yan Taru groups are found among African-American Muslims who identify with the particular Qadiriyya Sufi brotherhood and heritage of the Fodio family of West Africa.[1] Even so, the racial and ethnic identity of some 'Yan Taru chapters is changing as they reflect the Latina identity of some new converts/reverts in the communities. There is one new Latina convert in the Hartford CT 'Yan Taru organization, and several Latinas in the Pittsburgh PA 'Yan Taru group. As the news item above about San Diego indicated, the numbers of Latinas in that 'Yan Taru group appear to be higher still. As the ethnic profile of 'Yan Taru communities changes, whether the 'Yan Taru concept will remain within these communities of Muslims or grow beyond the limits of the Qadiriyya-affiliated groups remains to be seen.

On the other hand, while these 'Yan Taru chapters appear to be growing with the increase of their respective communities,

---

1   This historical connection is so strong that there are families in Georgia who have assumed the dan Fodio surname in honour of the illustrious West African family, without any evidence of lineal connections.

the truth is that their vitality is threatened by the pace and distractedness of twenty-first century life, in which economic pressures often require every adult in a household to go out to work. Added to a schedule of adult jobs and children's educational and activity schedules, is the need to observe daily prayer times, and to accomplish all this without the benefit of extended families in residence to relieve daily pressures. This leaves little time, energy, or opportunity for undertaking the perpetuation of discretionary educational meetings like those which the 'Yan Taru organization involves. Wherever a 'Yan Taru chapter exists, the women who seek to orchestrate it struggle to find the time and opportunity to fit educational and social welfare work meetings into their busy lives.

Meanwhile, the 'Yan Taru tradition remains intact and active in its place of origin, Sokoto, Nigeria, but there is not yet an awareness there of the American 'Yan Taru movement. It is too expensive and time-consuming for American 'Yan Taru women to be able easily to visit Sokoto, and electronic communication with Nigeria is inconsistent, so there has been little communication among them. However, with the publication of another volume on Nana Asma'u, in which the American 'Yan Taru story is told, it is possible that women involved in 'Yan Taru groups on both continents will have the chance to know about one another and perhaps eventually work together.

It is significant that Nana Asma'u's written works have given substance to her legacy internationally. The written materials contained in her collected works provide the blueprint for social action. They are preserved as written documents, and used in oral form. What cannot be easily quantified is the use to which they are put, since these are not literature lessons, but social and ethical directives. Even when the poems are merely referenced, and not actively used, they represent their author symbolically. Nana Asma'u constitutes a model of intellectual engagement, ethical values, productivity, and activism for women of another age and culture, whose only certain shared circumstance is that of being Muslimas, and whose comfort is being connected by heritage to the Fodio family legacy. Through Asma'u's nineteenth-century example, twenty-first century women in both West Africa and North America confirm their Islamic right to pursue education and social welfare work in the community.[1] They teach Asma'u's poems as a blueprint for organizing her students to be actively involved in social welfare projects. That is the foundational message of these works. The preservation and dissemination of Asma'u's works explain Asma'u's and her community's ethos to women of another age and place, who receive these words via means of transmission unimagined in Asma'u's time. In a way never before realized, technology allows for the preservation and transmission of knowledge, and the inspiration of human behaviour.

---

1   These rights are clarified in the Qur'an, as confirmed by contemporary scholars such as Asma Barlas (Believing Women in Islam [Austin, TX: University of Texas Press, 2002]), Amina Wadud (Qur'an and Woman (Oxford: Oxford University Press, 1999), Jamal Badawi (Gender Equity in Islam (Plainfield, IN: American Trust Publications, 1995).

APPENDIX

In 1997 the supervisor of the Hubbare (*Mai Hubbare*) visited with Jean Boyd and provided information about the women who had lived in these residences since the time of Asma'u. The information may be incomplete, but it is the best available to us and we are deeply appreciative that we were entrusted with it:

Rukaya, the daughter of Sultan Abubakar III, and wife of Waziri Junaidu lived in Asma'u's room, where Gidaɗo's *kaya* (effects) were kept, including his sword *Gagarau* ('difficult to handle') and his bow, quiver, and ring. The sword has been used in a symbolic way to help women suffering prolonged birth pangs. The unsheathed sword is washed and the water given to the sufferer to drink. The ring was given to Gidaɗo by the Shehu's brother Abdullahi ɗan Fodio.

A. In the home of Hauwa ('Dakin Hauwa), the house of Abdurahman Atiku ɗan Shehu (b. 1782, r. 1838–1842), lived:

1. Ummu, daughter of Mai Garin Jabbo, ɗan Sarkin Musulmi Abdu ɗan Atiku
2. Innama, daughter of Sarkin Musulmi Abdu ɗan Atiku
3. Kulu, daughter of Sarkin Musulmi Abdu
4. Uniya, daughter of Mai Garin Jabbo ɗan Sarkin Musulmi Abdu[1]
5. Hannatu, daughter of Mai Garin Jabbo ɗan Sarkin Musulmi Abdu[1]
6. Antu, daughter of Sarkin Musulmi Muhammad Ahmadu Mai Turare (r. 1915–24)

---

1   Nos. 1–4 in the list appear to have the same father. This is possible but not certain. Hannatu (5) was the *Modibo* in 1997; her father died in 1924.

232

APPENDIX

B. In the home of Shatura ('Dakin Shatura), House of Ahmadu Rufai ɗan Shehu (born *ca.* 1812, r. 1867–73), lived:

1. Dede, daughter of Sarkin Musulmi Ahmadu Rufai
2. Nana, daughter of Sarkin Musulmi Ahmadu Rufai
3. Goggo Inna Wuro, daughter of Sarkin Musulmi Ahmadu Rufai
4. Garka, daughter of Sarkin Kebbin Silame Lili ɗan Sarkin Musulmi Ahmadu Rufai
5. Kubra, daughter of Sarkin Kebbin Silame Umaru ɗan Sarkin Musulmi Ahamadu Rufai
6. Ige , daughter of Lada ɗan Sarkin Musulmi Ahmadu Rufai
7. Bajina Jikanyar Sarkin Musulmi A Rufai
8. Ige, daughter of Sarkin Kebbi Ahmadu [1997]

C. In the home of Hajjo (aka Tabaraya), ('Dakin Hajjo), House of Abdulkadir ɗan Shehu, born *ca.* 1807, died at Anka [1836] (No sarauta, died a martyr) lived:

1. Nana, daughter of Bayero [no sarauta] ɗan Abdulkadir
2. Dudu, daughter of Bayero [no sarauta] ɗan Abdulkadir
3. Amiru, daughter of Bayero [no sarauta] ɗan Abdulkadir
4. Tage, daughter of Bayero [no sarauta] ɗan Abdulkadir
5. *Modibo* Giwa, daughter of Iliyasu ɗan Abdulkadir
6. Utiya[1]
7. Abu[1]
8. Jaba[1]
9. Hawa'u [current, 1997][1]

D. In the home of Aisha (aka Gabdo), ('Dakin Aisha), lived:

1. *Modibo* Abu
2. *Modibo* Haizarana
3. *Modibo* Umanatu [current, 1997]

When Boyd went to Salame where Hadija (eldest daughter of the Shehu) had lived, she was informed by the male descendants that they were Tijaniyya, a puzzling observation, since the Shehu

---

1   We do not know the names of the fathers of nos. 6,7, 8, and 9.

and his family were Qadiriyya Sufis. When she interviewed the *Modibo* in 2003, she was told that Aisha, the wife of the Shehu, was buried in a grave adjacent to the room they were sitting in and that her successors lie near her. That is all the information Boyd was given on this matter.

E. Mariya, in the House of Isa ɗan Shehu (last-born of the Shehu), Sarauta Sarkin Yamma Kware, lived:

1. Mariyam *Uwar Deji*
2. Matar Modi
3. Autaju
4. Hajara
5. *Modibo* Dikko, daughter of Mallam Bayero ɗan Isa
6. *Modibo* Habsatu [current, 1997]

Boyd interviewed *Modibo* Habsatu in 1981, who was then reluctant to be forthcoming on these matters even though Boyd had been sent to her by Waziri Junaidu. This circumstance demonstrates that inquiry into these matters entails complications too deep for those outside the circle to have access to. Investigating these histories is quite personal, and a sensitive problem.

The Mai Hubbare explained to Jean Boyd in 1997 that the identities of the Shehu's widows were:

Hauwa, of the house of Bello ('Dakin Bello)[1]
Shatura, of the house of Rufa'i ('Dakin Rufa'i)
Hajjo, of the house of Abdulkadir ('Dakin Abdulkadir)
Gabdo, of the house of Hadijatu ('Dakin Hadijatu)[1]
Mai Riga, a concubine of the house of Isa

---

1 Is 'Dakin Bello the same as 'Dakin Atiku? Presumably Hauwa died in Atiku's reign. 'Dakin Bello is the preferred name today; these two were full brothers. As for 'Dakin Hadijatu, Boyd does not know its identity.

REFERENCES

Note. A number of the works consulted have not yet been formally catalogued, let alone edited to the standard scholars might wish for. We have presented titles in the form in which they are usually identified in the region, rather than in formal transliteration. The information provided is the best available to us at the time of writing. More information on some of the works referred to, with discussion and full or partial translations in English, has been written up by Shaykh Muhammed Shareef and posted on the web-site, www.siiasi.org.

Manuscripts in the private archives of Sokoto scholars, principally Waziri Junaidu

ABDULLAHI 'DAN FODIO, first Emir of Gwandu, *Annasa'ihu fi Ahammil-Masalihi.* Translation in Hausa by Muhammadu Isa Talata Mafara (Sokoto History Bureau). Arabic title: *al-Naṣāʾiḥ fī ahamm al-maṣāliḥ* (advice on the most important matters of social welfare). Typescript copy in Jean Boyd's collection.

—, *Kitabun Niyyat fil Aimalil Dunyawiyyat Waddiniyyati* Translation into Hausa by Muhammadu Isa Talata Mafara (Sokoto History Bureau). 39 pp. typescript. Arabic title: *al-Niyyāt fī l-ʾaʿmāl al-dunyawiyya wa-l-dīniyya* (intentions relating to worldly and religious works). This is an abridgement of the first section of the famous *Kitāb al-Madkhal fī tanmiya l-ʾaʿmāl...* by the famous Maliki scholar Abū ʿAbdillāh Ibn al-Ḥājj (d. 1347). It contains, as well as advice about prayer and ritual ablutions, advice on market procedures and trades such as farming and weaving. The author, Abdullahi, said on p. 39: 'We have taken only excerpts from the *Madkhal* by Ibn al-Hajj. If you are interested and want to read more, do so.'

—, *Lubabul Madkhali.* Translation in Hausa by Malam Sidi Sayudi (Ubandoman Sokoto), and English by Jean Boyd, 19 June 1977.

Arabic title: *Lubāb al-Madkhal fī adāb ahl al-dīn wa-l-faḍl* (epitome of *al-Madkhal* on the etiquette of the people of religion and grace). It contains discussion of the best manners of religious teachers and how students should follow their example. (As John Hunwick pointed out in many of his writings and lectures, Ibn al-Ḥājj arguably had the greatest influence upon the reform movement initiated by the Shehu and his colleagues.)

—, *Fara'idal Jalila,* Chapter 4. Translation in Hausa by Mallam Boyi, in English by Jean Boyd, unpublished manuscript. Arabic title: *al-Farā'id al-jalīla wasā'iṭ al-fawā'id al-jamīla* (sublime pearls [of verse], the means to beautiful [moral] gains). Its subject is the best way to introduce the young to the sciences of the Qur'an and its exegesis. This text is actually a versification of part of the famous *al-Itqān fī ʿulūm al-Qurʾān* of ʿAbd al-Raḥmān al-Suyūṭī (d. 1505).

ABUBAKAR III, Sultan of Sokoto (r. 1938–1988), *Dokokin Ayukken Uwayen Kasar Sokoto Division* (Regulations covering the work of District Heads in Sokoto Division). Examples of topics covered: collection of cattle tax, care of receipt books, land disputes, building maintenance. Always known as '*Mai Rigar Fata*' because all copies were protected by leather covers. 28 pp., 18 sections, 1951. Untranslated. Jean Boyd, SOAS Archive: PPMS 36, 1998.

ASMA'U 'YAR SHEHU ᴅAN FODIO. Sixty poems in the private collection of Waziri Junaidu, loaned by him to Jean Boyd. The poems are written in Arabic, Hausa or Fulfulde. The originals were returned to the Waziri's private library. Hand-written copies, edited by Alhaji Muhammad Magaji; Jean Boyd, SOAS Archives: PPMS 36, 1991. (For the print edition and English translation of these poems, see BOYD and MACK, 1997.)

GIᴅAᴅO ᴅAN LAIMA (Waziri Gidaɗo), *Al Kashful Bayan.* Translation in Hausa by Malam Sidi Sayuɗi. Arabic title: *al-Kashf wa-l-bayān an baʿd ahwāl al-Sayyid Muhammad Bello* (discovery and exposition of some situations [during the life] of Muhammad Bello). This contains an account of Bello's special qualities and of events in his life before and after the hijra. Unpublished ms. (See LAST, 1967, p. 210, n. 136.)

—, *Al Majmu fi Ashab Bello.* Translation in Hausa by Malam Sidi Sayuɗi. Arabic title: *Majmūʿ aṣhāb al-sayyid* (compendium on the companions of the Sayyid [Bello]). This is a list of Bello's companions, viziers, servants, wives, sons and daughters. Undated (probably 1840; see LAST, 1967, pp. 210 f.) unpublished ms.

—, *Al Majmu yasir illa hisal Shaikh Usuman*. Translated into Hausa by Malam Sidi Sayuɗi. Arabic title: *Majmū^c yashīr nashīr fīhi ilā ba^cḍ khiṣāl al-Shaykh ^cUthmān* (compendium, wherein a sketch of some of the particular qualities of the Shehu Usman). There are only three folios but it includes a map of the neighbourhood of the Shehu in Degel and a list of all his neighbours. The Arabic and English of this work are posted at www.siiasi.org.

—, *Raud al Jinan* Translation in Hausa by Malam Sidi Sayuɗi. Arabic title: *Rawḍ al-jinān fī ba^cḍ karāmāt al-Shaykh ^cUthmān* (the meadows of paradise regarding some of the miracles of Shehu Usman). Undated (possibly 1838–9; see LAST, 1967). The book gives an account of the Shehu and his qualities, which the author, Giɗaɗo, had witnessed. The English of the entire text is posted at www.siiasi. org.

JUNAIDU ꞌDAN MUHAMMADU BUHARI, Waziri of Sokoto, *Arfuraihani* Translation in Hausa by the author. Arabic title: *^cArf al-rayḥān fī dhikr ba^cḍ awlād al-Shaykh ^cUthmān* (the fragrance of repose in remembrance of some of the children of the Shehu Usman). Unpublished, undated ms. On the virtues of the children (nine sons and four daughters) of Shehu Usman ɗan Fodio, this work contains much detailed biographical data.

—, *Nailul Arabi*. Translation in Hausa by the author. Arabic title: *Nayl al-ꞌarab fī istiqṣāꞌ al-nasab* (the attainment of proficiency in profound study of ancestry). Unpublished, undated, handwritten ms. This work contains lists of the descendants of Giɗaɗo ɗan Laima and Nana Asma'u in northern Nigeria, Niger, and Sudan. Copy of handwritten manuscript in Jean Boyd's private papers/mss. in Waziri's private collection. Along with the mss. of Nana Asma'u's poems (see above), several poems by her sisters were copied out and placed in the SOAS Archives: PPMS 36, 1990. These poems are undated; they are: by Hadija, seven poems; by Faɗima, one poem; by Hafsatu, one poem; by Safiya, one poem; by Maryam, three poems and a letter to the Emir of Kano.

MUHAMMAD BELLO ꞌDAN SHEHU ꞌDAN FODIO, First Caliph, *Al Gaith al Wabli*. Arabic title: *al-Ghayth al-wabl fī sīrat al-imām al-^cadl* (the [blessing as of] abundance of rainfall in the life-way of the just leader). Undated (LAST, 1967, suggests 1820) ms. This work, on the duties of leaders in time of war, is arranged in twelve chapters after an introduction. The whole of it was edited, annotated and translated by Dr. Omar Bello for his PhD dissertation at SOAS. A partial translation can be downloaded from www.siiasi.org.

—, *Kitab al Nasihati*. Translation in Hausa by Malam Sidi Sayudi. Arabic title: *al-Naṣīḥa al-waḍīᶜa fī bayān inna ḥubb al-dunyā raᵓs kulli khaṭīᵓa* (well-placed advice in explanation of [the fact] that love of the world is the source [head] of every mistake). Bello produced this work from the books at his disposal, one of which was *Sifat al-Safwa* by Ibn al-Jawzi (d.1200). He then asked Nana Asma'u to translate and versify *Kitab al Nasihati* into Fulfulde and Hausa. To the lists of examples of exemplary womanhood, he added the names of women in the Shehu's community and that of his own mother. (See below for details of the book *Sufi Women,* a translation of *Sifat al-Safwa* by Javad Nurbakhsh.)

SHEHU ʻDAN FODIO. Early Fulfulde poems (unpublished, handwritten manuscripts, no date except for one indicated):

Untitled, 18 vv. Verse 3: 'This poem is about married men who have become rogues.'

Untitled, 48 vv. Verse 3: 'This poem is about married women who irritate their husbands.'

Untitled, 18 vv. Verse 6: 'This poem is about married couples who are in error.'

Untitled, 35 vv. Verses 3 and 13: 'I intend to tell you what the regulations are concerning a man's duties to his wife and a wife's duties to her husband.'

Untitled, 79 vv. (dated 1789). Verse 77: 'This poem is to awaken, alert you to the causes of the bad situation that obtains in Hausaland.'

Bonoji Hausa, 102 vv. The title may be translated as 'The ills of Hausaland are many and obvious'.

Mudinori. The title may be translated as 'What a pious scholar teaches'. Twenty chapters on topics such as alms, fasting, pilgrimage and marriage. The Shehu said: 'Listen to this poem which is to teach you about the Shariᶜa...' The poems were translated from Fulfulde into Hausa by Malam Muhammadu Magaji and from Hausa into English by Jean Boyd. Copies are in Jean Boyd's private collection.

REFERENCES

Published works and archives

ADAMU, LADI S., *Hafsatu Ahmadu Bello: The Unsung Hero*. Zaria: Ahmadu Bello University Press, 1995.

ADULLAHI 'DAN FODIO, *Liya'ul Hukkam* Translated into Hausa by Alhaji Haliru Binji, Zaria: Gaskiya Corporation, *ca.* 1966. (This is book of guidance for law makers and the administration of the law; Arabic title: *Ḍiyā' al-ḥukkām* (light for magistrates).)

—, *Tazyin al-warakat*. Dated 14 October 1813 by the author, who explains the title (p. 84) as 'The adornment of the papers by the collection of my verses'. (Poems written before, during and after the Jihad with the history that accompanied them. See below: HISKETT.)

ABDULLAH YUSUF ALI (transl.), *The Holy Qur'an*. Elmhurst, NY: Tahrike Tarsile Qur'an Inc., 2nd US edn.,1988.

AHMED, LEILA, 'Western Ethnocentrism and Perceptions of the Harem', *Feminist Studies*, 8/3 (1982), pp. 521–34.

ALKALI, NUR *et al.* (eds.), *'Daʿwa* and Contemporary Challenges Facing Muslim Women in Secular States – A Nigerian Case Study' in *Islam in Africa: Proceedings of the Islam in Africa Conference*. Ibadan: Spectrum Books, 1989.

BADAWI, JAMAL, *Gender Equity in Islam*. Plainfield, IN: American Trust Publications, 1995.

BARLAS, ASMA, *Believing Women in Islam*. Austin, TX: University of Texas Press, 2002.

BARTH, HEINRICH, *Travels and Discoveries in North and Central Africa 1849–1855*. New York: Harper and Brothers, 5 vols., 1857–58.

BATTEN, T. R., *A Handbook on the Teaching of the Elementary History and Geography Syllabus in Nigeria*. Lagos: CMS Bookshop, 1934.

BESMER, FREMONT, *Horses, Musicians, and Gods*. South Hadley, MA: Bergin and Garvey, 1983.

BLAIR, SHEILA, 'Arabic Calligraphy in West Africa' in Shamil Jeppie and Soulemayne B. Diagne (eds.), *The Meanings of Timbuktu*. Cape Town: Human Sciences Research Council, 2008, ch. 5.

BOYD, JEAN, *The Caliph's Sister*. London: Frank Cass, 1989.

—, Archival material SOAS, PPMS 36. Deposited July 1991: title: 'Women in Northern Nigeria 1790–1990', Catalogue pp. 136.

Deposited March 1998: title: 'Sokoto papers and postcard collection', Catalogue pp. 105. Deposited August 2006: title: 'Supplement to Women in Northern Nigeria', Catalogue pp. 105.

BOYD, JEAN, and BEVERLY MACK, *The Collected Works of Nana Asma'u, Daughter of Usman dan Fodiyo 1793–1864*. East Lansing, MI: Michigan State University Press, 1997. (Nigerian edition: Ibadan: Sam Bookman Publishers, 1999.)

BRUCE-LOCKHART, JAMIE, *A Sailor in the Sahara: the Life and Travels of Hugh Clapperton, Commander RN*. London: I.B. Tauris, 2008.

CALLOWAY, HELEN, *Gender, Culture and Empire: European women in colonial Nigeria*. Urbana, IL: University of Illinois Press, 1987.

CLAPPERTON, HUGH, Vol.1. Major Denham, Captain Clapperton and the late Dr. Oudney, *by Major Denham, Captain Clapperton, and the late Doctor Oudney, extending across the great desert to the tenth degree of northern latitude, and from Kouka in Bornou, to Sackatoo, the capital of the Fellatah empire. Narrative of Travels and Discoveries in Northern and Central Africa*. London: John Murray, 1826. Vol. 2. *Journal of a second expedition into the interior of Africa from the Bight of Benin to Soccatoo, to which is added the journal of Richard Lander from Kano to the sea coast*. London: John Murray, 1829. Reprinted London: Frank Cass, 1967.

COLONIAL ANNUAL REPORTS, Annual Report No. 346, 1900–11. 877 pp., case-bound. Unpublished. SOAS reference VW 351: 34 7698.

CROWDER, MICHAEL, *West Africa under Colonial Rule*. London: Hutchinson, 1968.

CURTIS, EDWARD E. IV, *Islam in Black America: Identity, Liberation, and Difference in African Thought*. Binghamton, NY: State University of New York Press, 2002.

KANYA-FORSTNER, A. S. and PAUL LOVEJOY, *Pilgrims, Interpreters and Agents. French Reconnaissance Report on the Sokoto Caliphate and Bornu 1891–1895*. Madison, WI: University of Wisconsin Press, 1997.

GOMEZ, MICHAEL A., *Black Crescent: The Experience and Legacy of African American Muslims in the Americas*. New York: Cambridge University Press, 2005.

HISKETT, MERVYN (ed. and transl.), *Tazyin al-warakat of Abdullah dan Fodio*. Ibadan: Ibadan University Press, 1963.

HOGBEN, S. J. and A. H. M. KIRK-GREENE, *The Emirates of Northern Nigeria*,

London: Oxford University Press, 1966. (A revised edition of S. J. Hogben's *Muhammadan Emirates of Nigeria* (London 1930).)

IBRAHIM DAN JUNAIDU, *Rayuwar Wazirin Sakkwato* (A biography of Waziri Junaidu). Sokoto: Fadama Printing Works, 1993.

IMAM, AYESHA (ed.), *The WIN Document: The Conditions of Women in Nigeria.* Zaria: WIN, 1985.

—, (ed.), Policy *Recommendations to 2,000 AD.* Zaria: WIN, 1985.

—, (ed.), *Women in Nigeria Today.* London: Zed Books, 1985.

JOHNSTON, H. A. S., *Fulani Empire of Sokoto.* London: Oxford University Press, 1967.

JUNAIDU DAN MUHAMMAD BUHARI, Waziri of Sokoto, *Tarihin Fulani* (A Fulani history: a chronicle of the events that occurred during the reigns of each caliph from the time of the Shehu to Abubakar III). Zaria: Northern Region Literacy Agency (NORLA), 1957.

—, *The Relevance of the University to Our Society.* Ahmadu Bello University Press, 1972.

—, *Bughyat ar-raghibin bi-ziyadi is'afi z-za'irin. Handbook for Pilgrims.* Translation in Hausa by Kadi Haliru Binji. Sokoto: Sifawa Printing Enterprise, 1961.

KANYA-FORSTNER, A. S. and PAUL LOVEJOY, *Pilgrims, Interpreters and Agents, French Reconnaissance Report on the Sokoto Caliphate and Bornu 1891-1895,* Madison, WI: University of Wisconsin Press, 1997.

LAST, MURRAY, *The Sokoto Caliphate.* London: Longman, Green & Co., 1967.

LEMU, AISHA, *A Degree Above Them: Observations on the Condition of Northern Nigerian Women.* Zaria: Gaskiya Corporation, 1983.

MACK, BEVERLY, *Muslim Women Sing: Hausa Popular Song.* Bloomington, IN: Indiana University Press, 2004.

—, 'Muslim Women Scholars in 19th and 20th Century: Morocco to Nigeria' in Shamil Jeppie and Souleyman Bashir Diagne_(eds.), *The Meanings of Timbuktu.* Cape Town: Human Sciences Research Council of South Africa, 2008, pp. 165–79.

MACK, BEVERLY and JEAN BOYD, *One Woman's Jihad: Nana Asma'u, Scholar and Scribe,* Bloomington, IN: Indiana University Press, 2000.

MARABLE, MANNING and HISHAAM D. AIDI (eds.), *Black Routes to Islam.*

New York: Palgrave Macmillan, 2009.

MILLER, WALTER, *An Autobiography* (Zaria, n.d.). See private papers ACC237 Walter S Miller, CMS Archives Heslop Room, University of Birmingham Library.

MOHAMED, ALTINE and BENE MADUNAGU, 'WIN: A Militant Approach to the Mobilisation of Women', *Review of African Political Economy*, 37, Oil Debts and Democracy Nigeria (Dec., 1986), pp. 103–05.

MUHAMMAD BELLO ʾDAN SHEHU ʾDAN FODIO, First Caliph, Sokoto Caliphate, *Infakul Maisuri*. Dated 14 Muharram 1236 (1821). Arabic title: *Infāq al-maysūr fī taʾrīkh bilādi Takrūr,* a history of the Jihad, the war with Gobir. Published Arabic versions: ed. C. E. J. Whitting (London: Luzac & Co., 1951); ed. Abubakar M. Gummi (Cairo, 1964); ed. Bahija al-Shadhili (Rabat, 1996). Version in English by E. J. Arnett, *The Rise of the Sokoto Fulani, Being a Paraphrase and in Some Parts a Translation of the Infaku'l Maisuri of Sultan Mohammed Bello* (London: SOAS, 1922).) Version in Hausa: *Infakul Maisuri* (transl. by Jean Boyd and Sidi Sayuɗi; ed. Alhaji Haliru Binji and Waziri Junaidu. Sokoto History Bureau, 1975).

MUFFETT, DAVID J. M., *Concerning Brave Captains, being a history of the British occupation of Kano and Sokoto and of the last stand of the Fulani forces. With a foreword by Alhaji Sir Ahmadu Bello*. London: André Deutsch, 1964.

MUHAMMAD, AMIR NASHI ALI, *Muslims in America: Seven Centuries of History 1312–2000*. Beltsville, MD: Amana, 2001.

NURBAKHSH, JAVAD, *Sufi Women*. London: Khaniqahi Nimatullahi Publications, 1st edn., 1983; revised 2nd edn., 1990.

PERHAM, MARGERY, *Lugard, the Years of Authority 1898–1945*. Vol. 1: *The Years of Adventure, 1858–1898*. Vol. 2: *The Years of Authority 1898–1945*. London: Collins, 1956–60.

SHAGARI, SHEHU, *Beckoned to Serve*. Ibadan: Heinemann, 2001.

SHARWOOD-SMITH, JOAN, *Diary of a Colonial Wife: An African Experience*. London: Radcliffe Press, 1992.

SHAW, FLORA (LADY LUGARD), *A Tropical Dependency; an outline of the ancient history of the western Sudan with an account of the modern settlement of Northern Nigeria*. London: James Nisbet. 1905. Republished by Biblio Life, Charleston, SC, *ca.* 2008. Recently (2010) reissued in paperback by Cambridge University Press in the series 'Cambridge Library Collection – Women's Writing'.

SHEHU USMAN 'DAN FODIO, *Bayan Wujub*. Arabic title: *Bayān wujūb al-hijra ᶜala l-ᶜibād*, 1806. The Shehu's explanation of the title: 'Exposition of the obligations upon the servants of God of emigration and appointing an imam and understanding jihad.' Transl. F. H. el-Masri, Oxford: Oxford University Press, printed in the Sudan at Khartoum University Press, 1978. Subject: a comprehensive explanation of 'jihad'; 63 chapters under headings such as the division of booty, the qualities of the Commander of the Faithful.

—, *Nurul albab*. Arabic title: *Nūr al-albāb* (light for the hearts; on the reasons why misfortune has spread across Hausaland). Translated from Arabic into Hausa by Sidi Sayudi, from Hausa into English by Jean Boyd, edited by Alhaji Haliru Binji and Waziri Junaidu.

—, *Handbook on Islam: Iman, Ihsan*. Dated 1809. A translation by Aisha Abdar-Rahman of *Kitāb Usūl al-dīn*. Printed in Zaria, no details, 2 pp., with *Kitāb ᶜUlūm al-Muāᵓmala*, 44 pp. by Sheikh Usman dan Fodio. Bungay, Suffolk: Diwan Press, 1984. Covers a wide range of beliefs, obligations and Sufism; listed in LAST, 1967.

—, *Islam and Women* in Thomas Hodgkin, *Nigerian Perspectives: An Historical Anthology* (London: Oxford University Press, 1960), pp. 194–5. Translated from *Nour el-albab de Cheikh Otmane ben Mohammed ben Otmane dit Ibn-Foudiou* in *Revue Africaine*, 41 (Algiers, 1897–8), pp. 227–8.

SULAIMAN, IBRAHEEM, 'The Agony of a Complacent Nation', *Radiance* (1983). Published by Muslim Students Society.

SULE, BALARABA B. M. and PRISCILLA STARRATT, 'Islamic Leadership Positions for Women in contemporary Kano Society' in Catherine Coles and Beverly Mack (eds.), *Hausa Women in the Twentieth Century*. Madison, WI: University of Wisconsin Press, 1991, pp. 29–49.

TILHO, Documents Scientifiques de la Mission Tilho, Vol. 2 (Paris 1911); typescript extract CELHTO, Niamey. (Oral traditions and histories collected in Niger Republic by French colonial officials.)

TREVOR, JEAN. Papers relating to a study of the education of Muslim Hausa women of Sokoto, 1930–974. ms Thesis, Rhodes House, Oxford. RH SSS ARSS 1757.

TROLLOPE, JOANNA, *Britannia's Daughters: Women of the British Empire*. London: Hutchinson, 1983.

WADUD, AMINA, *Qur'an and Woman*. Oxford: Oxford University Press, 1999.

YUSUF, BALA, 'The State of Learning, the State of Society: from the Jihad to the S.A.P. [Structural Adjustment Programme]' in Isma'ila A. Tsiga and Abdalla U. Adamu (eds.), *Islam and the History of Leearning in Katsina* (Ibadan: Spectrum Books, 1997).

YUSUF, HAJIYA BILKISU, '*Da'wa* and Contemporary Challenges Facing Muslim Women in Secular States – A Nigerian Case Study' in Nur Alƙali *et al.* (eds.), *Islam in Africa: Proceedings of the Islam in Africa Conference*. Ibadan: Spectrum Books, 1989, pp. 276–95.

News items

'King Hassan of Morocco'. Obituary, *The Guardian* (London), 26 July, 1999.

BOYD, JEAN, 'An Account of the Life of Nana Asma'u, Daughter of Shehu Usman ɗan Fodio', *Gaskiya Ta Fi Kwabo*, and *Sunday Triumph* (Nigeria), circa April 1984.

SHAKUR, ZAID, 'Traditional Islam for the Hip-Hop Generation', *In Focus* article, 3 March 2007.

YUSUF, HAJIYA BILKISU. Article concerning WIN conference, 29 May 1983, on 'Women and the Family'. Title not available. *Sunday Triumph* (Nigeria), 13 June 1982.

Alhaji Shehu Kangiwa, Governor of Sokoto State. Interview, *New Times* (Nigeria), 26 April 1981.

Non-print media sources

FOMWAN website: http://www.fomwan.org/index.php

SPECIFIC PICTURES, *New Muslim Cool* (DVD) narrated by Hamza Perez, 2009.

SANKORE INSTITUTE: http://www.siiasi.org.

YUSUFU, HAJIYA BILKISU, *Nigeria: FOMWAN – Lesson from the Sokoto Caliphate*, 28 August 2008, http://allafrica.com/stories/200808280883.html

WILLIAM, FRANK (director), *Nana Asma'u*. Documentary film for NMO (Dutch Muslim Broadcasting Corporation), 2003. Screened in Sokoto 2004.

INDEXES

Geographical terms

Persons, peoples and associations

Concepts, keywords, themes